A Woman's Guide to
Muscle
and
Strength

Irene Lewis-McCormick

Human Kinetics

A Woman's Guide to

Muscle

and

Strength

Library of Congress Cataloging-in-Publication Data

Lewis-McCormick, Irene, 1967-
   A woman's guide to muscle and strength / Irene Lewis-McCormick.
      p. cm.
   Includes bibliographical references.
   ISBN 978-0-7360-9035-3 (soft cover) -- ISBN 0-7360-9035-5 (soft cover)
   1. Exercise for women. 2. Weight lifting. 3. Bodybuilding for women. I. Title.
   GV482.L49 2012
   613.7'045--dc23
                           2011048020
ISBN-10: 0-7360-9035-5 (print)
ISBN-13: 978-0-7360-9035-3 (print)

Acquisitions Editor: Justin Klug; **Developmental Editor:** Laura Floch; **Assistant Editor:** Elizabeth Evans; **Copyeditor:** Patsy Fortney; **Permissions Manager:** Martha Gullo; **Graphic Designers:** Nancy Rasmus and Joe Buck; **Graphic Artist:** Kim McFarland; **Cover Designer:** Keith Blomberg; **Photographer (cover and interior):** Neil Bernstein; **Visual Production Assistant:** Joyce Brumfield; **Photo Production Manager:** Jason Allen; **Art Manager:** Kelly Hendren; **Associate Art Manager:** Alan L. Wilborn; **Illustrations:** © Human Kinetics; **Printer:** Sheridan Books

We thank Fitness World Ankeny in Ankeny, Iowa, for assistance in providing the location for the photo shoot for this book.

Human Kinetics books are available at special discounts for bulk purchase. Special editions or book excerpts can also be created to specification. For details, contact the Special Sales Manager at Human Kinetics.

Printed in the United States of America   10 9 8 7 6 5 4 3 2 1

The paper in this book is certified under a sustainable forestry program.

Human Kinetics
Website: www.HumanKinetics.com

United States: Human Kinetics
P.O. Box 5076
Champaign, IL 61825-5076
800-747-4457
e-mail: humank@hkusa.com

Canada: Human Kinetics
475 Devonshire Road Unit 100
Windsor, ON N8Y 2L5
800-465-7301 (in Canada only)
e-mail: info@hkcanada.com

Europe: Human Kinetics
107 Bradford Road
Stanningley
Leeds LS28 6AT, United Kingdom
+44 (0) 113 255 5665
e-mail: hk@hkeurope.com

Australia: Human Kinetics
57A Price Avenue
Lower Mitcham, South Australia 5062
08 8372 0999
e-mail: info@hkaustralia.com

New Zealand: Human Kinetics
P.O. Box 80
Torrens Park, South Australia 5062
0800 222 062
e-mail: info@hknewzealand.com

E5063

To my mother, Maire Agnes Lewis

Contents

Exercise Finder

	Pg. #	Equipment used	Exercise focus
Warm-up (chapter 4)			
Lateral stretch	46	None	Lengthens the spinal muscles
Spinal extension	46	None	Lengthen the back muscles and hamstring stretch
Standing knee flexion and extension with ankle dorsiflexion	47	None	Active stretch for the hamstrings and low back and also a balance skill
Standing figure four	47	None	Stretch the gluteals and IT Band
Front lunge with lateral squat	48	None	Warms up the large muscles of the lower body with active ranges of motion
Standing cat and cow	49	None	Stretches the spinal muscles including the neck
Standing shoulder horizontal adduction	49	None	Stretches the shoulder and middle back muscles
Seated pelvic tilt on stability ball	50	Stability ball	Lubricates the low back and focuses on pelvic tilts in preparation for exercise
Seated hip circles on stability ball	50	Stability ball	Lubricates the low back and focuses on pelvic rotation in preparation for exercise
Knee lift with medicine ball	51	Medicine ball	Warms the body up and engages the muscles of the core
Body ball reach	51	Medicine ball	Warms the body up and engages the muscles of the core
Plié with medicine ball lift	52	Medicine ball	Warm up move and works the gluteal muscles
Shoulder rotation with bands	52	Therapy band	Warm up for shoulder joint
Cool-down (chapter 4)			
Full-body stretch	56	Mat	Lengthens the whole body and allows for deeper relaxation
Bridge	56	Mat	Lubricates the spinal segments and helps with core control
Low back stretch	57	Mat	Stretches the spinal and gluteal muscles
Hamstring stretch	57	Mat	Lengthens the hamstring muscles
Spinal twist	58	Mat	Stretches the low back
Quadruped cat and cow	58	Mat	Strengthen the core muscles and lengthens the spine via lengthening the arms and legs
Child's pose	59	Mat	Stretches the low back and shoulders

(continued)

Exercise Finder, *continued*

	Pg. #	Equipment used	Exercise focus
Downward-facing dog	59	Mat	Lengthens the spine and stretches the posterior legs
Forward bend	60	None	Stretches the back and hamstrings
Forward bend with a twist	60	None	Stretches the low back and hamstrings adding rotation which increases the stretch intensity
Foam roller spinal alignment	61	Foam roller, mat	Lengthens and relaxes the spinal segments
Foam roller shoulder extension	61	Foam roller, mat	Lengthens and relaxes the spinal segments and allows for range of motion stretches at the shoulders and chest
Upper body (chapter 5)			
Dumbbell chest press	74	Dumbbells, flat bench	Chest, triceps, and anterior shoulder muscles
Barbell chest press	74	Barbell, bench	Chest and triceps
Dumbbell chest fly	75	Dumbbells, flat bench	Chest and shoulders
Standing cable chest fly	76	Cable machine	Anterior shoulder, chest, core and triceps
Decline barbell press	77	Decline bench, barbell	Chest and triceps
Push-up	78	Mat	Core, chest, triceps
Incline push-up	78	Mat, bench	Core, chest, triceps
Decline push-up	79	Mat, bench	Core, chest, triceps
Front raise	80	Dumbbells	Anterior and middle shoulder
Front cable raise	80	Cable machine	Core, anterior and middle shoulder
Lateral raise	81	Dumbbells	Middle shoulder
Seated shoulder press	81	Dumbbells	Middle shoulder, triceps
Dumbbell upright row	82	Dumbbells	Middle shoulder
Bent-over dumbbell row	82	Dumbbells	Middle shoulder
Straight bar upright row	83	Barbell	Core, lats, rhomboids, biceps
Lat pulldown	84	Lat pulldown machine	Lats, biceps
Pull-up	84	Pull-up bar	Biceps, shoulders, core,
Pullover	85	Dumbbells	Lats, shoulders
Shrug	85	Dumbbells	Trapezius
Rear deltoid fly	86	Dumbbells	Posterior shoulder
Seated low row	86	Rowing machine	Lats, biceps
Spinal extension	87	Mat	Spinal muscles
Pilates swimming	87	Mat	Shoulders, back, gluteals
Quadruped spinal extension	88	Mat	Shoulders, back, gluteals
Biceps curl with EZ Curl Bar	88	EZ Curl Bar	Biceps

	Pg. #	Equipment used	Exercise focus
Hammer curl	89	Dumbbells	Biceps
Preacher curl	89	Dumbbells	Biceps
Reverse curl	90	Dumbbells	Biceps, forearms
Triceps kickback	90	Dumbbells	Triceps
Triceps dip	91	Dip machine	Triceps, core
TRX chest press	91	Suspension trainer	Chest, front shoulder, core
TRX mid row	92	Suspension trainer	Middle back, core
TRX atomic push-up	93	Suspension trainer	Chest, triceps, core, abdominal muscles
TRX Y deltoid fly	94	Suspension trainer	Posterior shoulder, core
Lower body (chapter 6)			
Dumbbell front squat	103	Dumbbells	Legs
Good morning	103	Dumbbells	Hamstring, gluteals
Seated hamstring curl	104	Hamcurl machine	Hamstrings
Supine stability ball bridge	104	Stability ball	Gluteals
Stability ball gluteal squeeze	105	Stability ball	Gluteals
Front lunge	106	Dumbbells	Quadriceps
Reverse lunge	106	Dumbbells	Gluteals
Walking lunge	107	Dumbbells	Legs, gluteals
Side lunge	107	Dumbbells	Quadriceps, gluteals
Dumbbell squat	108	Dumbbells	Legs
Single-leg squat	108	Kettlebell	Quadriceps, hamstrings
Seated leg press	109	Machine	Legs, gluteals
Seated leg extension	109	Machine	Quadriceps
Seated calf raise	110	Machine	Calves
Kettlebell squat	110	Kettlebell	Legs, core, shoulders
Angle kettlebell squat	111	Kettlebell	Legs, core, shoulders
Kettlebell hip hinge	111	Kettlebell	Hamstring
Squat sequence with curtsy lunge	112	Dumbbell or medicine ball	Legs, gluteals
TRX squat	113	Suspension trainer	Legs, core
TRX single-leg squat	113	Suspension trainer	Legs, gluteals, core
TRX step back lunge	114	Suspension trainer	Hamstring, gluteals, core

(continued)

	Pg. #	Equipment used	Exercise focus
TRX balance lunge	114	Suspension trainer	Quadriceps, gluteals, hamstrings, core
TRX hip press	115	Suspension trainer	Gluteals, core
TRX hamstring curl	116	Suspension trainer	Hamstrings, calves, core
Core (chapter 7)			
Abdominal progression series	122	Mat	Anterior abdominal wall
Pilates roll-up	123	Mat	Anterior abdominal wall, spine
V-sit (boat pose)	124	Mat	Abdominal wall, hip flexors
Standing Russian twist	124	Medicine ball	Core
Side plank	125	Mat	Core, shoulder complex
Supine bicycle	125	Mat	Anterior abdominal wall, obliques, hip flexors
Supine contralateral bicycle	126	Mat	Obliques, hip flexors
Windshield wipers	126	Mat	Core
Supine clocking	127	Mat	Core
Stability ball roll-out	127	Stability ball, mat	Shoulder complex, core
Oblique stability ball roll-out	128	Stability ball, mat	Obliques, shoulder complex
Plank	128	Mat	Chest, core
Push-up to plank	129	Mat	Chest, core, triceps
Supine plank	129	Mat	Shoulder complex, core
TRX plank	130	Suspension trainer	Core, shoulder complex, chest
TRX side plank	130	Suspension trainer	Core, shoulder complex
TRX pike	131	Suspension trainer	Abdominal wall, hip flexors, core
TRX crunch	131	Suspension trainer	Abdominal wall, hip flexors, core
TRX oblique crunch	132	Suspension trainer	Obliques, hip flexors, shoulder complex

Acknowledgments

I would like to thank Ann Mooney, Jen Krakau, Ara May Hubbard, Taylor Hilbrands, and Holly Shirbroun for their time and talent.

PART I

Basics of Strength Training for Women

Strength Training and the Female Body

Many women have used fitness equipment and free weights in a weight room, in group fitness classes, or at home with little or no result. The strong, toned arms and legs desired through weight training never come to fruition—even when they use the correct exercises and proper lifting techniques. The likely culprit dates back to strength training beliefs touted in the not-so-distant past, which probably affect a majority of women's attitudes about strength training today.

Self-proclaimed fitness experts Jane Fonda, Jackie Sorenson, and Jack LaLanne dominated the exercise scene in the 1970s and 1980s. They were instrumental in the development of the fitness movement and should be thanked for that. However, they encouraged women to perform aerobic activity and to lift only light weights using a dizzying amount of repetitions. This supported the misguided concept that lifting heavy weights resulted in brawny, masculine muscles. As a result, a majority of women today are fearful that lifting heavy weights will result in muscles that are bulky like men's. Moreover, they do not realize the positive impact that strength training will have on their bodies.

Strength training doesn't have to mean bodybuilding. Consider the 30-something woman who comes into the gym, maybe as frequently as five days a week. She alternates cardio machines for up to 90 minutes and then leaves the facility without doing any flexibility or strength training. She typically isn't overweight, but neither is she as toned as she desires. She is your typical example of a "skinny fat" woman. Yes, skinny and fat can coexist when women don't perform resistance training to increase their lean musculature.

If you want to increase your muscle strength and size, sculpt your body into a well-developed form, or train for performance enhancement for a specific sport or activity, you will need to use a combination of training tools and methods. Also, the weight you lift must be heavy enough to create a physiological response in your muscle tissue; light hand weights and hundreds of repetitions just aren't going to cut it. Machines are a good start, and group classes labeled strength training can help you master basic strength training lifting techniques (if the instructor is trained properly, of course), but learning exercise progression and periodization training in addition to these techniques is important for success.

This book will help you examine your current level of fitness and establish training goals, detail the variety of strength training exercises that will help you achieve your goals, and teach you how to apply the training technique known as periodization to get results for life. Additionally, the book provides photos and detailed descriptions of how to perform many exercises so you can achieve fantastic fitness results.

Fortunately, today's fitness professionals know much more about strength training than those of the past. They rely on peer-reviewed research conducted in laboratories in universities around the globe, as well as practical education from certification and continuing education programs. As a result of this increased knowledge, today's strength training includes functional training (exercises that improve health and function in our daily lives), metabolic training (training that improves our capacity to burn calories), and resistance training (exercises that actually sculpt and change the musculature of our bodies).

HEALTH-RELATED BENEFITS OF STRENGTH TRAINING

Strength training is an important component of a complete exercise regimen for women. As a personal trainer, I see women who are initially hesitant to venture into the weight area of the fitness center, thinking it primarily a masculine domain. But they've since experienced the incredible benefits weight training provides, such as increased muscle strength and endurance, stronger bones, definition, and leaner bodies. Being strong and having more fat-free mass is important for health as well as aesthetics. Strong is the new skinny!

Weight training is exercise that adds resistance to the body's natural movements to make those movements more difficult and construct muscles that are bigger and stronger. I encourage clients to develop balanced fitness programs that combine aerobic exercise, which builds endurance and benefits the heart and lungs, with resistance training, which develops muscle hypertrophy and strength. Weight work can be particularly rewarding for women who have weak upper bodies. Most women haven't trained the way their male counterparts have, and have strength imbalances between their upper and lower bodies. Many women have participated in group fitness classes or walking or running programs, so their legs may be relatively strong compared to their arms, shoulders, and back, which tend to be underdeveloped. Also at issue are the increased postural issues that come with increasing age. Working out with resistance heavy enough to create a physiological response develops upper body strength, which can make many tasks of daily living such as lifting and carrying heavy objects much easier, as well as improve posture.

Exercise is also an important component of any healthy lifestyle. All overweight woman can benefit from daily, consistent aerobic and anaerobic (resistance training) exercise. Aerobic activities such as using an elliptical trainer, treadmill walking, jogging, and running burn calories more quickly than resistance training does, but resistance training burns calories longer after the exercise session has ended. For this reason, it is part of a positive general lifestyle change from inactive to active, which is where the biggest payoff is.

Metabolism and Exercise

In my role as a fitness professional, clients often ask me if they are burning fat during strength training. Ormsbee and colleagues (2007) concluded that muscle contributes significantly to resting metabolic rate, which is the energy expended to maintain all bodily functions at rest. Their research demonstrated that the body continues to use fat as a fuel source, both during and after a resistance training session. Additionally, Donnelly and colleagues (2009) stated that resistance training plays an important role in weight loss.

None of this research is a surprise, considering that both resistance training and aerobic activity play a big role in fat and weight loss as a result of an easily explained physiological condition called excess postexercise oxygen consumption (EPOC). EPOC is the measurable increased rate of oxygen consumption following strenuous aerobic or anaerobic activity, and plays a huge role in postexercise caloric consumption. This is so because exercise results in the breakdown of fat stores and the release of fatty acids (FFA) into the bloodstream. During recovery from either aerobic or anaerobic exercise, EPOC is accompanied by an elevated consumption of fuel, meaning that you continue to burn fat calories even after your exercise session is completed.

Inactivity is a major cause of many disease conditions, medical complications, overfat body composition, and obesity. Women who appear skinny, or thin, often carry the same or more amount of fat on their frames as obese women. Research has shown that resistance training creates meaningful changes in body composition (Marx et al. 2001). Thus, one of the noteworthy benefits of resistance exercise is the maintenance or increase of fat-free body mass while decreasing fat. As this research demonstrates, the quality of the tissue (fat versus fat-free) is more important than how small or large someone is, or what her clothing size indicates. For example, being a size 2 with a 40 percent body fat reading is extremely unhealthy.

There is a growing consensus in the medical community that physical activity, specifically resistance training exercise, positively affects the cardiovascular and musculoskeletal systems, and even increases bone mineral density. Significant health benefits can be obtained by being physically active on most, and preferably all, days of the week; fitness programs involving progressively increasing intensities have even greater protective benefits.

Elevated systolic and diastolic blood pressures are associated with a higher risk of developing coronary heart disease (CHD), congestive heart failure, stroke, and kidney failure. There is a marked increase in developing these diseases when blood pressure is 140/90 mmHg. People who regularly perform progressive resistance exercise training experienced about a 2 percent reduction in resting systolic blood pressure and a 4 percent reduction in resting diastolic blood pressure (Fagard 2001).

Arthritis, characterized by stiffness, pain, and loss of joint function, affects people of all ages, of both sexes, and in all ethnic groups. It may jeopardize people's physical, psychological, social, and economic well-being, depriving them of their independence. Physicians commonly prescribe exercise as a treatment for arthritis. Consistent exercise improves aerobic capacity, muscle strength, joint mobility, functional ability, and mood, without apparent increases in joint symptoms or disease. Increased lean mass can take stress off these vulnerable joints. Because the muscle tissue absorbs shock, the increased development of muscle around the knee and shoulder decreases joint stress. Although exercise doesn't cure arthritis, it may significantly improve symptoms.

Progressive resistance training actually strengthens bones, too. Current research on osteoporosis suggests that strength training can both prevent and treat the condition. Osteoporosis is a degenerative disease characterized by a loss of bone mineral density resulting in a susceptibility to bone fractures and health problems. Osteoporosis, which literally means "porous bones," causes calcium losses that weaken bone structure. About 40 percent of all fractures occur in the spine, resulting in a loss of height and a stooped posture (kyphosis). Twenty-five percent of fractures occur at the hip, most often in the femur. It is clear that increased strength levels not only help conserve bone mass, but also maintain muscle mass (lean mass) and improve balance, both of which are important in the prevention of falls.

Research has demonstrated that resistance training and weight-bearing aerobic exercise may provide the needed stimulus for bone formation. Strength training allows the body to build new bone. Resistance training programs undertaken before age 30 can prevent major bone losses, thereby warding off or even preventing osteoporosis (Kohrt et al. 2004).

SCIENCE BEHIND STRENGTH TRAINING

The information on strength training provided to this point has been on a general level, the type of information you might see in a women's magazine or in a pamphlet advocating the benefits of strength training for women. However, to understand how strength training really works, let's dig a little deeper into the bona fide science behind increased lean mass and what this means for a woman and her body.

Muscles and Their Response to Strength Training

Strength training focuses on skeletal muscles because these are the muscles you can control during activity. Skeletal muscles themselves are a complex arrangement of fibers organized into bundles surrounded by connective tissues. These connective tissues transmit the force of muscle contraction to the tendons, which are attached to bones, which ultimately cause movement when stimulated via nervous impulses. Therefore, direct stimulation from the central nervous system via muscles ultimately moves limbs and creates joint actions, or body movements, to occur.

Human skeletal muscles come in two varieties. Slow-twitch muscles (also referred to as Type Ia) enable you to stand upright and walk. The muscles of the core are made up primarily of this type. The other variety, fast-twitch muscles, are divided into two categories: Type IIa and Type IIb. These provide the power for movements such as pushing, pulling, lifting, and throwing.

The term *muscle contraction* actually implies muscle shortening, but muscles can produce force while lengthening or maintaining a specific length. For example, to pick up an object, you bend (or flex) your elbow joint and use the biceps muscle to assist your hand in grasping the object to pick it up. The biceps muscle is contracted, or shortened, to produce the necessary force to accomplish this task. Likewise, when you are in a plank position (the up phase of a push-up), you are contracting many muscles to hold that position, but there is no change in muscle length. Therefore, you are producing force in the skeletal muscles without changing the length of the muscles. Because the word *contraction* can mean a variety of things, the term *muscle action* is actually more descriptive and more appropriate when discussing exercise and what muscles do in response to exercise. Isotonic muscle actions include concentric (muscle shortening) and eccentric (muscle lengthening). Isometric muscle actions involve the production of force without movement.

A concentric muscle action occurs when a muscle produces force, resulting in a shortening of the muscle fibers and the creation of torque. For example, when you flex your knee, your hamstring muscles shorten and produce force in the back of your thigh. *Torque* is yet another term for the force produced when a muscle is pushed, pulled, or twisted around a joint. *Torque* usually refers to twisting or rotating movements. Sometimes this is a good thing, but torque can be undesirable, resulting in an increased risk of injury. An eccentric muscle action occurs when torque is produced while the muscle is being lengthened. When the speed and the force of a muscle contraction are low, both slow- and fast-twitch muscle fibers are recruited. When the muscle contraction is fast and requires more force, the slow-twitch muscle is too slow to contribute as much, so the predominant fiber type is fast twitch.

Why Do Muscles Get Sore?

Delayed onset muscle soreness (DOMS) is the muscle pain or discomfort often felt from 24 to 72 hours after intense exercise. DOMS typically subsides within two or three days. Although the precise cause is unknown, the type of muscle contraction seems to be a factor in the development of DOMS. Exercises that involve many loaded, eccentric contractions can result in the most severe cases of DOMS. For example, think about the quadriceps when you are in a squat position. As you hold that squat, you can see that the thigh muscle is under tension and stretched. You may be able to assume this type of position every day without any soreness, but when you add external load (such as holding heavy weights or a heavy object above and beyond what you normally might carry in daily life), soreness occurs.

There is no need to be alarmed by the onset of DOMS. It generally subsides in a couple of days. Additionally, it is important not to measure the effectiveness or the success of your workout based on the appearance of DOMS. Typically, if you try a new exercise, perform it in a new sequence, use new patterns, or add additional loads, DOMS will be more likely to occur. If you do not experience DOMS, that is not an indication that your workout is not intense enough or unsuccessful. Training in a state of constant soreness would be uncomfortable, although you may be able to adapt to it.

The relationship among muscle soreness, rest, and hypertrophy can be a controversial topic where bodybuilding is concerned. Some have claimed that perpetual muscle soreness ensures muscle growth, but rest and recovery are required for optimal training results.

One possible way to reduce DOMS is by stretching before and after exercise. Warming up before and cooling down after exercise can also be beneficial. Other evidence, however, suggests that stretching has no impact on DOMS. Flexibility training is an extremely important component of fitness that should not be avoided or underemphasized. However, stretching after an intense workout will not decrease the onset of DOMS. Flexibility training is most beneficial when performed midway through and at the end of a workout, but it will not reduce your chances of experiencing DOMS. Some fitness experts have recommended contrast showers—alternating between cold and hot water—to increase circulation as a possible treatment for DOMS. However, the best way to recover from DOMS is simply to take time. You need about 24 to 48 hours to recover from this muscle rebuilding process.

Now that we have examined the types of muscles in the body, let's take a closer look at how muscles respond to a strength training program. Muscles adapt to resistance training by growing and developing—or in other words, by becoming stronger and larger. Scientifically speaking, the effects of resistance training occur as a result of hormonal responses in the body. The hormones essential to muscle development (called myogenesis) can be separated into two broad classes: catabolic hormones and anabolic hormones. Catabolic hormones break down muscle fibers to prepare them to be rebuilt stronger by anabolic hormones. Catabolic hormones play a vital role because muscle fibers must be broken down before they can be built back up.

Although many chemical reactions occur in the body at any given moment, at least one has a major influence on a woman's muscle development. Marks and Kravitz (2000) examined the function of hormones and the acute responses to resistance exercise in women. During strength training, the endocrine system releases hormones (which is actually its role in the body) that travel in the blood and target and influence almost all the tissues in the body. Although the process is complicated, it influences muscle growth in both men and women. Women, of course, do not produce as much testosterone as men do, and so the researchers of this study wanted to know how women increase their lean mass in the absence of significant amounts of testosterone. The answer lies in the influence of growth hormone (GH). The researchers found that women who strength train exert more GH than those who do not, and that they maintain the increased rise of GH in their body for longer periods of time than do women who do not strength train. What this means is that resistance training helps women grow and maintain lean mass, and the more lean mass they have, the less fat they have.

The process of muscle growth and development is called hypertrophy, or muscle enlargement, because it results in increases in the size and shape of muscle strands. Muscles tend to increase in size, or hypertrophy, as strength gains occur. Typically, larger muscles are stronger than smaller muscles, which may seem obvious. It is important to understand, however, that muscles tend to drive physical movement more effectively and to a greater degree (i.e., more intensely) when they are larger and stronger than when they are not developed to their full potential.

Let's say that you perform cardio exercises in addition to a strength training routine. Wouldn't it make sense that your gluteal muscles would facilitate more intense work and therefore provide more effective cardio and lower body strength training workouts if they were larger and stronger than they would if they were underdeveloped, atrophied (i.e., smaller because of disuse), and underused? When your muscles are fully engaged and hypertrophied with the maximum amount of muscle fibers being recruited and firing, you are working so much closer to your full potential. You burn more total calories because you are using more fat-free mass, and so you should expect better results from your routine, including more calorie burning, more strength, and weight loss, than someone who has not fully developed her muscles. So, essentially, strength training is used to hypertrophy the muscles. Following are the factors that are generally responsible for hypertrophy:

- *Overload* is the response of the muscles to loads (e.g., weights) that are heavier than what your body is already accustomed to lifting or moving. When you move more than your own body weight either by carrying heavy objects or lifting weights, you apply additional external loads to your body. As a result, your body has to respond by either failing to perform the task at hand or overcoming the load, thereby increasing muscle strength and size through the process of overload.

- *Muscle fiber recruitment* refers to the interaction between the muscles of the body and the central nervous system (CNS). For a muscle to move, the brain has to stimulate a nerve. When a physical activity is performed, motor neurons within the muscles contract to cause that movement. When more fat-free mass is created (as a result of resistance training), more nerve and muscle fibers must be recruited. As more motor units are recruited, and as the frequency of stimulus increases, greater levels of muscle tension occur (or the ability to create muscle tension is increased). The pattern of motor fiber unit recruitment also varies, depending on the inherent properties of specific motor neurons. Performing a variety of exercise for the same muscle group recruits the motor neurons in as many ways as possible. This ensures that the muscles do not stop responding to the exercise stimulus.

- *Adequate energy intake* is critical to both short- and long-term exercise and strength training success. Although this book does not include in-depth information on diet, energy consumption, and energy expenditure, this chapter addresses the body's energy systems and explains the role they play in programs and routines. Understanding nutrition and having a working knowledge of the body's energy systems will help you enhance your exercise performance; having adequate energy available for exercise is necessary to increase lean mass and lose body fat. If you want to be successful in fat loss and muscle gain, you have to eat the right foods.

Muscle endurance, by definition, is the ability to produce repeated muscle actions over and over without fatigue. Obviously, for this to occur repeatedly, the load or weight lifted must be light. However, increased strength and muscle hypertrophy will not occur if the weight is too light. Unfortunately, women often "lift light," performing too many repetitions with weights that do not create fatigue. This is the result of outdated beliefs that lifting light weights creates muscle tone as opposed to larger muscles. To see changes in your muscles, you need to lift weights that are heavy enough to induce a fatigue response, thus achieving overload. If you do not use loads heavy enough to feel local muscle fatigue after the set, you will not achieve the muscle definition you are seeking.

Calorie-Burning Energy for Exercise

We usually talk about *having* energy, as if it were something we either possess or don't. For example, we say, "I don't have a lot of energy today." But energy comes from very specific places in the body. It controls all of our thought processes, activities, and body movements. Burning energy is another way to talk about a desire to lose weight.

At rest, the body expends a lot of energy just to maintain the functions of cells that are essential for life. The continuous pumping of blood by the heart demands energy, as does the continuous movement of air into and out of the lungs. In addition, maintaining a life-supporting environment within and around cells requires constant energy production. This energy is used to form the molecules necessary for repairing cells, storing energy, fighting infections, and processing nutrients obtained from eating and digesting foods. These energy-demanding functions combine to form the body's basal metabolic rate (BMR), which can vary from 800 to 1,500 calories per day, depending on body size and total caloric intake.

The three energy pathways are the phosphagen system (ATP-PC), the glycolytic energy system (anaerobic glycolysis), and the aerobic energy system. As the fastest way to resynthesize ATP, the phosphagen system is the predominant energy source used for all-out exercise lasting up to about 10 seconds. This is the energy system you can feel when you perform an all-out sprint for a very short distance. Adenosine triphosphate (ATP) is the main molecule the body uses to perform cellular work in the phosphagen process. Exercise adds to the amount of calories the body burns, because muscle contractions require the repeated forming and breaking down of ATP. The energy released from the breakdown of ATP fuels the contraction of muscles, thereby adding to the energy demands of the body, and raising caloric expenditure.

During short-term, highly intense activities, the muscles need to produce a large amount of power, which results in a high demand for ATP. No carbohydrate or fat is used in this process. The regeneration of ATP comes solely from stored creatine phosphate (CP). Creatine phosphate is used to regenerate ADP back to ATP. This short-term energy process is crucial during quick burst of high-intensity movement. Because oxygen is not needed to resynthesize used ATP, the phosphagen process is considered anaerobic, or oxygen independent. A resting skeletal muscle fiber contains about six times as much creatine phosphate as ATP. But when a muscle fiber is undergoing a sustained contraction, these energy reserves are exhausted in about 15 seconds. Because a limited amount of stored CP and ATP is in skeletal muscles, fatigue occurs very rapidly. The muscle fiber must then rely on other mechanisms to convert ATP to ADP.

Glycolysis is the second energy system and the dominant one used for exercise that requires an all-out performance lasting from 30 seconds to about 2 minutes. This system is the second-fastest in resynthesizing ATP, or energy for muscle contractions. During glycolysis, carbohydrate—in the form of either blood glucose (sugar) or muscle glycogen (the stored form of glucose)—is broken down through a series of chemical reactions. Although only a little energy is produced through this pathway, the energy needed for powerful movement is available very quickly. However, when oxygen is not supplied fast enough to meet the muscles' needs, hydrogen ions (which cause the muscle pH to decrease, a condition called acidosis) and other metabolites accumulate causing a number of problems inside the muscles. A burning sensation occurs when exercise intensity inhibits the muscles' ability to pump enough blood to clear out the accumulated metabolites. As a result, muscles lose their ability to contract effectively, and muscle force production and exercise intensity decrease.

The third system, the aerobic system, or what is also called the oxygen system, is primarily engaged when exercising aerobically at low intensities (keep in mind that the definition of low-intensity exercise depends on the person). This system can continue indefinitely, assuming the body has enough glucose (sugar broken down from glycogen), fat, and oxygen. The main source of energy for this system is carbohydrate, which comes from muscle stores, the bloodstream, and fat stored all around the body.

The aerobic system requires oxygen. When you exercise at lower intensities, your body relies more on the production of glucose from amino acids, fat, and other noncarbohydrate substances (referred to as gluconeogenesis) and the production of energy from carbohydrate (called glycolysis) to meet the greater demand for energy (ATP, or adenosine triphosphate). When you are exercising just below the lactate threshold, you are using mostly carbohydrate. Exercising just below lactate threshold means that you are working at the point at which the exercise intensity is almost purely aerobic, but nearing the point at which it will become anaerobic and the body increases oxygen consumption and the muscles start to feel fatigued. Once the intensity of exercise has risen above the lactate threshold, you are using only carbohydrate as a fuel source. If you were to exercise long enough (over two hours), your muscle carbohydrate content and blood glucose concentration would become low. Because carbohydrate is the muscles' preferred fuel source, this metabolic state presents a threat to the survival of the muscles.

When carbohydrate is not available, the muscles are forced to rely on fat as fuel. However, although only a small amount of fat is used when exercising below the lactate threshold, the rate of caloric expenditure and the total number of calories expended are much greater than they are when exercising at a lower intensity, so the total amount of fat used is also greater. This is one of the reasons people believe that exercising in the lower intensity zones is best for burning fat. This is partly true. Yes, there is a larger reliance on fat for energy production. However, when it comes to weight loss, total caloric expenditure is more important than the amount of fat used. We will take at look at this fitness myth in more detail in chapter 2.

As you learned, the first two energy systems are of shorter duration, can be activated almost instantaneously, are very powerful, and require no oxygen. Examples of exercises performed using these two systems are plyometrics (jump exercises) and short-duration, high-intensity intervals of running, pushing, or pressing a weight load. The third system, the aerobic energy system, lasts longer, offering greater energy sources, but it takes more time to be activated and offers less power. This is the energy system that is primarily activated during long runs. It is important to understand that no single system works alone. All three systems are in play all the time regardless of the activity. However, the duration and intensity of the activity determines which system is being used primarily.

Sources of Energy in the Body

Understanding how energy is produced for physical activity (cardio workouts and strength training, specifically) is important when it comes to setting up and establishing an exercise program. Understanding how the energy systems work and when they kick in will help you work at the proper intensity and duration to meet your goals. Following are sample activities that target each energy system:

- The *ATC/PC energy system* can be trained by doing very fast sprints on the treadmill at quick speeds for 5 to 15 seconds with three to five minutes of rest between them. The longer rest periods allow for complete replenishment of creatine phosphate in the muscles so it can be reused for the next interval. Without the rest periods, performance in this energy system would be compromised.

- The *glycolytic energy system* can be trained using fast intervals lasting 30 seconds to 2 minutes with an active recovery period twice as long as the work period (1:2 work-to-rest ratio).

- The *aerobic energy system* can be trained with both continuous exercise and intervals. For example, treadmill running at an intensity that is manageable (i.e., not too uncomfortable, but you certainly know you are exercising) for 30 or more minutes uses the aerobic energy system.

Body Composition

The difference between being thin and being healthy lies in body composition. A "skinny fat" woman might be thin, but she has lots of body fat because she does not exercise and actively maintain her lean muscle mass. Regardless of your clothing size, having more lean mass than fat is important to good health. Lean mass is simply your muscles, bones, connective tissue, and organs—anything in your body that is not fat. Anything that is not lean falls into the fat category.

Your body does require a certain percentage of fat to function, but that's only a percent of your total body weight. To determine healthy body composition, consider your percentage of body fat in proportion to muscle mass. Understandably, many women measure their ideal weight with a scale. A scale will help you obtain an accurate measurement of your weight, but you do not know how much is lean mass and how much is fat. For years, insurance companies and medical professionals have used height versus weight (body mass index, or BMI) to determine levels of body fat and overall health in both men and women. However, BMI measures are not always suitably informative because they fail to determine whether a person is lean or fat. Neither scales nor BMI measurements differentiate between lean tissue (muscle, bones, internal organs, blood) and fat.

The ideal body fat level for most women is 18 to 22 percent. The average woman today, who is healthy and looks okay in her jeans, likely has about 25 percent body fat. A woman with 29 to 35 percent fat is considered "overfat" in body composition, and a woman with greater than 39 percent fat is considered obese. The ideal percentage of body fat will vary from one person to the next because body fat is determined by factors such as body type, heredity, age, activity level, and diet. A woman should not have more than 25 percent body fat if her general lifestyle involves adequate aerobic activity, proper nutrition, and strength training.

Given these limitations, a BMI chart still may be a good overall measure of whether you are in a healthy BMI category. A high body mass index on the chart indicates that you are overweight, but it doesn't determine whether that weight is fat or muscle—or where any extra fat is located. Extremely muscular people may fall into an overweight category simply because muscle weighs a lot. For people with BMIs between 25 and 35 (overweight to obese), a larger waist (more than 35 inches for women) adds risk factors for diseases on top of those associated with the BMI.

You can calculate your BMI by dividing your weight in pounds by your height in inches squared, and then multiplying this by 703. Once you figure your BMI, you can use the chart in figure 1.1 to find out which category you fall into. For example, if you were 5 feet, 7 inches tall (67 inches, or 170 cm) and weighed 220 pounds (100 kg), the calculation for your BMI would look like this:

$$220 / 4,489 \text{ (67 in.} \times \text{67 in.)} \times 703 = 34.45 \text{ (your BMI)}$$

Many measuring devices are available for monitoring where you rank and the progress you are making in losing body fat. Some body fat monitors use bioelectrical impedance analysis (BIA) technology, whereas others require skinfold calipers and a fitness professional to perform the assessment. The body fat monitors work by sending a low-level electrical signal through the body from two footpads on the scale or through a handheld device. The signal passes more quickly through muscle than through fat because of muscle's high water content. The monitor analyzes the readings from this signal with stored personal data (e.g., height, weight, gender, activity level). This information is converted to a body fat percentage in seconds.

FIGURE 1.1 Body mass index (BMI) calculator.

Body weight (pounds)

Height (inches) \ BMI	Normal						Overweight					Obese										Extreme Obesity														
BMI	19	20	21	22	23	24	25	26	27	28	29	30	31	32	33	34	35	36	37	38	39	40	41	42	43	44	45	46	47	48	49	50	51	52	53	54
58	91	96	100	105	110	115	119	124	129	134	138	143	148	153	158	162	167	172	177	181	186	191	196	201	205	210	215	220	224	229	234	239	244	248	253	258
59	94	99	104	109	114	119	124	128	133	138	143	148	153	158	163	168	173	178	183	188	193	198	203	208	212	217	222	227	232	237	242	247	252	257	262	267
60	97	102	107	112	118	123	128	133	138	143	148	153	158	163	168	174	179	184	189	194	199	204	209	215	220	225	230	235	240	245	250	255	261	266	271	276
61	100	106	111	116	122	127	132	137	143	148	153	158	164	169	174	180	185	190	195	201	206	211	217	222	227	232	238	243	248	254	259	264	269	275	280	285
62	104	109	115	120	126	131	136	142	147	153	158	164	169	175	180	186	191	196	202	207	213	218	224	229	235	240	246	251	256	262	267	273	278	284	289	295
63	107	113	118	124	130	135	141	146	152	158	163	169	175	180	186	191	197	203	208	214	220	225	231	237	242	248	254	259	265	270	278	282	287	293	299	304
64	110	116	122	128	134	140	145	151	157	163	169	174	180	186	192	197	204	209	215	221	227	232	238	244	250	256	262	267	273	279	285	291	296	302	308	314
65	114	120	126	132	138	144	150	156	162	168	174	180	186	192	198	204	210	216	222	228	234	240	246	252	258	264	270	276	282	288	294	300	306	312	318	324
66	118	124	130	136	142	148	155	161	167	173	179	186	192	198	204	210	216	223	229	235	241	247	253	260	266	272	278	284	291	297	303	309	315	322	328	334
67	121	127	134	140	146	153	159	166	172	178	185	191	198	204	211	217	223	230	236	242	249	255	261	268	274	280	287	293	299	306	312	319	325	331	338	344
68	125	131	138	144	151	158	164	171	177	184	190	197	203	210	216	223	230	236	243	249	256	262	269	276	282	289	295	302	308	315	322	328	335	341	348	354
69	128	135	142	149	155	162	169	176	182	189	196	203	209	216	223	230	236	243	250	257	263	270	277	284	291	297	304	311	318	324	331	338	345	351	358	365
70	132	139	146	153	160	167	174	181	188	195	202	209	216	222	229	236	243	250	257	264	271	278	285	292	299	306	313	320	327	334	341	348	355	362	369	376
71	136	143	150	157	165	172	179	186	193	200	208	215	222	229	236	243	250	257	265	272	279	286	293	301	308	315	322	329	338	343	351	358	365	372	379	386
72	140	147	154	162	169	177	184	191	199	206	213	221	228	235	242	250	258	265	272	279	287	294	302	309	316	324	331	338	346	353	361	368	375	383	390	397
73	144	151	159	166	174	182	189	197	204	212	219	227	235	242	250	257	265	272	280	288	295	302	310	318	325	333	340	348	355	363	371	378	386	393	401	408
74	148	155	163	171	179	186	194	202	210	218	225	233	241	249	256	264	272	280	287	295	303	311	319	326	334	342	350	358	365	373	381	389	396	404	412	420
75	152	160	168	176	184	192	200	208	216	224	232	240	248	256	264	272	279	287	295	303	311	319	327	335	343	351	359	367	375	383	391	399	407	415	423	431
76	156	164	172	180	189	197	205	213	221	230	238	246	254	263	271	279	287	295	304	312	320	328	336	344	353	361	369	377	385	394	402	410	418	426	435	443

Reprinted from U.S. Department of Health and Human Services, National Heart, Lung, and Blood Institute, 1998, *Clinical guidelines on the identification, evaluation, and treatment of overweight and obesity in adults: The evidence report.* [Online]. Available: www.nhlbi.nih.gov/guidelines/obesity/bmi_tbl.pdf [September 20, 2011].

The BIA device provides a good ballpark figure of where you stand in relation to body composition. The gold standard of body composition measurement is underwater weighing. This technique, although highly reliable, is often performed only in university lab settings and hospitals, so access is often a problem. Most personal trainers are able to measure a client's body fat using either skinfold calipers or a BIA device free of charge or for a nominal fee.

Although fat storage primarily depends on genetic factors, subcutaneous fat is responsible for the appearance of cellulite. Subcutaneous fat (i.e., under the skin) is the most visible and the most difficult to get rid of. Cosmetic companies have made millions of dollars promising women that their products will help reduce the appearance of cellulite. It is scientifically impossible to reduce cellulite with a lotion or a cream, however. There is no substitute for diet, exercise, and genetics.

Subcutaneous fat also plays an important role in health and safety. It serves as a cushion for the body as well as an energy storehouse for the aerobic energy system. Men generally store more subcutaneous fat around the abdominal area and in the calves, whereas women usually store this type of fat around the hips, buttocks, and thighs.

Visceral fat is the fat that surrounds the internal organs, mostly in the abdominal region, and is the reason so many people have large, protruding bellies. This is the really dangerous fat directly linked to diabetes, heart attacks, high blood pressure, stroke, and some cancers. Visceral fat is full of hormones and toxins, which, when released, go directly to the liver or into the bloodstream. The more visceral fat your body carries, the more likely you are to develop diseases or health conditions that can incapacitate or even kill you.

The good news is that although visceral fat is the easiest fat to put on, it's also the easiest to take off. Dieting alone won't rid your body of visceral fat, however, because it must be burned off through exercise. To keep off visceral fat, you must make adequate aerobic activity and resistance training part of your daily life. Weight loss diets accompanied by sufficient aerobic and muscle strengthening exercise may cause weight loss, but unless strength training is part of the exercise regimen, most of what is lost is lean muscle tissue and not stored fat.

Loss of muscle mass typically begins for women in their 30s or 40s and continues as they age. As the muscles atrophy, fat levels increase, which leads to a slowdown in metabolism and weight gain, even if caloric intake and expenditure remain the same. It's up to you to convince your body that your lean muscle tissue is too precious to sacrifice so that it will resort to burning fat for its fuel source. Weight training can reverse this process, putting back muscle (which uses more calories and takes up less room than fat) and diminishes fat stores. So even if you don't lose weight, by strengthening your muscles, you can lose inches and sizes. You can preserve your lean muscle tissue through resistance training, which creates strength and takes inches off your body through the combination of fat loss and muscle strengthening.

So many factors are important to muscle growth and development and ultimately reshaping or recomposing your body. With everything you need to keep in mind when developing a program for yourself, it's no wonder some women fail to incorporate some of the principles of a solid training program. Sometimes they lose sight of the most basic concepts responsible for increased muscle and fat loss. Being aware of your energy needs but also understanding how the body uses energy are key factors to increasing fat-free mass and getting what you want and need from your exercise experience.

KEYS TO MUSCLE GROWTH AND DEVELOPMENT

Clearly, changing your body composition is a complex task involving many body systems. Not only must you build more lean mass and decrease fat by lifting weights, but you must also understand the energy systems, muscles, and types of fat to create safe, effective, long-term strength training programs. Because muscle development is part of a progression of training principles, understanding and following the principles of strength training, which is covered in chapter 9, will guide you in developing your exercise program and help you determine which method of training will deliver the results you are looking for.

To achieve your fitness goals, you must make the right choices about exercise on a daily basis and assess your progress regularly. Later in the book we will look at several techniques for determining your current fitness level and creating short-term and long-term fitness goals. Balancing specificity, overload, intensity, and rest (described in the following sections) will help you achieve optimal muscle development as well as overall fitness. The appropriate combination will depend on your goals, your fitness level, and probably most important, your ability to follow a program consistently.

Specificity

Specificity dictates that to improve a particular component of fitness (examples include cardio, strength, flexibility), you have to address that component in your training program specifically. You need to determine your goals and then establish a method of training that will support them. For example, if you want to increase the strength and size of a particular muscle group, your strength training exercises must be site specific (not to be confused with spot reduction, which is addressed in chapter 2). If you desire a greater capacity for anaerobic power, you must specifically target that energy system in training. If you have want to lose fat, you must train specifically for this goal by performing at least six, one-hour exercise sessions weekly that focus on using the aerobic energy system. Power walks of 60 minutes or longer at a strong pace with intervals of short-duration jogging or striding would be appropriate for losing body fat. If you wanted to increase flexibility, you would need to stretch daily, particularly the muscles where you would like to see flexibility improvements.

Overload

Overload dictates that for any physiological system (e.g., heart, skeletal muscles, lungs) to improve its function, it must be exposed to a load that is greater than normal. If you are lifting loads that are about the same that you perform in your everyday life, you will not achieve overload, or any strength gains. For muscles to get bigger, stronger, and more defined, the loads must be great enough to cause physiological fatigue (within a predetermined amount of time) and require recovery.

Intensity

Intensity refers to how hard you work in the weight room and determines how effective you are at recruiting all of your muscle fibers. The greater the number of fibers you recruit, the greater the growth stimulus will be, assuming recovery is adequate. As discussed earlier, larger muscles are usually stronger than smaller ones because they tend to work harder. When you recruit more muscle fibers, you increase the strength and size of your muscles while also burning more total calories. This is because larger, stronger muscles are metabolically expensive— meaning that they cost your body a lot of calories to keep them in tip-top working order. Working at higher intensity levels should decrease fat and increase lean mass.

Rest

Most athletes know that getting enough rest after exercise is essential to high-level performance, but many still overtrain and feel guilty when they take a day off. Because the body repairs and strengthens itself in the time between workouts, continuous training can weaken even the strongest athletes. Rest days are critical to sport performance for a variety of reasons—some physiological and some psychological.

Rest is physically necessary so that the muscles can repair, rebuild, and strengthen. Sleep, a major function of rest, is critical for muscle strength and development. In general, one or two nights of little or poor sleep won't have much impact on performance, but consistently getting inadequate sleep can result in subtle changes in hormone levels, muscle recovery, and mood. The body performs most of its recovery while sleeping, which is why getting adequate amounts of sleep as well as building in rest days between workouts can maintain a healthy balance of home, work, and fitness goals. The amount of sleep you need depends on your personal history and your particular needs. Determine how many hours of sleep are best for you, and then aim to achieve them as frequently as possible.

Obviously, strength training does more than just change you aesthetically. It also affects your health and everyday functional capacity. You are in better physical condition when you incorporate a strength training routine into your daily life. Understanding the way fat affects your body and how to determine whether you are carrying too much fat offers a reference point from which you can set out to effect change. Determining your current health and fitness status and learning about the importance of recovery and the roles of intensity and specificity are crucial to designing an optimal exercise program, workout, or training schedule that you can adhere to, and that will deliver results.

Designing a program that adheres to all of these guidelines can be challenging. So, you can see why many athletes turn to coaches or trainers for help with the details so they can focus on the workouts. This book can serve the same function—providing programs that are safe and effective and taking the guesswork out of results-based training.

Myths and Pitfalls of Strength Training

Myths and misinformation about strength training for women never seem to disappear. You will hear that lifting weights will bulk you up like a linebacker. And then you will read an article that promises supermodel limbs in as little as 10 minutes a day. Hearsay, fitness fads, and offbeat diets often make up a significant portion of the information women have used over the years to try to achieve greater strength and muscle definition.

The fear that hulky muscles will result from lifting too heavy has been the belief for a long time now. However, the proper methods to achieve greater strength and muscle size come from research and properly applied exercise science techniques, not pop culture. Increased metabolism (when combined with cardio exercise), decreased body fat percentage, increased muscle definition, enhanced energy production, decreased risk of some serious health conditions, and enhanced personal confidence are just some of the benefits of strength training.

Strength training will not bulk you up; actually, if you do not lift loads that are heavy enough, you will not see any results at all. This chapter examines some of the misconceptions that keep many women from making strength training part of their regular fitness routines. It addresses the facts about lifting heavy, describes cardio training that is best for your fitness goals, and explains why muscle soreness is not a predictor of successful workouts. We will also take a look at excuses women often have about why they have flabby bellies and no "lower abs," and the misconceptions that surround these issues.

WOMEN'S FITNESS MYTHS

Before you begin your strength training program, you need to understand the facts about many aspects of exercise, including cardio training, flexibility, and to some extent, the role diet plays in helping you reach your fitness goals. It takes more than just lifting weights to own the ideal female physique—one that is strong, low in body fat, and high in lean mass, that provides muscle definition, and that functions well in everyday life. Some of the most common misconceptions, or myths, that women believe about exercise are covered here. The following answers to common questions provide simple, unbiased advice about exercise fads, fitness hype, magic bullets, and false promises, as well as information that every female exerciser should know.

IF I WANT TO LOSE WEIGHT AND TONE UP, SHOULD I BE DOING MORE WEIGHTS OR MORE CARDIO?

Cardiorespiratory exercise that promotes adequate caloric expenditure is necessary for fat loss, weight management, and overall fitness. But myths about aerobic exercise and energy expenditure abound, as do those about strength training. You probably already know that to lose weight you need to address both diet and exercise. Exercise must include both cardio and strength training. Many women believe that only cardio exercise is needed to lose weight, but nothing could be further from the truth.

We will go into detail about the value of strength training for weight loss throughout this book, but let me say here that cardio exercise is a vital component to any strength training program and weight loss effort. The reason is that it ups the ante on caloric expenditure and improves the health of your heart, blood vessels, brain tissues, and other vital organs. Significant amounts of scientific evidence clearly show that cardio exercise (as well as strength training) can help prevent and manage hypertension, coronary heart disease, stroke, type 2 diabetes, osteoporosis, arthritis, stress, colon cancer, abnormal cholesterol levels, and depression (Hillman et al. 2008).

HOW DO I KNOW WHEN I AM IN THE FAT-BURNING ZONE?

Perhaps the most popular myth about aerobic exercise is that there is a specific heart rate range in which you must exercise to burn fat as the primary fuel source. *Target heart rate* has become a buzz phrase. Many cardio machines even display a fat-burning zone on their panels, encouraging people to exercise in a specific heart rate range to burn fat specifically. Because more fat is used at lower exercise intensities, many people assume that low-intensity exercise is best for burning fat.

The truth is that we use both fat and carbohydrate (as well as some protein) for energy during exercise. These fuels provide energy as the body needs it, sort of on a sliding scale. During exercise at very low intensities (e.g., walking at a moderate pace), fat accounts for most of the energy being used. As exercise intensity increases, the contribution from fat decreases, and the contribution from carbohydrate and protein increases. What matters here, however, is the rate of energy expenditure. Where the calories come from is really not the point. When exercising at higher intensities (i.e., closer to the lactate threshold), you are burning more total calories from all energy sources. For fat and weight loss, what matters most is the difference between the number of calories you expend and the number of calories you consume. For the purpose of losing weight, it matters little whether the calories burned during exercise come from fat or carbohydrate. Fat and weight loss is really all about burning lots of calories and cutting back on the number of calories consumed.

CAN I STRENGTH TRAIN TO GET RID OF MY BELLY FAT OR TIGHTEN MY UPPER ARMS?

Ask any woman what her "trouble" spots are, and she will probably give you a list of all the well-known areas women like to approach through exercise, including

Selecting Appropriate Cardio Exercises

Including enough cardio exercise in your program is a big part of the equation, although selecting the right type is equally important. Many choices exist. The key is to work smarter, not longer, and in this case, smarter means harder.

You can easily increase your exercise intensity performing cardio exercise. All you have to do is make small changes to your regular cardio routine (this, of course, is assuming that you are currently performing a cardio routine). For example, you can increase the speed at which you walk or run, add hills for more intensity, or change your normal routine by trying the treadmill over the recumbent bike or getting on the elliptical trainer instead of walking. You might even try short sprints during your outside jogs or runs, simply to increase the caloric expenditure.

I understand that some women are leery about performing high-impact cardio exercises to increase caloric expenditure. *High impact* refers to the amount of jarring your body might experience performing certain cardio exercises such as jumping or running. It is undeniable that high-impact exercise burns more calories than low-impact exercises such as walking or cycling, but keep in mind that it is not necessary to perform high-impact exercise over and over for minutes on end. Try adding three 1-minute jump rope sequences during your 30-minute walk. Or run for 30 to 45 seconds on the treadmill three or four times during a 30- or 45-minute walking session. I am not saying that you shouldn't bother with low-impact exercise; I am just encouraging you to include both types of cardio exercise into your existing routine. Doing both offers caloric burning within a balanced program.

glutes, thighs, waist, belly, and upper arms. Spot reduction is the mythical belief that fat can be lost in specific areas or muscle groups. However, fat is lost throughout the body in a pattern dependent on genetics, gender, hormones, and age. Overall body fat must be reduced to lose fat in any particular area. Although fat is lost or gained throughout the body, it seems that the first areas to get fat or the last areas to become lean are the abdominals, hips, and thighs. But, although you cannot spot reduce, you can spot train, meaning that you can strengthen a specific muscle group through aerobic activity and resistance training.

IF I LIFT TOO HEAVY OF A WEIGHT, WILL I GET BULKY MUSCLES?

Contrary to many women's concerns, strength training using heavy weights won't result in large, bodybuilder-type physiques. However, some women still fear that it will bulk them up in unfeminine ways. Women who strive to become competitive bodybuilders work out for several hours a day using a variety of exercise techniques, and a large percentage of their training combines very heavy weight loads. Some women also take hormones and steroids to increase their muscle mass.

Muscle strength is improved primarily by increasing muscle size (hypertrophy) and the number of muscle fibers recruited. Muscles experience hypertrophy when the muscle fibers increase in size. Increases in muscle size are highly dependent on diet, genetics, muscle fiber types, and the kind of training performed.

Circulating hormones such as testosterone play a large role in the development of large muscles. Men have between 20 and 30 times more circulating testosterone than women, and it is for this reason, as well as the fact that men have more numerous and larger muscle fibers, that men can develop much bigger muscles than women. Keep in mind that genetics and individual differences play a role in the rate and degree to which muscles mass increases in either gender. Men and women who train similarly can increase their muscle strength, but because women have lower levels of testosterone and fewer and smaller muscle fibers than men do, they cannot increase muscle size the way men can.

CAN SUPPLEMENTS HELP ME GET STRONGER OR LEANER, DEVELOP MORE TONE, OR LOSE WEIGHT?

Millions of people rely on dietary supplements for everything from enhancing their sex lives to improving their athletic performances. There is essentially no systematic regulation of the dietary supplement industry, so there is no guarantee that any supplement will live up to its claims. More important, there is no guarantee that any supplement is safe. Some dietary supplements are probably safe and effective if consumed according to the manufacturers' instructions. An example is the traditional use of vitamin and mineral supplements. Although the recommended doses can improve a deficiency resulting from a poor diet, megadoses can have toxic effects. Because dietary supplements are not regulated by the U.S. Food and Drug Administration (FDA), there is no guarantee that what is stated on the label is actually in the supplement.

WILL CERTAIN TYPES OF CARDIO HELP ME BURN MORE CALORIES?

The type of exercise you select will determine the amount of energy you expend and, thus, how many total calories you burn. Many exercise modalities are marketed to women with the claim that they burn more calories, and the fitness consumer is left to wonder just what determines the number of calories burned during exercise. Just because you may sweat more in a particular workout (e.g., a cycle class or a hot yoga class) doesn't necessarily mean that you are burning more calories. Additionally, acute bouts of exercise do not burn a huge number of calories. It is the consistency of the exercise that results in weight loss.

Understanding what determines how many calories your body burns during exercise and why your body obeys certain rules that dictate the magnitude of caloric expenditure is important when selecting exercises. With this knowledge you can create realistic goals for yourself with respect to fat loss and increased lean mass. In addition, you will be in a better position to discern the truth regarding many of the advertising claims that suggest that a particular exercise modality is best for caloric expenditure and weight loss. The fact is, the more you exercise, the more fit you will become. You will burn more total calories walking briskly or running 5 miles (8 km) than you will just 1 mile (1.6 km). So instead of burning 100 calories for 1 mile, you burn about 500, and that's a lot more calories burned than if you had stayed on the couch. Bottom line: the harder you work, the more calories you expend, and you have to do this on a regular (ideally, daily) basis.

PITFALLS OF STRENGTH TRAINING

Beginning a strength training program can be a confusing endeavor for many women to take on. The following sections address a few of the most common strength training pitfalls and how you can overcome or avoid them.

Diminished Return

Muscles adapt to stress quickly and adjust to a particular workout within six to eight workouts. This concept is referred to as the principle of diminished returns—an economics term that can be applied to exercise and, for our purposes, strength training in particular. Diminished returns refer to the fact that expected outcomes begin to decrease despite an increase in labor or effort. Eventually, muscles become very efficient at a particular exercise; they learn to perform the movements using less energy and less stress, making the routine less effective. This is why changing the exercises, even for the same muscle group, every few workouts is important to consider when developing a long-term workout routine. This is also why so many options exist for each muscle group and why periodization techniques are so important.

Muscle Soreness and Fatigue

As discussed in chapter 1, the muscle pain experienced after intense workouts, called delayed onset muscle soreness (DOMS), is the result of the intense loads placed on the muscles. Two types of soreness occur from lifting weights: one that is felt during the immediate experience of intense exercise, and one that is felt a few days afterward. The likelihood of experiencing DOMS is high if strength training is new for you, you have not worked out in a while, or the weights (or loads) and movement patterns are new to your body. Immediate muscle fatigue, the fatigue felt when performing a powerful or maximal effort that lasts about 30 seconds to 3 minutes, is related to metabolite accumulation. The presence of metabolites (e.g., hydrogen and lactic acid) keeps the muscle cell from contracting. The produced excess metabolites are removed rather quickly when the exercise session is completed. The excess is metabolized in the muscle cells where it was produced during exercise, and the metabolites that are not cleared by the muscle cells are carried to the liver for metabolization.

New exercisers should not be alarmed by DOMS as it is often a response to intense exercise. When DOMS occurs, the muscles recover and increase in size, leading to greater stamina. However, the acute, sudden, and sharp pain of injuries such as a muscle strain or sprain is not to be confused with the aches from DOMS. These injuries can often cause swelling or bruising. DOMS is always the most painful two days following new, intense exercise, and the soreness will subside over the next few days. It is important to allow adequate recovery between workouts, particularly if your workout was intense enough to cause DOMS. Recovery is critical to increased muscle mass and improved strength.

It is okay to exercise a muscle group (e.g., perform cardio or endurance and flexibility exercises such as yoga or Pilates) when you are experiencing DOMS. However, do not lift heavy or intense loads when experiencing DOMS. Allow for recovery, and then resume exercises for that particular muscle group once soreness subsides.

Risk of Injury

Exercise of all types can place extraordinary demands on your body. When strength training, in particular, lifting too heavy or choosing inappropriate exercises for your current level of fitness may place you at risk for certain injuries. Injuries may be an issue in even the most conscientious exercisers and can manifest in many places including the feet, knees, shins, hips, shoulders, and low back. A good rule of thumb is to attend to all injuries quickly. Don't avoid dealing with an injury because you don't want to admit you have one, or you believe that if you admit to the injury, you will not be able to continue your training. Modifications are required when injuries occur.

Use the following guidelines for general injury prevention during exercise:

- Warm up appropriately for the exercise you will be engaging in.
- Cool down until the body has reached its preexercise state, and include stretches for improved flexibility.
- Wear adequate footwear that is appropriate for your activity (see the sidebar Selecting the Proper Footwear for more information).
- Do not increase the pace, intensity, or duration of your training program too quickly. Follow the 10 percent rule: When beginning a new activity, start gradually and increase by no more than 10 percent per week.
- Be sure to have enough glucose available to your working muscles. At least two hours preexercise, eat a meal or snack that contains both carbohydrate and protein.

Selecting the Proper Footwear

Strength training puts extra stress on your feet, so be sure to wear a shoe that provides support and traction and is comfortable. Professional weightlifters are not allowed to compete without the proper shoes. Although special weightlifting shoes are not necessary for the average exerciser, footwear does matter. You want to wear the best shoe for your specific activity. Therefore, consider your foot size, shape, arch, and other details about how you land on your foot when you walk, jump, or run. If you will be wearing these shoes for your run as well as your strength training sessions, make sure they are comfortable and supportive for both activities.

Before purchasing shoes, try them on in the store and walk around in them. If they do not feel completely comfortable right then and there, they are not right for you. Try shoes on late in the day. Your foot is smaller and tighter in the morning than it is after a day of walking, and you do not want to end up with a shoe that is too small. Also, make sure you take the socks you will wear when you exercise to the store with you. The right fit must take sock size into account.

It is also helpful to know a few terms related to feet and shoes no matter what your choice of exercise. Pronation describes the movement of the ankle. A neutral foot strike means that the heel and ball land evenly, with no rotation of the ankle. Overpronators (i.e., those with flat or fallen arches) tend to roll the ankle too far inward. Underpronators (i.e., those with high arches and stiff feet) don't have enough flexion in their stride. Ankle and arch issues permeate all sports, so have an expert watch you as you walk and, if possible, your running stride.

If you have high arches, investigate cushioning shoes. These shoes are built on a curved last, with padding in the heel or under the ball of the foot (or both places) to encourage a rolling motion through the heel strike to the ball push-off. If you are a neutral strider, you can find excellent shoes offering a middle level of cushioning, motion control, and stability that will encourage an efficient running motion without providing too much extra support. Stability shoes are lighter than motion-control runners, but a little heavier than cushioning runners.

Whatever you choose, make comfort the ultimate factor in your final decision, and be sure to change your shoes every six weeks or so. Shoes' natural cushioning and support break down in about six weeks. Even though a shoe may look as though it is in good condition, the supportive structures that are so crucial to protection are diminished. Make a regular investment in your athletic footwear and keep your shoes up to the task.

- Drink plenty of water before, during, and after exercise.
- Listen to your body and take a break from exercise if you need one.

In addition, always visit a health care provider if pain persists for more than 10 days, there is bleeding or severe bruising, you suspect a sprain or a broken bone, dizziness or light-headedness upon standing persists and seems unusual to you, or you experience any other symptom that seems unusual to your normal state of wellness.

Body Image

Your body image is the conception or picture that you have of your own body. We are not born with a body image. The way we feel about how we look is learned and influenced by family, friends, and the media. It is also influenced either positively or negatively by our race and gender and the culture in which we are raised. Research by the American College of Sports Medicine (2007) has shown that a negative body image is linked to serious health and emotional problems. People with poor body image are more likely than those with good body image to experience depression, disordered eating, and anxiety disorders. They are also more likely to go to unhealthy lengths to change their bodies and appearance.

With respect to exercise and strength training specifically, it is critical to recognize and accept your body type. Genetics and other lifestyle factors play huge roles in how you will respond to strength training, even more than the training techniques you use. Let's take a look at the following somatotypes, which are categories that are based purely on genetic body types:

- *Endomorph*—a softer, rounder body with a high percentages of body fat
- *Mesomorph*—a muscular physique with an athletic build
- *Ectomorph*—a slender, lean physique with low levels of body fat

Do any of these somatotypes fit your body type? If you have difficulty figuring out which one describes you, think about the type of body you had as a child or a teen. That image will be reflective of your genetic body type. Identifying your type does not mean that you cannot make changes to your levels of body fat or fat-free mass. It simply will help you understand why you may respond to exercise differently from the way a friend or family member responds. If you ignore the facts about your body type, you may find yourself trying to make changes to your body that are unrealistic or even impossible. Whatever your body type is, never allow it to become a reason to avoid exercise.

The following tips will help ensure that you are on the right path toward establishing and maintaining a positive body image with respect to exercise:

- Care for and value your body at all times.
- Dress in a way that makes you feel good right now.
- Exercise boosts self-esteem, so make sure to engage in daily exercise.
- Look in the mirror without judging yourself.
- Set your goals in terms of achieving physical health and emotional well-being rather than obsessing about your physical appearance.

If you match your exercise expectations with your genetics, you will likely enjoy the exercise and its benefits much more.

Female Athlete Triad

Most women have concerns about the size and shape of their bodies, but those who engage in extreme levels of exercise are at risk for developing a health crisis known as the female athlete triad.

Women who develop the triad have certain risk factors that set them apart from other exercising females. Identified almost 25 years ago, the triad initially consisted of disordered eating, amenorrhea, and osteoporosis. Women could have one, two, or all three components of the triad. Today, the triad is defined by energy deficiency associated with disordered eating and the development of menstrual disturbances. Both energy deficiency and low levels of the hormone estrogen are associated with amenorrhea, and also play a role in bone loss (i.e., osteopenia).

Each component of the triad exists on a continuum of severity, from healthy to more severe and even disease. Many female athletes do not demonstrate extreme ends of the continuum, but rather, show signs of one or more of the conditions, which progress along the three continuums. This can occur at different rates, meaning that a female can have one, two, or all three components of the triad at varying degrees. Although one condition may occur independent of the other two, it is more likely that a woman experiencing one component of the triad is also experiencing the others.

Common signs that a female fitness enthusiast or athlete may be suffering from one or more components of the triad include the following:

- Having irregular or absent menstrual cycles
- Always feeling tired and fatigued
- Having problems sleeping
- Experiencing stress fractures and frequent or recurrent injuries
- Often restricting food intake
- Constantly striving to be thin
- Eating less than needed to improve performance or physical appearance
- Having cold hands and feet

If you experience irregular menstrual cycles, increased stress, stress fractures, or severely restrictive eating patterns, it is important that you visit your physician and inquire about testing and treatment. Keep in mind that even moderate restrictions of food intake (with or without weight loss) or subtle irregular menstruation cycle changes can be early indicators of the progression to serious complications. The bottom line is to pay attention to any changes in your menstrual cycle and to be mindful of the fact that female exercisers need adequate caloric intake, recovery periods, and regular physical exams by a qualified health care provider.

As more and more women become interested in strength training, it is crucial that they be able to discern truth from the fiction concerning female strength training. Because strength training offers so many health and fitness benefits, it is a solid choice to begin to implement regularly. Although many women believe strength training is only for males, this isn't the case at all. If anything, strength training is more important for women because it provides a maximum opportunity to maintain weight control while also conferring many other long-term benefits.

CHAPTER 3

Essentials of Excellent Strength Training

Good posture is extremely important to your overall fitness, health, and well-being. Although many people are aware of the importance of good posture, it is still one of the most neglected aspects of health. Poor posture is a common cause of improper lifting techniques and can lead to poor breathing techniques, decreased self-esteem, and a heavier or overfat appearance, as well as being a potential cause of injury during strength training. By developing a keener awareness of your posture, you can identify areas of your body that need increased strength and flexibility. Additionally, choosing the right strength training equipment will promote muscle balance and increase your overall physical function.

This chapter examines the essentials of excellent strength training by looking closely at chronic poor posture and how it affects you, as well as techniques you can use to improve your posture. It also outlines strength training equipment and exercise options and helps you choose exercises based on your goals and the equipment available to you.

ESTABLISHING CORRECT POSTURE

Have you ever noticed the distinct posture of a gymnast, a dancer, or a person who sits at a desk all day? For example, one can usually identify a gymnast by the particular way they stand, walk, or carry themselves. A gymnast is an athlete who needs to assume a totally different posture to be able to compete well. The reason for this severely arched lower back (a spinal deviation known as lordosis) results from the "hand-based" orientation of her particular athletic activities. The severely arched lower back is part of the sport's proper form. But, constant training in this posture leads to the same posture in the daily course of her life, which is frequently a cause for serious injuries in the knee, shoulder, neck and lower back. Although the posture of a dancer or someone who sits all day may have different spinal misalignments, the end result is the same—poor daily posture and often pain and injury as a consequence. Poor postures are reflections of deviations in the spine and muscles, and can be seen to a certain extent in most all men and women in Western cultures. Therefore, arming yourself with knowledge about posture makes it possible to correct poor posture and increase core strength through strength training.

Exercise is best performed when the joints are aligned and the spine is in its most natural and ideal position. Your posture affects everything you do in your daily life—sitting, standing, or moving on your feet all day can do a number on your back. Gravity is pulling you down all the time! As you get tired, your body responds by tightening up; muscles and other soft tissues compress, and your posture must compensate to keep you upright and functional. Poor posture and improper body alignment strain your joints and can lead to headaches, neck and shoulder tension, sciatica, and hip and knee pain, as well as decreased self-esteem. When the body is out of proper alignment, it puts stress on the joints and spine. Whether you are lifting weights or just walking the dog, proper posture and alignment is imperative to counteract the constant force of gravity on the body, reduce stress on the spine and low back, and ensure that the joints are working effectively.

The most common indications of improper posture are a forward head tilt, rounded shoulders (also known as kyphosis), a protruding abdomen, excessive curve in the low back (lordosis), and hyperextended knees. Most women have a natural tendency toward muscle imbalance, with certain muscles being prone to shortening and others to lengthening and weakness. For example, some women tend to hunch forward at the shoulders, due to either a lack of flexibility in the shoulders and chest or a lack of strength. Exercises that strengthen the muscles of the midback and chest, as well as opening up the shoulders, will go a long way in improving posture and correcting imbalances. Good posture also lends itself to the appearance of looking more muscularly balanced between the upper and lower body, and can even create the illusion of weight loss.

Posture can be improved with self-awareness, increased core strength, and overall total-body strength training. This means that the right strength training exercises and properly applied training techniques can result in fewer backaches, a decreased risk of injuries, a stronger midsection and core musculature, and increased self-esteem that is directly or indirectly the result of improved posture.

The best way to know what is going on in your body is to become your own postural specialist. Knowing your posture profile is the first step to making the necessary changes in your body alignment. The correct way to stand is with all of the body's segments stacked, from head to shoulders to hips, knees, and feet. To assess your posture easily and reliably, you can either take a look your body in a mirror from a side view or grab a friend and take the plumb line test to see where you stack up. For the plumb line test, create a plumb, or straight, line (e.g., tie a key ring to a piece of string and hang it from inside a doorjamb). When you stand next to it sideways, the center of your ear, shoulder, hip, knee, and ankle should be in a straight line (see figure 3.1).

Postural imbalances indicate that certain muscles are doing most of the work when you move. If your posture is not tall and correct according to the natural curves in your spine (referred to as neutral spine), overpowering muscles kick in and start working for the weak ones. This is called muscle compensation and may be why you might feel your neck hurting during certain back or abdominal exercises. If this happens to you as you perform any of the strength exercises prescribed in this book, stop and correct your form and posture. For example, use a lighter weight or even do a different exercise that puts you in a better postural position. If you fail to make these postural changes during the exercises, you could be making your postural problems worse!

FIGURE 3.1   Proper posture and alignment using the plumb line test.

To adopt the correct working positions during exercise, you should understand neutral spine and how to find it in your body. To find your neutral spine, lie on your back with your knees bent and your arms resting down by your sides. Move your pelvis into a posterior pelvic tilt by pressing your back into the floor (see figure 3.2a) and then into an anterior pelvic tilt by arching your low back off the floor (see figure 3.2b). The place where your low back feels neutral, as shown in figure 3.4, is somewhere between the exaggerated positions of the anterior and posterior pelvic tilts.

FIGURE 3.2   Moving your pelvis into exaggerated (a) posterior and (b) anterior tilt.

Wall Test for Improved Posture

Both good and poor posture develop from habits of repeated movements, so getting into the routine of performing a simple self-exam to assess your spine will help you greatly improve and correct poor posture. To figure out what postural compensations you may be making, try this postural self-exam.

1. Stand with your back against a wall and your feet about 4 inches (10 cm) away. Check that your shoulder blades and buttocks are both touching the wall (see figure 3.3a).

2. Now pull your head back to touch the wall and level your chin with the floor. Pull your shoulder blades toward each other and flatten them on the wall. Press your arms to the wall with your thumbs pointing forward, pinky fingers touching the wall, and reach your fingertips toward the floor (see figure 3.3b).

3. Pull your belly button in and check that there is a space about two fingers wide between your low back and the wall. Make sure your knees are not locked out and your feet are pointing forward and are directly under your hips (see figure 3.3c).

4. Stand as tall and still as you possibly can and breathe there for about one minute. Have a mirror in front of you or have a friend watch that you are not moving, just breathing.

5. After standing as tall as you can, step away from the wall and relax.

Do you feel taller? What part of that was hard? Pulling your head back? Pulling your shoulders back? Creating a space between the wall and your low back, or maybe pulling your belly in enough to make that space smaller? Keeping your knees from locking? Or keeping your feet straight with toes pointing forward? Where you had the hardest time holding yourself straight is where your postural weakness is, or will be in the future unless you correct it now.

FIGURE 3.3   The wall test.

FIGURE 3.4 Your neutral spine is generally somewhere between the exaggerated pelvic tilt positions.

Posture plays a huge role in accessing the muscles that form the core musculature; correct posture and core strength work hand in hand. If your core is weak, you will have difficulty maintaining ideal spinal alignment. If you're following the current trends in exercise and fitness, you've probably heard the phrase *core strength*, which many confuse with "abs." The terms *core* and *core strength* refer to the muscles of your abdominal wall and back, and their ability to support your spine and keep your body stable and balanced. The core muscles also play a major role in maintaining the length of the torso and the upright posture of the spinal column. But, both the abdominal muscles and the back muscles work together to improve posture and core stabilization. Core exercises strengthen the front and back of the torso, offering strength and support for the spine as well as improving posture.

USING PROPER LIFTING TECHNIQUES

In part II, Strength Training Exercises for Women, each exercise is described in a way that makes it as safe and effective as possible. Remember, though, that you can always make modifications to accommodate your current fitness level, preexisting injuries, muscle compensations within a range of motion, or other biomechanical limitations. But, overall, proper body positioning, along with correct posture as we discussed in the previous section, will be the important consideration with all of the exercises. To highlight this a little further, let's take a look at the proper body positioning for standing exercises.

- Stand with your feet parallel, hip-width apart. Hip-width apart is also referred to as ASIS (anterior superior iliac spine) joint apart. The ASIS joints are the bony prominences located on your pelvis at the top of the hip area. To find these, palpate the area until you locate the hip bones and then place your hands or fingers on them. The line that you could draw between those two hip bones should be level. See figure 3.5a for an example of this location.

- While standing with your feet hip-width apart, check to see that your body weight is evenly distributed between both feet. Feel your weight on the balls, heels, and outer edges of your feet. Stand so that you could lift up easily through the arches.

- Use your hands to once again palpate the ASIS joints by placing your little fingers on the hip bones and your thumbs on the bottom of your rib cage (see figure 3.5b). This test can help you make sure your rib cage is stacked directly

FIGURE 3.5 Proper body position for standing lifts.

on top of your hips, and that your pelvis is in neutral, not tilted backward in posterior pelvic tilt or forward in anterior pelvic tilt.

- Lift your chest and separate your rib cage from your pelvis by drawing in your abdominal muscles and drawing in and sliding your shoulder blades down your back. Center your head right on top of your spinal column and flush with the ceiling, and set your chin level with the floor.

Lifting in front of a mirror, as shown in figure 3.6, is a good way to determine that your alignment and form are correct while performing the exercises. Although some of the established Olympic-style lifts adhere to strict lifting protocols, there is no perfect lifting technique for any of the strength exercises described in this book. People move differently, have different goals and different anatomical structures, and need to respect their bodies accordingly. However, you should adhere to specific body positions to create the safest lifting environment possible. This is why I encourage proper lifting techniques using proper posture. Using proper lifting techniques can contribute to a stronger core and better overall posture with a decreased risk of injury.

Finally, you should keep a few basic body positioning cues in mind overall—not just for standing exercises, but also for exercises performed while seated or lying down. The following tips will help you get into the correct positions while performing the exercises in this book. Use your knowledge of neutral spine and the guidelines offered when selecting and executing exercises.

- Use back support to remind you to sit and stand tall when exercising. When you lie on a weight bench, use the flat surface to set your posture before you

FIGURE 3.6 Lifting in front of a mirror can help you ensure that your alignment and posture are correct.

lift the weight. When you are performing standing strength exercises, try using a wall, if possible, to correct your posture and keep you in perfect form. When you perform seated exercises, use a bench with back support while you are training to keep your spine tall and erect and to remind you to always maintain proper posture.

- Stand tall and relax your shoulders during your lifts so they don't hunch up by your ears. Try not to allow your shoulder blades to creep up to your ears. When this happens, the trapezius muscles are usually forced to work too hard. This takes away from the stress, or stimulus, to the muscle group that you are performing the exercise for.

- Don't rock your body back and forth to help you move the weights up and down. Although momentum may help you move more weight, the rocking motion places additional stress on joints and the low back and may increase your risk for overuse injuries.

- Don't arch your back or hunch through your back when performing any of the exercises or lifts. Again, the spine comes out of neutral alignment when doing this, which can add to your risk of injury.

- Keep your wrists in neutral alignment, extended from the forearm, not broken or flexed. When you flex at the wrist when lifting a weight, for example, you place stress in the wrist joint that can cause injuries.

- Keep your abdominal muscles pulled in and your rib cage separated from the hips. This is important in maintaining neutral spine during exercises.

- Breathe through the exercises. Maintain a constant, continuous breathing rate. Exhaling on the exertion will actually increase intrathoracic pressure that can help you get through the hard part of the lift or movement pattern by increasing the strength effort coming from your core.

- And finally, in every strength exercise or activity that you do, always check that your spine is tall, your ears are in line with your shoulders, your abs are lifted, your chest is open, your shoulders are pulled away from your ears, and your shoulder blades are pulled toward each other in scapular retraction. The more you practice correct posture, the more you will notice your posture changing in the rest of your life.

Strength Training and Breathing Techniques

Breathing during strength training is an important principle and should be a focus during your workouts. You can use breathing to control the speed of your movements, as well as to lift safely.

Holding your breath during intense exercise can cause your blood pressure to spike. This can be very dangerous, especially if you already have high blood pressure (many people don't realize that they do). Holding your breath can also result in ruptured blood vessels, particularly in the retina of the eye. It can also cause you to pass out. For this reason, be aware of your breathing patterns during exercise. When strength training, breathing properly involves inhaling and exhaling, depending on where the hardest part of the exercise is. As a general rule, exhale on the contraction and inhale on the return. For example, when performing a biceps curl with an EZ Bar, exhale as you curl the bar toward your body, and then inhale as you stretch your arm out, returning the bar to the starting position.

Establishing a rhythm during your weight training routine will also help you perform at the correct tempo. Use your breathing to dictate the speed at which you move during each exercise. For example, if it takes you three seconds to exhale during the hardest part of the lift, that is how long it should take you to perform that portion of the lift. Some exercises will go a little faster than others when using this method, but you will always be performing the lifts at the correct speed if you can match the movement speed to your rate of breathing—both inhalations and exhalations.

Another benefit of using your breath during strength training is that it increases intra-abdominal pressure. One muscle that engages when breathing properly is the transversus abdominis. This muscle contracts when you exhale. Try it—notice how as you exhale, your abdominal wall contracts and then acts to solidify the muscles of the core, which in turn helps to support the spine. Power lifters and other advanced strength trainers intentionally hold their breath during very heavy lifts to increase intra-abdominal pressure. I do not recommend that you hold your breath during strength training. Make sure you are breathing during your exercises, and try to use the breath to help you perform the lifts. Try to keep this rhythm throughout every set. In the beginning, it will take some concentration, but after a while, it will become a habit.

KNOWING THE TYPES OF STRENGTH TRAINING EXERCISES

You have most likely heard the terms *open-chain exercises* and *closed-chain exercises*, but perhaps you have never understood what these terms mean or the difference between the two. First of all, a kinetic chain is a chain of joints exercised together. For example, the hip, knee, and ankle joints, when performing a particular exercise all together, make up the lower-extremity kinetic chain. Likewise, when the shoulders, elbows, and wrists all work together along with the spine to perform an exercise, this is an example of a movement in the upper-extremity kinetic chain. There are benefits to doing both open- and closed-chain exercises. The following information will help you understand the differences and the pros and cons of each type of exercise.

Closed-Chain Exercises

The chain referred to is the kinetic chain, which simply means that all your bones and muscles are connected in a chain; therefore, the movements you make are also part of that kinetic chain. You perform closed-chain exercises on a daily basis, because they are a natural part of daily life. Another term for closed-chain exercise could be functional exercise.

During closed-chain exercises, your hands or feet are in a constant, fixed position (usually on the ground) during the exercise. Closed-chain exercises work multiple joints and multiple muscle groups at once. For example, a squat involves the knee, hip, and ankle joints as well as multiple muscle groups (quadriceps, hamstrings, hip flexors, calves, and gluteal muscles). This is great because most of the movements that occur in daily life happen using large muscle groups in multijoint patterns. Using more muscles at once expends more calories and increases overall strength and endurance. Closed-chain exercises can be done with body weight alone, with added weight (in the form of free weights, medicine balls, kettlebells, or other external resistance), or with the use of a TRX Suspension Trainer. Examples of closed-chain exercises are push-ups, squats, plank poses, and lunges, all of which can be done with or without added weight.

Again, closed-chain exercises are very functional, meaning they have the potential to mimic activities of daily living. Very few movements in daily life or in athletics isolate joints and muscles the way open-chain exercises do. (Open-chain exercises occur in isolation from other muscles or joints in the body.) The downside of closed-chain exercises is that many are too challenging for beginning or novice exercisers because they require a certain amount of both body and postural awareness. This is why open-chain exercises may be helpful in improving strength in isolated muscle groups or when just starting strength training. For example, performing an exercise on a machine that isolates the chest muscles may bring more awareness and focus to them. There would be no need to support your own body because the machine does that for you. If you are a novice exerciser, you might need this type of support and feedback before attempting to perform more complex movements that do not offer any support or assistance, such as a flat-bench chest press using a barbell or dumbbells. The chest press requires more body awareness and strength than a chest machine does.

Open-Chain Exercises

Simply stated, exercises in the open kinetic chain involve the body being supported while the hands or feet are free to move during the exercise (as in a chest fly or a leg curl on a machine). Your body is supported by a piece of equipment so that you do not have to stabilize yourself or work to support your body weight during the exercise. You also have to overcome a fixed resistance when performing open-chain exercise. On a leg press machine, you have to overcome the resistance selected to get the machine to move and correspondingly increase strength in the targeted muscle or muscle group. These types of exercise machines facilitate movements that tend to isolate a single muscle group or a single joint. For example, the one joint involved during a leg extension is the knee; this exercise isolates one muscle—the quadriceps.

Open-chain exercises can be done with or without added weight, but when weight is added, it's usually placed at the distal (far) portion of the limb (such as the ankle). Examples of open-chain exercises are chest presses, biceps curls, and leg extensions. The disadvantage of open-chain exercises (e.g., knee extensions or hamstring curl exercises performed on machines) is that they can produce shear forces (speed × distance = force), which stress the knee joint (including the vulnerable ligaments such as the ACL, or anterior cruciate ligament) and are more likely to result in injury to vulnerable joints including the knee, shoulder, and hip.

Open-chain exercises are a good choice for beginners, older adults who may need additional support during exercise, and those who are looking to increase the size or strength of a particular muscle. For example, a female bodybuilder may spend more time in open-chain exercise than someone who has a more functional goal and therefore wants a functional approach to a fitness routine.

If you have joint pain (such as knee pain) or a previous injury to a joint, it may be in your best interest to avoid certain types of open-chain exercises on that particular joint. For example, if your knees are bad, you should perform closed-chain exercises such as squats and lunges instead of machine-based leg extensions or leg curls, which are open-chain exercises. If you have injured your elbow or shoulder joint, you may want to perform push-ups (closed kinetic chain) instead of the flat-bench chest presses (open kinetic chain) or pull-ups in lieu of overhead presses. Although both open- and closed-chain exercises increase strength, there are benefits to open-chain exercises. For example, if you were injured and your arm were placed into a cast, the muscles of the arm (biceps and triceps) would atrophy (become smaller). Performing open-chain exercises such as seated biceps curls or machine biceps curls would be effective for increasing strength and size in that specific muscle. These types of exercises are often selected in rehabilitation programs, beginning strength training programs, and programs geared at increasing size and strength in a particular muscle group.

CHOOSING AMONG STRENGTH TRAINING EQUIPMENT OPTIONS

So many equipment options are available for fitness pursuits and performance enhancement today. Because you invest valuable time and energy in your exercise routines, selecting the right equipment is important. However, deciding what fitness equipment to use and when can be difficult. The following sections discuss both the pros and cons of a variety of resistance training equipment. Most important for increasing muscle strength and endurance is to increase resistance incrementally. These equipment suggestions will help you determine what equipment to use, when to use it, and how to use it, as well as direct you toward the pieces that will provide maximal training benefits based on your goals.

Free Weights

Free weight exercises, which include both dumbbell and barbell exercises, are characterized by a broad range of motion. Because they incorporate the stabilizing muscles, free weight exercises may be more effective in producing overall muscle strength and power gains than weight machines.

Body Weight Exercises

Body weight exercises are an important type of resistance training. Exercises such as plank pose, pull-ups, dips, and push-ups, as well as many core exercises that require some type of torso flexion or extension are the most practical exercises to incorporate into your strength training routine. Not only do most body weight exercises not require any additional equipment, but they are also very effective for increasing both muscle strength and endurance. Body weight progressions are accomplished through increased repetitions as opposed to added resistance. The progressive-repetition approach works until the exercise duration exceeds one minute and a half to about two minutes. Once you can perform the move continuously in good form for longer than that, the strength-building stimulus diminishes.

Performing body weight exercises will also help you move your body through space with precision. Being able to perform exercises correctly and with optimal technique is important for exercise safety. Movement precision is a fundamental aspect of proper exercise form and technique. A body that does not move well needs to be reeducated about movement patterns and joint action mechanics. Adding weight loads to dysfunctional movement pattern is an injury waiting to happen. Moving with clean, clear-cut, strict guidelines is imperative for proper exercise technique.

Additional loads can be incorporated to increase the difficulty of body weight exercises, and some exercises do require some sort of apparatus to lean on or hang from (such as a suspension trainer), but the majority of body weight exercises require only a floor. It is also possible to enhance the difficulty of a body weight exercise by wearing a weighted vest. Some people use belts to strap additional weight plates to their bodies when performing dips and pull-ups. Other solutions include Pilates and yoga-based movements, which connect flexibility and range of motion to the strength and endurance component of body weight training. A myriad of body weight equipment and exercise options exist, from simple to complex.

Dumbbells in particular are very versatile. Dumbbell exercises require an equal application of force by both hands. The muscles are completely engaged as you lift and balance the weight. The negative side to this is that you must learn to balance the weight while exerting force. This can be difficult and potentially dangerous if you are lifting weights overhead or performing certain difficult lifts without the assistance of a spotter.

Isolating specific muscles can be difficult with free weights. To target the muscles you want, you need to use very precise techniques. For example, free weights can be swung for momentum rather than lifted slowly and steadily. In some cases, a lack of control can lead to injury if you don't use proper technique. However, with a knowledge of safe lifting techniques, you can perform a wide variety of dumbbell exercises that will work your muscles in distinctive ways.

When using barbells, you must maintain proper form and engage your muscles to their fullest extent. With barbells, you can typically lift more weight than you can with dumbbells because the bar and the support pins allow for heavier loads to be placed on the bar and the racks. Because the weight of the barbell and additional plates (when used) are spread along the line of the bar, it is easier to lift and control heavier loads than it is with free weights, even when the weight loads are equal. Barbells are frequently used for heavier lifts such as front and back squats, flat and incline bench presses, and some overhead presses.

Weight Machines

Weight machines, also referred to as selectorized equipment, are well suited for beginners because they provide body support, and the movement patterns are predetermined. They aren't as intimidating as free weights and are much easier to use. Selecting an appropriate weight is also very easy. Just follow the machine's range of motion to guarantee that you hit your target muscle group or groups. Weight machines may also help prevent injuries. Injuries are more likely to occur when we go out of our body's preferred range of motion; weight machines keep this from happening by controlling the movements and the range of motion.

Typically, many weight machines are arranged in exercise stations set up to work each muscle in the body. You sit on, stand at, or lie in a weight machine, allowing it guide your body through the movement while it provides resistance. Once you select a weight load, you can progress through your workout quickly, easily performing sets of exercises by moving from one machine to another without having to readjust dumbbells or find ones that are the appropriate weight.

Exercises particularly well suited for weight machines are trunk rotation, trunk extension, knee flexion and extension, and hip adduction and abduction exercises. These joint actions and corresponding muscle groups can be difficult to isolate using free weights alone.

Unfortunately, there is a downside to the use of selectorized equipment. Although machines may decrease your risk of injury by helping you control the movements and the range of motion, they also result in performing the same range of motion over and over, workout after workout for many weeks at a time. When you work the same muscles, tendons, and ligaments each time you exercise, you set yourself up for strength plateaus and a false sense of increased strength. Performing an exercise on a machine (open-chain exercise) and lifting something, like free weights, (closed-chain exercise) are significantly different.

You may find that although your weights are increasing at the gym, you aren't particularly stronger outside of the gym. For example, when you bend over to pick up a heavy box, you don't have the opportunity to rest the nonworking parts of your body (as you do when using a machine, isolating all your force to the working muscles). You need to incorporate more muscles, such as the muscles in the center of the body known as the core muscles, to stabilize yourself while picking up the box. If these other muscles aren't strong, you may have a hard time performing closed-chain exercises in which you have to stabilize your body with your own muscles, joints, and spine. Even if you are following the right range of motion, you can still overload your muscles with too much weight, causing a muscle strain or tear that can leave you sidelined for weeks.

Cables

Cable machines have similar properties to weight machines, but allow for significantly more movement freedom than traditional weight machines do. Like selectorized equipment, cables are attached to vertical weight stacks that move when pulled against the force of gravity. Therefore, the resistance force remains constant throughout the entire range of motion during almost all of the cable exercise actions. Popular cable exercises are triceps press-downs, lat pulldowns, and shoulder, chest, and back exercises.

Medicine Balls

Medicine balls are available in a large variety of weights, shapes, and sizes and can be used for a variety of standing, seated, prone, and supine exercises. If dropped, they are not as dangerous as free weights are, and they can be passed from one person to another. One of the greatest benefits of medicine balls is that they can be passed and released very quickly (tossed or thrown and released), allowing for powerful movement patterns that do not necessarily stress the joints structures at the end of the range of motion.

Resistance Tubing

Resistance tubing offers an inexpensive and portable way to perform both specific muscle group exercises and full-body strength training workouts. Tubing requires little space and can be easily adapted to almost any exercise. Most tubing is color coded, allowing you to select a resistance that is best suited to your fitness level. As the tubing is stretched, it provides a resistance force, so it works particularly well for exercises such as chest presses, squats, biceps curls, and shoulder presses. The downside of tubing is that it can break and cause injury. For this reason, it's important to check for holes or worn spots in the tubing and to replace the tube if you see any signs of wear. Make sure the tubing is secure, either under a foot (wear athletic shoes when exercising with tubing), or anchored to a secure surface.

Suspension Training

Suspension training is a relative newcomer to the fitness industry with respect to mass use. It helps tremendously with the goal of increasing muscle strength and endurance in a closed-chain format. Although the concept of weight training using suspension concepts (and even free weights) dates as far back as the Roman Empire, today's options are far less primitive and much easier to incorporate into strength training routines.

The TRX Suspension Trainer is a system of straps with a single anchor point attached by a carabiner; it is used for closed-chain exercises. This system allows you to maximize core muscle use, which demands stability during every exercise. The suspension trainer has foot cradles and handles that allow you to perform a broad spectrum of unique exercises such as push-ups with your feet off the floor and crunches that use the spine and adjacent core muscles to perform the exercise. Because the feet or hands are generally supported by the single anchor point while the opposite end of the body is in contact with the ground, the training is very challenging. Body weight is balanced with gravity, and is loaded onto the body through a selection of vectors (angles), mixing support and mobility to train for strength, endurance, flexibility, range of motion, core strength, and coordination through a range of resistance. This equipment allows you to focus on specific body parts, muscle groups, and planes of motion. This unique concept allows for an unsupported and, more often than not, unstable exercising environment to build functional strength while also enhancing muscle balance in the legs, hips, arms, and core.

Kettlebells

With roots in the former Soviet Union, kettlebells have made a huge comeback in the modern American strength training scene. Kettlebells, which resemble cannonballs with handles, come in a huge variety of weight loads and can be used for both traditional strength training exercises and nontraditional lifts.

Balance Training and Equipment

Movement is essential for performing all activities of daily living, and moving efficiently requires balance, also known as postural alignment. Balance is a component of core strength and stability and frequently accompanies exercises and programming that aligns with core training. Often, when you are practicing balance exercises, you are also performing core training. Training for balance can involve equipment or just the manipulation of body positions. For example, standing with your feet wider than your hips increases your body's center of gravity and base of support. A wide foot stance creates more stability and hence better balance, and can be adopted to control heavier loads. Narrowing your foot stance decreases your center of gravity and your body's base of support. For example, during lunges or squats, if the exercise is too difficult, you can decrease the intensity simply by widening your foot stance. These are simple examples of manipulating balance as part of the exercise program, but they are important principles.

The following sections describe various balance equipment options.

BOSU

The BOSU (Both Sides Utilized) Balance Trainer is a piece if fitness equipment that challenges core stability and dynamic balance during a variety of strength exercises. This type of training is another aspect of functional training, because of the focus on integrated movement, balance, and body awareness. Using the BOSU in conjunction with free weights or body weight exercises challenges both mind and muscles as you work to respond to these unique movement challenges.

Many of the exercises included in this book can easily be performed on the BOSU instead of the floor. When stepping on a BOSU, try to place your feet on center of the dome. Use caution when stepping onto and off the BOSU. Standing or kneeling on the BOSU will challenge your core stability in coordination with the muscles you are exercising. BOSU exercises involve lying, standing, kneeling, and even lying sideways on the BOSU. Squats, biceps curls, shoulder presses, and upright rows can be done while standing on the BOSU. Many of these exercises can also be done while kneeling. Crunches or holding a V-sit can be done lying faceup on the BOSU. You can also hold a medicine ball and pass it to another person while on the BOSU.

Stability Ball

Popular today in all fitness settings, the stability ball (also called a Swiss ball) is ideal for performing exercises that you can also do on the floor or a bench. The stability ball offers a dynamic environment in which you need to control the body. This challenges the core through all the microadjustments your body has to make to stay on top of the ball while doing the exercises. Stability balls come in two popular sizes: 55 centimeters and 65 centimeters. To determine whether a ball is the correct size for your height, sit on top of the ball with your feet on the floor and your knees bent. If your knees are higher than your hips in this seated position, the ball is too small for you. Your knees should extend from the hips—not higher or lower than. Adjusting the size of the ball is easy to do. If you have a 65-centimeter ball and it is too big, simply let some air out of it. High-quality balls are burst resistant, meaning that they will not pop like a balloon if they are pierced, but the air will slowly come out them.

Foam Roller

A foam roller is appropriate for many training and conditioning exercises for developing core strength and stability. Foam rollers also assist with stretching, self-massage, postural alignment, and balance exercises. In the exercises for the core, described in chapter 7, a few exercises incorporate foam rollers. Most foam rollers in the fitness setting are about 3 feet (91 cm) long and about 12 inches (30.5 cm) in diameter. Some rollers are very soft, and others are more firm; firmer ones are best for self-massage.

Additionally, the TRX Suspension Trainer can be used to develop balance by challenging stability, mobility, and strength.

Kettlebells are a unique training tool because of their shape and the way they are lifted. Because of their shape, they are more aerodynamic than traditional dumbbells and are actually designed to be swung as oppose to simply lifted. The swinging introduces the elements of both acceleration and deceleration which are important components for advanced exercisers, especially if you are training for any type of athletic goal. Learning to perform acceleration promotes power in strength training. Deacceleration offers the ability to control movement, which can be helpful for decreasing injury risk as it teaches one how to control a weight. It is important to realize that both acceleration and deceleration training techniques are also more likely to result in delayed onset muscle soreness (DOMS) than typical free weight and machine training techniques are. Developing explosive power may be a result of kettlebell training if the correct techniques are implemented. Power, one of five secondary components of fitness, can result in greater muscle strength and speed of movement as well as the development of Type II muscle fibers.

Fitness Trampoline

A fitness trampoline can offer you the opportunity to incorporate high-intensity, fat-burning cardio exercises into your strength workout. Trampoline exercise is a low-impact form of exercise that you can adjust to your current fitness level by decreasing the depth of your jumps, changing the position of your feet on the trampoline bed, or changing the intensity of your movements. Trampoline exercises are easier on your joints and back than other high-impact cardio exercises such as running or jumping rope. Although running and jumping rope are great cardio options and should be incorporated into your cardio workouts, the trampoline can offer an alternative to the constant demand that high-impact running can place on the joints.

A fitness trampoline is not the same as a child's playground trampoline; it is used differently than traditional trampolines. The mini-trampoline, or fitness trampoline, is used by pressing into the mesh bed with the feet in quick, purposeful bursts, not by jumping high on it. This pressing into the trampoline is referred to as "loading down." Most people enjoy the extra intensity the trampoline offers in a surprisingly easy way.

Try using the trampoline to perform running, high-knee jogging, jumping jack, cross-country ski, twisting, and other bounding movements in intervals during your strength training sessions to burn more calories during your workout. Try one to three minutes of trampoline exercise every 10 to 15 minutes of strength training as a cardio interval.

Now you understand the relationship between posture and exercise, as well as equipment selection—all three of these components influence your overall workout. By improving posture, you will gain noticeable strength in your core, simply as a result of improving your ability to lifts weights with better form and technique. Enhancing your core strength will enable you to use exercise equipment in a much more effective way. If you understand how to hold your body through a variety of exercise positions, you will notice that you are able to move more weight, which will increase your exercise intensity. This, in turn, will create more intensity in your training. Greater intensity will result in the ability to lift heavier weight, perform more repetitions, or increase the number of exercise sets you can perform. Increased intensity will also get you where you want to be faster—strong, lean, fit, and healthy.

In addition to improving your exercise technique (making you a safer, more efficient exerciser), improved posture will enable you to incorporate a large variety of equipment and exercise options into your strength training program without the risk of injury. This variety will result in more enjoyment of your program. Being able to perform a large variety of exercises is also better for you in the long run, because it will decrease your risk of burnout, stagnation, and ultimately, boredom.

PART II

Strength Training Exercises for Women

Warming Up and Cooling Down

Two important aspects of your strength training program are the warm-up and the cool-down. Warming up gives your body time to adjust to the demands of the upcoming exercise, and a good warm-up prepares your body for more intense activity. It gets your blood flowing, raises your core body and muscle temperature, and increases your breathing rate. This can improve your performance and help you get the results you want. Just as the warm-up prepares your body for exercise, an effective cool-down gives your body time to recover. Your cool-down begins as you gradually decrease your intensity level at the end of your exercise session and allows you to transition out of the exercise session as the warm-up did to ease you in.

Stretching: Good or Bad?

There is some controversy about including stretching as part of the warm-up. The argument has to do with the muscles' ability to generate force. Some people believe that too much stretching during the warm-up increases muscle elasticity to a point, which lowers force-generating capacity. So, it's probably a good idea to perform some form of rhythmic or range of motion (ROM) stretches toward the end of your warm-up. The muscles and joints at this point are more receptive to brief stretching, as long as you have adequately increased your core body temperature. However, stretching before increasing your core body temperature is not recommended.

A stretching routine following the cool-down increases flexibility and ROM, which are critical for muscle balance, posture, and the ability to perform exercises using proper techniques as discussed in chapter 3. Stretching, however, will not decrease your risk of delayed onset muscle soreness (DOMS), as popular folklore asserts.

WARM-UP

It is imperative that you warm up before you work out. A thorough warm-up prepares your body for the upcoming demands of more intense exercise. This means that your warm-up should be active and rhythmic, which makes the muscles more pliable and less susceptible to injury. Many women believe they need to perform a stretching routine before beginning a strength training workout, but this is not true. Static stretching is actually counterproductive because it decreases the muscles' ability to create power.

A thorough warm-up raises the core body temperature, increases blood flow to the heart and working muscles, rehearses forthcoming movements, and lubricates the synovial joints. For each degree of increased internal temperature, the metabolic rate of cells increases by about 13 percent (Astrand and Rodahl 2003). The increased temperature of the body decreases the potential for injury because neuromuscular coordination increases, fatigue is delayed, and tissues are less susceptible to injury or trauma. The American Council on Exercise (2007) listed the following additional physiological benefits of a warm-up:

- *Increased metabolic rate.* When the body temperature begins to increase in preparation for exercise, the metabolic rate increases and the endocrine system begins to unload hormones that help the body prepare for exercise and activity (cortisol, insulin, and adrenaline). This increases the rate at which energy production occurs.

- *Higher rate of oxygen exchange between blood and muscles.* As part of the warm-up process, the lungs take oxygen from the red blood cells faster, which increases the rate of exchange between the muscles and the blood. Also, waste products such as carbon dioxide and other toxins are exchanged for oxygen at a faster rate.

- *Increased muscle elasticity and flexibility.* The soft tissues of the body (muscles, tendons, and ligaments) become more pliable and are more easily moved into a variety of positions when the body temperature increases because of the increased blood flow to those tissues. Muscles, tendons, and ligaments that are more responsive to sudden changes in position are much less likely to become injured during exercise.

A thorough warm-up has two parts: the general warm-up and the dynamic warm-up. The general warm-up focuses on increasing joint lubrication, heart rate, and core body temperature. Activities that are appropriate here generally prepare the body for the upcoming exercise session and increased physical movement. The dynamic warm-up is more specific to the activity you are performing the warm-up for. For example, if you were about to start a 3-mile (4.8 km) run, you might begin by jogging slowly to specifically warm up for the activity of running. If you were strength training, the dynamic warm-up might include ROM activities. For example, if you are going to perform squats, you should go through some squats without any additional load (weights), focusing on the ROM that you want to go through while squatting. (Later, we outline some dynamic stretches that are appropriate for most strength training workouts.)

A general warm-up should increase your core body temperature to the point of sweating. Breaking a sweat is a good measure of the quality of your general warm-up. You can use the treadmill, elliptical trainer, recumbent cycle, or stair climber, or just take a walk or jog around the track to break a sweat. This should take three to five minutes or longer depending on the physical environment, current injuries, or your medical conditions.

Once you have broken a sweat, you are ready to engage in the second part of the warm-up, which includes dynamic flexibility and core engagement. These activities should continue to increase your core body temperature and further prepare you physically and mentally for the upcoming workout. Dynamic flexibility should engage your core, increase the length of your muscles, and increase your joint ROM. Remember, these are dynamic moves, so once you get into position, move with control in and out of each posture in flowing sequences for the prescribed number of repetitions. I recommend that you perform three to five of the following dynamic flexibility exercises to prepare for a workout.

LATERAL STRETCH

Standing with feet under hips, toes forward, reach your arm straight up toward the ceiling, the opposite hand moving down toward the lateral aspect of the knee (see figure). Inhale into the stretch, and then exhale, switching sides. Perform three to five times on both the right and left sides.

SPINAL EXTENSION

With feet hip-width apart, inhale reaching both hands upward, lengthening through the lateral spine and shoulders (see figure a). Form fists with your hands, and then place them in the small of your back for support (see figure b). Extend your spine by gazing up with your eyes, raising your chin, opening your throat, and extending the cervical and thoracic vertebrae (see figure c). Exhale back to an upright standing position. Perform two or three times.

STANDING KNEE FLEXION AND EXTENSION WITH ANKLE DORSIFLEXION

Standing upright, draw one knee up toward your torso and into your hands in a flexed position (see figure a). Hold your thigh as you maintain a neutral hip height, extend your knee and leg, and point your toes up (see figure b). Flex your quadriceps as you extend the knee joint, and then draw the leg back in and flex the ankle (see figure c). Extend and flex the knee joint three to five times on each leg.

STANDING FIGURE FOUR

Balance your body weight on one foot as you draw the opposite leg up on your thigh as if you were sitting in a chair (see figure a). Balance your body weight by extending your arms slightly, and slowly lower your chest down toward your thigh (see figure b). Go as low as you can, reaching with your fingers toward the floor, if possible. Hold for 5 to 10 seconds and then switch legs.

FRONT LUNGE WITH LATERAL SQUAT

From an upright standing position, step forward with your right leg (see figure *a*) into a front lunge. Land on your whole foot, flex your knees, and lower your back knee toward the floor as you flex your front knee to about a 90-degree angle (see figure *b*). Raise your body upward, pushing off the front leg (see figure *c*), and return to a standing position (see figure *d*). Follow immediately into the squat using the right leg by stepping laterally into a wide stance (see figure *e*) and lowering your center of gravity into a squat (see figure *f*). Raise your body back up by pushing off the right leg and returning to an upright stance (see figure *g*). Repeat this pattern on both legs for a total of five front lunges and lateral squats.

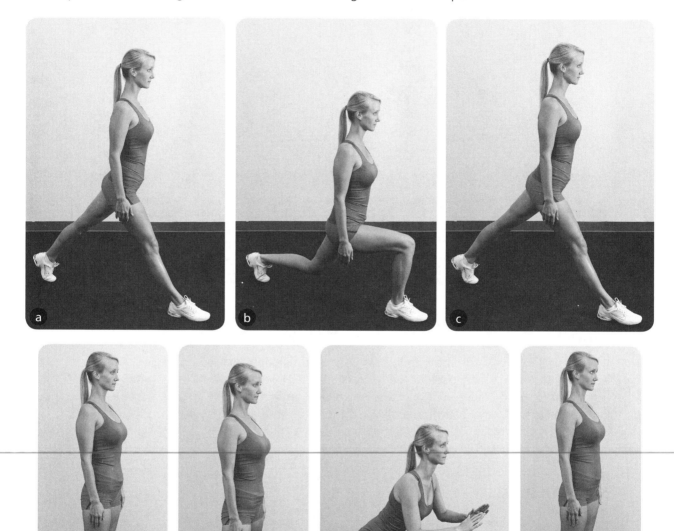

STANDING CAT AND COW

From a standing position, place your hands on your thighs with your hips at an anterior tilt (see figure a). Keep your chest open and your shoulders down, away from your ears. Alternate tilting your pelvis by drawing your abdominal wall in and rounding your spine (see figure b). Arch your back by lifting your tailbone backward and opening your neck by lifting your chin (see figure c). All movement should be pain free, so be mindful of the cervical motions. Alternate these two spinal positions three to five times each.

STANDING SHOULDER HORIZONTAL ADDUCTION

Stand with your feet hip-width apart, with upright posture. Reach one arm across the midline of your body, slightly flexing the elbow joint (see figure a). Place the opposite hand on the elbow joint (see figure b). This stretches the medial deltoid, rhomboids, and lower trapezius muscles located across the front of the shoulder and through the middle part of the back. Hold the stretch for three to five seconds, and then switch arms. Perform this stretch two or three times on each arm.

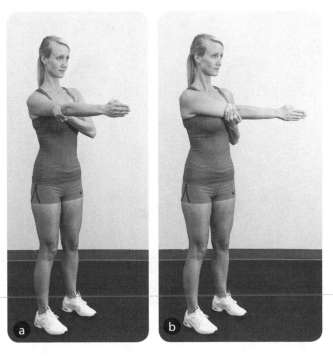

SEATED PELVIC TILT ON STABILITY BALL

Sit on a 55-centimeter or 65-centimeter stability ball, with your feet on the floor, hip-width apart (see figure *a*). Place your hands on the sides of the ball, and with your hips only, move forward and backward (see figures *b* and *c*), focusing on tilting the pelvis forward and back. Perform three to five times, both forward and backward.

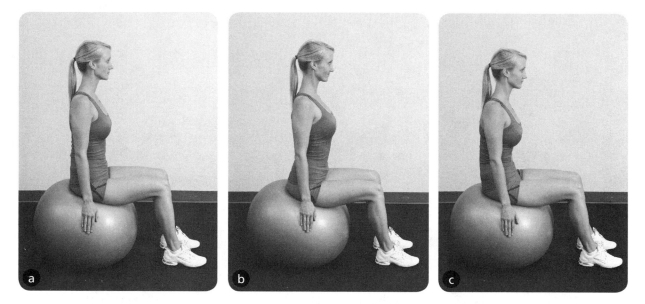

SEATED HIP CIRCLES ON STABILITY BALL

Sit on a 55-centimeter or 65-centimeter stability ball, with your feet placed on the floor, hip-width apart (see figure *a*). Place your hands on the sides of the ball, and with your hips only, move in a full circle through the pelvis to the right and then the left (see figures *b* and *c*). Perform three to five times, both to the right and to the left.

KNEE LIFT WITH MEDICINE BALL

Stand with your feet hip-width apart. Tighten your torso to stabilize your spine. Hold a 4-pound (2 kg) medicine ball overhead with both hands (see figure *a*). Lower the ball to chest height, and at the same time, bring one knee up (see figure *b*). Return to the start position and switch legs. Repeat alternating sides until you have performed 10 to 15 repetitions on each side.

BODY BALL REACH

Stand with your feet hip-width apart in a slight squat position. Hold a 4-pound (2 kg) medicine ball in your hands at chest level and close to your body with your elbows bent (see figure *a*). Raise your body up, lifting your arms overhead, leaning on a diagonal and reaching the ball to one side, and coming up on the toes on the opposite leg (see figure *b*). Return to the squat position and repeat on the other side; perform 8 to 10 repetitions on each side.

PLIÉ WITH MEDICINE BALL LIFT

Start with your legs wider than hip-width apart, pelvis tucked, and spine straight. The hips and feet are turned out, or externally rotated with straight legs. Hold the ball in front of your hips with your arms extended (see figure a). Flex your knees and lower your body in a plié squat while raising the ball up in front of your chest and keeping your arms long in front of your body (see figure b). As you return to the start position, squeeze your glutes and inner thighs. Repeat 10 to 15 times.

SHOULDER ROTATION WITH BANDS

This stretch focuses on increasing ROM about the shoulder joint. Using a resistance band or rubber tubing, place tension on the band by stretching it (be sure to hold it securely) and hold it in front of you at shoulder height, arms wide (see figure a). Keep your palms prone (facing down) and your wrists straight. Raise your arms up overhead (see figure b). You will feel a pull in the front of your shoulders. Continue to move your arms, lowering them behind your back (see figure c) and all the way down to your hips while keeping your elbows locked. Reverse the direction of the movement, returning the band to the starting position. Repeat six to eight times in each direction.

COOL-DOWN

Equally as important as the warm-up, the cool-down should be less intense and facilitate recovery. The cool-down does not have to be as specific as the warm-up in stimulating activity, but it does need to occur to allow the body the physiological opportunity to return to a preexercise state. If you have performed a fast-paced workout, you need to complete it with 5 to 10 minutes of slow movements such as stretching or low-intensity exercise. During strength training, a cool-down naturally occurs within the exercise session as a result of the intervals of work to recovery that are mixed into the workout. Although blood pressure and heart rate rise during strength bouts, they quickly return to preexercise levels during the naturally occurring recovery periods. Stretching after strength training, however, is a good idea because the body temperature is up and the joints are lubricated. Therefore, the body is in a good physiological state to increase muscle length.

As a general rule of thumb, the more intense and exhausting the activity is, the more gradual the tapering of the cool-down period should be. Therefore, an active cool-down is imperative following a cardio workout. Just slow down in increments of 30 seconds to one minute until you are at a complete stop. This would be an ideal time to stretch because your body temperature is up, but your heart rate is down.

The cool-down can be as simple as walking on a treadmill and performing a handful of stretches, or decreasing the intensity level of the activity you are performing with accompanying stretches. No matter what, do not skip the cool-down because returning to preexercise levels is important for recovery. An indicator that your cool-down segment was not long enough or adequate to achieve recovery is continued sweating. When clients tell me that they were still sweating after a shower, I know that they did not cool down adequately.

A cool-down helps blood to continue to flow and not pool in the extremities. It also prevents significant changes in blood pressure that occur when intense exercise is stopped too abruptly. A cool-down also helps to remove metabolic waste from the muscles so that it can either be used by other tissues in other chemical processes in the body or expelled in the form of water (sweat) or CO_2 release (exhaling breath).

Deep, sustained stretching to improve flexibility should follow strength training and cardio workouts because warm muscle tissue accepts stretch stimuli much easier than cold tissue does. This is why stretching at the end of a workout is more advantageous than stretching at the start. Flexibility is characterized by the ability to move joints through their normal, full ROM. Adequate flexibility prevents injury and maintains correct posture and body alignment. With specific flexibility training, the muscles, tendons, and ligaments adapt by elongating and increasing their ROM. The only way to increase ROM is to alter the muscles and tendons that control the joint. In some people, these structures become extremely tight, which results in a reduction of the normal ROM. Following are the three types of stretching techniques that increase ROM and lengthen muscles and connective tissues:

- Static stretching (including passive static and dynamic static)
- Ballistic stretching
- Proprioceptive neuromuscular facilitation (PNF stretching)

Static Stretching

Static stretching involves holding a static, nonmoving position for 10 to 30 seconds so that a joint is immobilized in a position that places muscles and connective tissues at their greatest possible length. Static stretches are best characterized as low-force, long-duration stretches. This technique has resulted in increased flexibility with little risk of injury. During static stretching, the component within the muscle belly called the Golgi tendon organ is stimulated. When stimulated, this component inhibits the entire muscle group, reducing muscle tension and consequently relaxing the entire muscle.

Passive static stretching involves performing a held stretch, often using an outside aid to assist the stretch (e.g., a towel, another body part such as your hand, or gravity). For example, when you pull your knee up toward your body to stretch your hamstring and low back, you use your hand to hold the knee up and close to your body. Because you are holding the leg or knee, it is called a passive stretch. If you were to flex the knee and bring it toward your body in the same stretch, but use only your own muscles to do so, it would be called an active stretch.

When performing a passive static stretch, the idea is to relax the body part and use the outside assistance to hold the stretch in place (e.g., with your hand or a towel). This is a common form of stretching because it's easy and relatively comfortable. Passive static stretches do increase ROM about a joint, but unfortunately, they do not help that much with movements that require dynamic movement. So for example, if you move your body through ranges of motion that require a certain amount of flexibility at that joint (e.g., performing a chest press and being able to go through a really big, full ROM because you have the flexibility and stability at the shoulder joint that allows for that motion), you are in essence increasing your ROM actively. This is a functional method to increase ROM.

No research currently exists that supports the notion that having passive ROM at a joint decreases the risk of injury, even though many believe that it does. The flexibility has to be joint and activity specific to decrease your risk of injury as well as work with current strength levels to ensure adequate stability. However, your ability to perform dynamic static stretches is a good predictor of injury risk because it is indicative of your ability to move through active ROMs during exercise or daily activity without assistance, which is how we typically move our bodies (i.e., functional movement).

With a *dynamic static stretch*, the outside assistance does not come from a towel, gravity, or another passive source. In dynamic static stretching, you are actively stretching one body part by using another. The outside force that assists with the dynamic stretch is usually an opposing muscle group or limb. For example, a static exercise to improve the length and function of the hamstring muscle group requires that you contract the quadriceps, lengthen the knee joint, hold the extended leg position for three to five seconds, and repeat the movement three to five times. For a dynamic static stretch using the same exercise, you would use your quadriceps muscles to lengthen the hamstring by extending the knee joint, but without using your hands to hold your leg up.

Dynamic static stretches are very common in sports and some fitness activities such as yoga and Pilates, but these stretches require more work and effort than passive static stretches do. They are very helpful for improving the function of real-life, dynamic movements as well as increasing joint stability.

Ballistic Stretching

Ballistic stretching is generally not used to increase muscle length. Ballistic stretching involves a rhythmic bobbing or bouncing motion that can invoke a stretch reflex that can actually cause a counter-contraction that opposes the desired outcome of achieving a stretch (remember those bouncy stretches from long-ago physical education classes?). This action can actually put the muscle at risk for injury. Muscle stretch reflexes are controlled by the muscle spindles located inside the muscle cells. These are involuntary responses propagated by the sensory nerves. When provoked, this action can result in a muscle contraction, causing increased muscle tension as opposed to muscle relaxation, the opposite of what a static stretch is designed to do.

There is a time and place for ballistic stretching. If you are a track and field athlete and you run in races that involve the steeple chase or hurdles, you should practice ballistic stretches in specific ranges of motion that lend themselves to those activities. In these cases (and others), ballistic stretching would help you perform these activities safely and efficiently, but they would only be performed when the body temperature is elevated.

Don't confuse ballistic stretching with dynamic stretching. Dynamic static stretching is controlled and deliberate, whereas ballistic stretching is jerky and uninhibited. Dynamic static stretches are held for about 6 to 10 seconds. Although a little movement may occur and they may look like ballistic stretches, there is more control and not as much of a bounce. Most stretching exercises should be performed without bouncing or jerking, because these actions may injure connective tissues and stimulate the stretch reflex.

PNF Stretching

Proprioceptive neuromuscular facilitation (PNF) stretching is a technique originally derived from rehabilitation settings such as physical therapy. Personal trainers often use this technique one on one with clients. PNF involves passively static stretching a muscle immediately after maximally contracting it against resistance. Research has found PNF stretching to be extremely effective at increasing passive ROM about a joint, but it is not always practical because it usually requires the assistance of a partner.

The following cool-down stretches include both types of static stretches (passive and dynamic). Along the way, it is a good idea to perform stretches within the context of the workout, particularly upper body stretches and stretches specific to the body part you have just worked. This way, by the time you get to the cool-down stretches, you can focus on full-body stretches that release tension from the major muscle groups.

FULL-BODY STRETCH

Lie on your back on an exercise mat. Take a deep breath in and stretch your arms and legs out, as if someone were pulling your ankles and your wrists away from your body gently and simultaneously (see figure). Stretch your arms and legs as far as you can. Exhale and let your muscles relax. Repeat three times (inhale and reach, exhale and release).

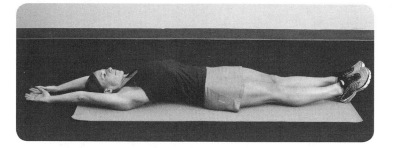

BRIDGE

While lying on your back with your feet hip-width apart and knees flexed, place your hands diagonally from your sides (see figure a). Start at the base of your spine and begin by peeling your spine off the mat one vertebra at a time, as shown in figure b, until your pelvis is raised up and your spine is lifted in a straight line from your shoulders to your knees (see figure c). As you release down, pay attention to rolling through the small of your back, touching down one vertebra at a time. Inhale as you expand your chest, and exhale as you lower down. Perform 8 to 10 repetitions.

LOW BACK STRETCH

While lying on your back, bring both knees up to your chest, separating them and grasping behind the thighs with your hands (see figure a). Exhale as you draw your knees upward toward your shoulders and your hips curl up slightly from the floor (see figure b). Inhale and release. Perform this three to five times.

HAMSTRING STRETCH

Lie on your back with your knees bent. Place your right foot firmly on the floor and extend your left knee, raising your leg to the ceiling (see figure a). Hold the extended leg with both hands, behind the thigh, and pull it toward your body gently (see figure b). If necessary, use a towel to hold the leg in the extended position. Try to keep your knee straight. Hold the stretch for 20 to 30 seconds, and then repeat with the other leg. Perform three to five times on each leg.

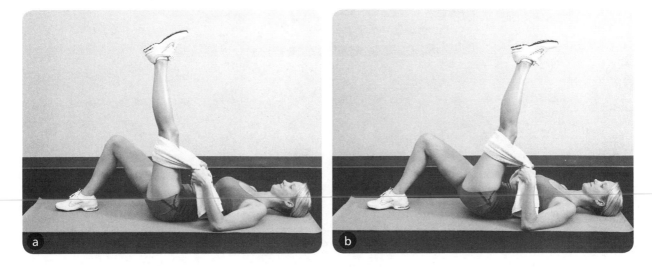

SPINAL TWIST

Lie on your back with your knees bent and your feet firmly on the floor. Reach your arms out in a T line, palms down at shoulder height (see figure *a*). Drop both knees to one side, turning your head in the opposite direction (see figure *b*). Try keeping your shoulders down as one hip lifts off the floor. Hold for 20 to 30 seconds and then change sides. When changing sides, draw in your abdominal muscles and brace your spine as you transition. Try this stretch three to five times on each side.

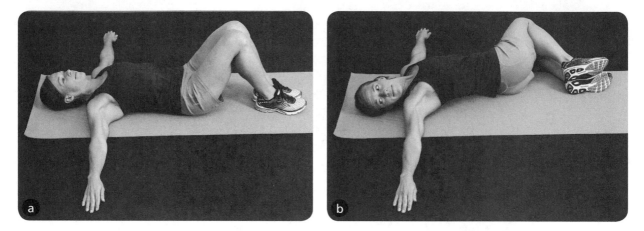

QUADRUPED CAT AND COW

Assume a quadruped position in which you are kneeling on all fours, hands under shoulders, fingers spread and facing forward, and knees on the floor under your hips (see figure *a*). Round your back up toward the ceiling, pulling your abdominal muscles into your spine, and exhale (see figure *b*). Reverse your spinal position by bringing your head up and arching your back so that your chest and throat open, and inhale (see figure *c*). Repeat each spinal position three times.

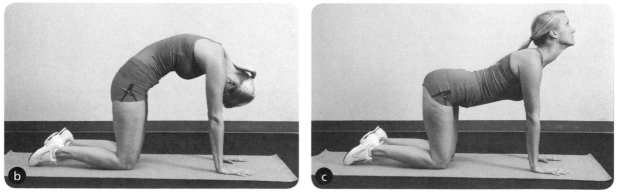

CHILD'S POSE

From a kneeling position, sit your hips back onto your heels (see figure *a*) and reach your arms forward. With your head between your elbows, rest your forehead on the mat (see figure *b*). Hold for 20 to 30 seconds feeling a good stretch in your shoulders, side, and low back. Repeat six to eight times.

DOWNWARD-FACING DOG

From a kneeling position, straighten your knees and press down through your heels into the balls of your feet (see figure *a*). Extend your arms fully and reach up and back with your hips, as if you were pressing them into the wall behind you, as you press your heels hip-width apart to the floor (see figure *b*). Maintain length through your spine. Drop your head between your biceps. Hold the stretch for 20 to 30 seconds. Perform this stretch six to eight times or as many times as you like.

FORWARD BEND

From a standing position, fold forward from your hips (see figure). You don't have to touch your toes with your hands; just reach down toward the floor and connect your hands with your ankles or shins (if you can't touch your toes). Allow your body to relax as you attempt to look through your legs at the wall behind you. Relax your head and neck, just allowing them to fall into the stretch. Hold the position for five to eight seconds.

FORWARD BEND WITH A TWIST

From the forward bend, place your left hand on the side of your right foot or ankle (see figure a). Take your right arm and reach up toward the ceiling, twisting through your torso as if you were wringing out a wet cloth, and keeping your wrists in line with one another (see figure b). Follow your hand with your eyes, gazing up if possible. Perform three to five times on each side, holding for 5 to 10 seconds each time; then, switch sides.

FOAM ROLLER SPINAL ALIGNMENT

Using a foam roller, lie faceup with your feet hip-width apart and your head and neck supported on the roller (see figure). Relax your body as you allow the weight of your spine to be fully supported by the foam roller. Just relax your body as you lie on the roller with your feet firmly anchored and your hands by your sides. If you need more stability on the roller, open your arms wider to allow for more stability to come from the hands. Breathe deeply.

FOAM ROLLER SHOULDER EXTENSION

After relaxing on the foam roller, maintain your body position on top of it, faceup, and move your shoulders through a full ROM over your head in an arc-type motion (see figures a and b). Try to keep your hands in contact with the ground as much as possible throughout the ROM. It's as if you were making a large circle with your arms and hands around the perimeter of your body. As you move through this ROM, notice the distinct increase in shoulder mobility and motion. Perform this exercise for 30 to 90 seconds. Just relax into the stretch and enjoy the break.

Jumping into your workout without preparing your body with a thorough warm-up could lead to muscle strain or injury. In addition, physiologically, it is not the smartest way to begin a workout. Remember, though, that the warm-up should not be so demanding that it creates undue fatigue and takes away from your ability to perform the workout. Also, properly cooling down after your workout will gradually reduce the temperature of your muscles, particularly if you've experienced an intense workout.

CHAPTER 5

Training the Upper Body

Upper body strength training exercises target the large muscle groups located in the upper part of the body—the chest, back, shoulders, and arms. Additional benefits of upper body strength include increased flexibility and improved performance of shoulder and arm movements, as well as reduced risk of injury, particularly in the shoulders and low back.

Upper body strength is the key to muscle balance between the upper and lower body. Many women neglect training the upper body (chest, back, shoulders, and arms), instead choosing to focus on the legs, hips, and thighs. Perhaps this is done to "slim down" the larger-looking legs. But remember, spot reduction is an ineffective method to lose weight and increase strength. In fact, the best way to slim the lower body is to increase overall lean mass. By adding lean mass to the upper and lower body simultaneously, most women experience a vast improvement in their overall appearance, because more lean mass in the upper body (stronger arms and shoulders) balances the look of the lower body (strong legs and thighs).

Without upper body strength, postural concerns also come into play, which can detract from an attractive and healthy physical appearance. This is particularly true as we age. A natural part of the aging process is a decrease in muscle mass (atrophy) and an increase in body fat. With upper body strength training, women can reduce muscle loss to maintain and even build up the fat-free upper body muscle, thus improving their overall strength and physical appearance. This is also important for maintaining a strong spine and correct, upright posture, as discussed thoroughly in chapter 3.

The loss of valuable strength in the shoulders, chest, and back results in poor posture and a vulnerability to the devastating effects of osteoporosis. Loss of bone mineral density in the neck and spine can create that rounded, hunched-spinal appearance called kyphosis. Kyphosis involves an exaggerated outward curve of the thoracic spine (middle back), as well as rounded shoulders, a sunken chest, and a hyperextended neck with a forward head position. To avoid spinal degeneration and postural issues, while enhancing muscle balance, make upper body strength training a priority.

ANATOMY OF THE UPPER BODY

The areas of the upper body (chest, back, shoulders, and arms) are further divided into muscle groups based on the joints they function with. It would be difficult to discuss the muscles of the upper body without taking a close look at the shoulder joint, so we'll cover this first. This is important because most of the muscles that can be trained in the upper body have some relationship with the shoulder joint.

Shoulder Joint

The shoulder joint is one of the most mobile in the body because the muscles and joints of the shoulder allow it to move through a wide range of motion. Although the shoulder joint is very mobile, it is also at a slightly higher risk of injury. For this reason, having good flexibility and strength in the deltoids, lats, and muscles of the arms is important for keeping that joint free of injury.

Three bones make up the shoulder joint: the clavicle (collarbone), the scapula (shoulder blade), and the humerus (upper arm bone) as well as various muscles, ligaments, and tendons. When discussing the shoulder, we will refer to it as the integrated unit that it is, which is the shoulder complex, but it is classified as a type of joint known as the shoulder joint, a ball-and-socket joint, also called the glenohumeral joint. This joint includes the top of the humerus, which is the round, knoblike bone at the top of the upper arm that fits into the shoulder girdle. The bone in the back that moves with the shoulder joint is called the *scapula*. It is a semiflat, spoon-shaped plate in which the knob sits. This structure allows for maximum rotation of the upper arm and shoulder. However, several muscles and tendons are required to put this joint into use.

The shoulder joint must be mobile enough for the wide range of actions that the arms and hands perform, but also stable enough to allow for other actions such as lifting, pushing, and pulling. Because of the mobility and stability it requires, the shoulder joint is at risk for several problems unlike other joints, such as the hip. The shoulder joint is highly mobile but unstable, whereas the hip is less mobile but very stable. The downside of the stability of the hips is that they can be very limited in their ranges of motion, which can lead to muscle tightness and inflexibility in the muscles and tendons at that joint. With this thought in mind, let's take a closer look at the muscles that allow for motion at the shoulder joint.

The *rotator cuff* (also called the rotor cuff) muscles are largely responsible for stabilizing the shoulder joint and allowing it to perform internal and external rotation. The group consists of the supraspinatus, the infraspinatus, the teres minor, and the subscapularis, as well as the deltoid and the teres major. All six muscles act to form the *scapulohumeral joint*. For our purposes, we examine just the first four rotator cuff muscles. See figure 5.1 for an illustration.

The supraspinatus lies just beneath the medial deltoid and assists in shoulder abduction (lifting the arms away from the sides of the body). The infraspinatus and the teres minor assist with external rotation, as when you flex your elbow and open your palm, allowing your arm to move away from your body. The subscapularis performs internal rotation, such as bringing the hand toward the abdomen with a flexed elbow. The infraspinatus is the only rotator cuff muscle that is externally visible. It looks like a triangle, back by the rear deltoid. The teres minor lies above the teres

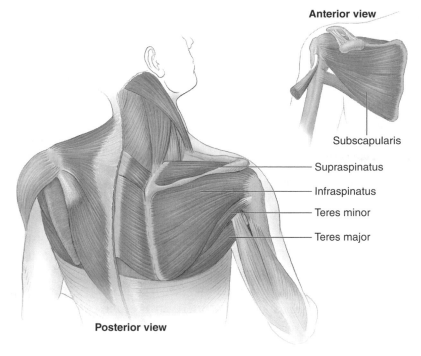

Anterior view

Subscapularis

Supraspinatus

Infraspinatus

Teres minor

Teres major

Posterior view

FIGURE 5.1 Muscular structure of the rotator cuff.

major, but it is not visually distinct from the infraspinatus. They actually appear to be the same muscle.

Internal and external shoulder rotations are important joint actions, and crucial for many sport activities that require throwing. Really, any activities in which the shoulder plays a role, including functional activities of everyday living, involve the use of the shoulder and the rotator cuff muscles. However, rotator cuff muscles are often overlooked in strength training programs. People who strength train on a regular basis have a natural tendency to perform exercises that involve internal shoulder rotation, such as those used to develop chest and back muscles. Exercises that engage the latissimus dorsi and the teres major require the internal rotation of the subscapularis. For example, when you perform a lat pulldown, you involve the latissimus dorsi, as well as the teres major, in the joint action. When these muscles act, working together in a strong and powerful unit, they can overwhelm the smaller, rotator cuff muscles. The result can be an imbalance between the actions of internal and external rotation. Aside from some exercises that involve the middle and rear deltoids, the external rotators of the shoulder joint need to be trained on their own, or within a totally different exercise at that shoulder joint. It is for this reason that performing just one or even two exercises for a joint is often not enough, as imbalances may occur from not performing exercises that engage all of the muscles and actions at that particular joint.

The other shoulder joint that comes into play during upper body strength training is the *scapulothoracic joint*. This is the bone in your back that moves with the shoulder joint. The scapula floats in the back, and because you have two shoulders, you have two scapulae. The scapulothoracic joint is the place where the two scapulae meet with the back of the rib cage. The scapulae are the human equivalent to wings; when you lift your arms out to the side (shoulder abduction) or bring them back into your sides (shoulder adduction), the scapulae rotate inward or outward, respectively.

Muscles of the Upper Body

The muscles of the upper body consist of muscles in the back, shoulders, chest, and arms. Let us take a closer look at their locations, their actions in the body, and how they affect your ability to move and function in everyday life. Note that even though we are examining the muscles independent of each other, muscles work together, depending on what joint action they are performing (e.g., pushing, planking, or pulling).

Chest and Deltoids

Despite the fact that the shoulder joints work together when performing upper body arm motions, two distinct groups of muscles influence the shoulders and their ability to perform movements—the chest and the deltoids.

Chest The *pectoralis major* and the *pectoralis minor* are the two major muscles that comprise the chest. See figure 5.2 for an illustration. These muscles originate in three places: the collarbone, the sternum, and the cartilage of the ribs nearest the sternum. They are both fan-shaped muscles that originate at the center of the chest (clavicle and sternum) and then stretch across each side of the chest, lying under the breast tissue. They then thin out to connect to the top of the humerus via a biceps tendon.

The pectoralis minor lies just underneath the pectoralis major. It is a thin, triangular-shaped muscle that is not easily visible. The pectoralis minor could be called a forgotten muscle, along with the *serratus anterior*. The serratus, which lies along the rib cage, is visible in only the leanest, most well-developed physiques. A tight pair of pectoralis minor muscles can pull the shoulder joints forward, creating a rounded-shoulder appearance and, consequently, poor posture.

To train these muscles, you don't have to isolate them because they are involved in most chest exercises. The pectoralis minor is largely involved in the pullover, whereas the serratus muscles are involved whenever the scapulae rotate upward and out (external rotation), such as during an upright row. The pectoralis major and minor muscle fibers all attach to the humerus. The fibers that start at the bottom of the chest attach to a higher point on the humerus. It should follow, then, that the fibers that start at the top of the chest attach to a lower portion on the humerus. This attachment causes the chest muscles to literally twist about the humerus. An understanding of how the pectoral muscles interact will help you select exercises to optimize chest development.

The main joint action that your chest performs is horizontal adduction, which occurs when moving your upper arm across the front of your torso, toward the midline of your body both inward and across at various angles, such as when performing a chest press or a fly. A variety of chest exercises are available for training the chest, using a variety of equipment options including dumbbells, cable machines, and body weight, as well as changing the angle of the body and the joint during the workout. (We will also explore alternative equipment such as stability balls, resistance tubing, suspension training, and the BOSU.)

Many strength trainers separate the muscles of the chest into upper, middle, and lower. However, if you were to examine the fiber arrangement of the chest muscles based on their origin (where they begin) and their insertion points (where they attach to), you may have a different view of the ability to truly separate these muscles into such groups. Some weightlifters believe that they must work the chest in an "upper, middle, and lower" fashion to achieve optimal muscle development,

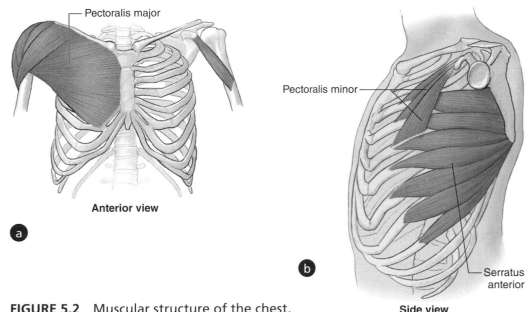

FIGURE 5.2 Muscular structure of the chest.

but they are partly mistaken. Although it is true that performing a chest press on an incline bench recruits more of the upper chest fibers, and that performing a chest press on a decline bench recruits the lower chest fibers more than the uppers, most of the chest muscle fibers work together, regardless of the body position.

Although variety in exercise selection is important to recruit muscle fibers differently, as indicated by the origin and attachment referred to earlier, the muscles of the pectoralis group twist. Because of this, most chest exercises engage the majority of the muscle fibers. So don't worry too much about upper, middle, and lower for optimal development. No matter which exercise you select, you will engage all the muscle fibers that comprise the chest.

Deltoids   The deltoids are located on the shoulder and are composed of three separate muscles. See figure 5.3 for an illustration. The *anterior deltoid* and *medial deltoid* are located on the front and tops of the shoulders, respectively, and make up part of the deltoid group. These muscles wrap around the cap of the shoulder joint and is largely responsible for moving the joint. The anterior deltoid originates on the outer third of the clavicle, whereas the upper pectoralis muscle originates in the other two thirds of the clavicle. This is why exercises for the chest most often engage the anterior deltoid. The medial deltoid originates at the *acromium process.* Simply referred to as the acromium, this point forms the summit of the shoulder and offers an attachment for the medial deltoid before it comes together with all the deltoid muscles to attach to the humerus, just underneath the biceps. The remaining shoulder muscle in the deltoids muscle group is the *posterior deltoid,* which consists of the back of the shoulder muscles and attaches to the spine of the upper third of the scapula.

The shoulders move the arms away from the body, and each muscle works differently from the others. The anterior deltoid lifts each arm up to the front of the body. That joint action is called shoulder flexion. The medial deltoid handles almost all the overhead movements (e.g., overhead press, upright row). The medial deltoid not only raises the arms overhead, but also, with the posterior deltoid, raises the arms out to the side of the body. This joint action is called shoulder abduction.

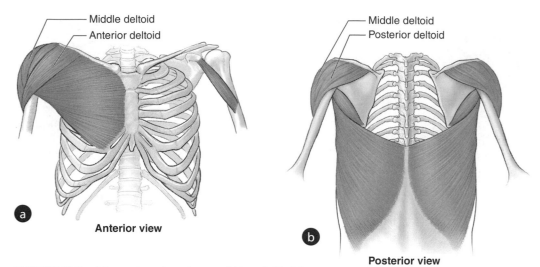

FIGURE 5.3 Muscular structure of the deltoids.

The supraspinatus, one of the four rotator cuff muscles that lie just beneath the deltoid, assists with this action. The posterior deltoid lifts the arm up and behind the body, and the joint action is called hyperextension. Because this muscle begins where the fibers of the upper and middle trapezius end, many of the rear deltoid's movements are associated with those of the trapezius and other scapular muscles involved in horizontal pulling, such as rowing exercises.

Back Muscles

The muscles of the back provide support for the entire body, as well as facilitating spinal, shoulder, and cervical (neck) movement. See figure 5.4 on page 71 for an illustration. Although the spine is bordered by several groups of muscles, we focus on what are termed the superficial muscles in this chapter. When we discuss the core in chapter 7, we examine the muscles that make up the core and further focus on the deeper spinal muscles as well as the abdominal wall.

The upper back muscle is referred to as the *trapezius*. This large muscle originates at the base of the skull and along the cervical and thoracic vertebrae (the cervical vertebrae form the neck, and the thoracic vertebrae form the spinal column that attaches to the ribs). The fibers of the trapezius run longitudinally from the base of the skull to the back of the collarbone and attach to the spiny ridge of the scapulae. The trapezius is one of the muscles in the back that moves the shoulder blades together, as well as pulling the shoulders down and supporting the arm. The muscle is large and broad, and actually supports each side of the vertebral column in the upper back.

Because the trapezius muscle fibers run in three directions, they are responsible for three functions. The uppermost fibers, referred to as the *upper trapezius*, are mostly involved in shrugging the shoulders. A smaller muscle called the *levator scapula* assists with this shrugging action and lies just beneath the bone in the back known as the scapulae. When this part of the trapezius is well developed (as in wrestlers and American football linemen), the neck begins to appears shorter, or disappears, an extremely unattractive look for both women and men. The fibers of the *middle trapezius* (aided by the rhomboids, which are described next) pull the scapulae in toward the spine, a joint action called scapular retraction. Scapular retraction is a very important action in maintaining good posture and safe lifting techniques. The lower trapezius also works with the rhomboids to tug the scapulae downward, as in vertical pulling exercises such as pull-ups and lat pulldowns.

Hidden directly beneath the middle trapezius are the *rhomboid* muscles. These muscles originate on the thoracic vertebrae, descending diagonally downward. These muscles lie directly between the shoulder blades and assist the trapezius in pulling the shoulder blades together (scapular retraction). Strong trapezius and rhomboid muscles are key to horizontal pulling exercises and are crucial for balancing strength between the chest and back. Imbalances in these two muscle groups can lead to significant shoulder problems, poor posture, and unnecessary pain during lifting exercises as well as in everyday life.

The *latissimus dorsi* (*latissimus* meaning "broadest") are the large fan-shaped muscles on the back, starting on the lower vertebral column, spreading across the width of the back, and attaching posterior to the arm. When looking at the size, the latissimus dorsi are certainly the body's largest muscles. Their fibers originate along the vertebrae of the lower half of the spine, along the posterior ridge of the hips, and along the last three ribs. They then twist together to attach to the humerus, forming the back of the armpit.

The lats are extremely busy muscles because they play many roles. They extend, abduct, horizontally abduct, flex, and internally rotate the shoulder joint. In short, the lats bring the arms down and toward the body (adduction). They also have a synergistic role, because they assist in lateral flexion of the spine. Everything that the lats do, however, is assisted by the *teres major*, a small strip of muscle that originates on the scapulae and attaches to the humerus, just above where the lats do. Because the lats are the largest muscle group on the posterior upper body, strengthening them will make a big difference in both functional performance and the aesthetics of your back.

The low back muscles consist of two sets of muscles referred to as the *erector spinae,* or spinal erectors. These muscles are recruited for most heavy lifting. Within these muscles are three additional sets that further consist of three muscles: the iliocostalis, the longissimus, and the spinalis. They span the entire length of the spinal cord, all the way up to the neck. These are the longest muscle groups in the human body, having the important job of stabilizing the spinal column. This muscle group is particularly important because it is required to carry and maintain all the weight of the body.

Viewing your body from the side, if you were to stand so that you could draw a straight line from your ear to your shoulder, down to your hip and straight to your lateral ankle bone, you would be standing in a natural, appropriate posture—spinal extension. When performing spinal flexion (a bent forward posture), these muscles bring your body back to an upright position known as spinal extension. These muscles also counterbalance spinal flexion and extension by taking your spine into hyperextension. Spinal hyperextension is nothing more than arching your back or leaning backward, which is a normal daily occurrence with typically no negative consequences.

In well-developed physiques, the spinal erectors appear as developed ridges that run along the spine all the way up the back. It is important to have well-developed spinal erectors because these muscles work hard to support the low back during heavy weightlifting exercises such as deadlifts and squats, which we will explore in chapter 6, and bent-over rows, which we explore in this chapter.

The *quadratus lumborum* (or QL) also assists the spinal erectors when the spine bends sideways (lateral flexion) or twists. Each set of these QL muscles lies under the spinal erectors and originates on the top of the pelvis and inserts on the lower lumbar vertebrae, attaching to the bottom rib. When the lower fibers of the erector spinae muscles are weak, the QL pick up the slack. As a result, the QL are often the source of low back pain (especially as a result of sitting for long periods of time at a computer or driving, or of overusing low back supports such as pillows or stability belts). Unfortunately, sitting for long periods can cause these muscles to be put into a state of constant contraction, resulting in muscle fatigue that can cause decreased blood flow to these muscles and adhesions in the muscle and fascia.

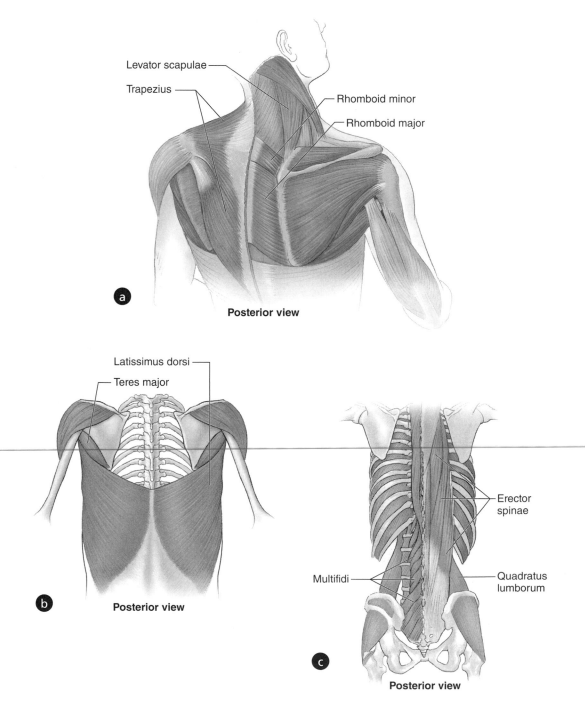

FIGURE 5.4 Muscular structure of the back.

These undersized muscles in particular may seem unimportant, but they are mighty important for maintaining spinal integrity and stability. All the muscles that support the spine (the core muscles and the many larger, superficial muscles, including the latissimus dorsi and trapezius, for example), should be trained for strength as well as endurance because their job is not always necessarily to move the spine, but to shore up any spinal weaknesses and to maintain structural integrity.

Arm Muscles

The muscles of the arm are related to the joint actions at the shoulder, elbow, and wrist. The shoulder, as discussed earlier, is a very complex joint involving several muscles. The elbow joint is simple to understand: its actions are flexion and extension. The forearm, however, is a bit more complex because of the long bones known as the radius and the ulna that form the *radioulnar joint*. See figure 5.5 for an illustration.

The forearm contains two sets of muscles that flex and extend the fingers and biceps; the flexors are located on the palm side, and the extensors are found along the side of the forearm. The forearm muscles, along with the biceps, also turn the hand faceup, a joint action called supination, as well as facedown, referred to as prone. The forearm flexors also pull the wrists forward or draw the hand down. The forearm extensors pull the wrists back. These muscles are small but important, especially when working the back and biceps muscle groups. They provide for a strong grip, critical for all the curling and pulling motions that most back and biceps exercises require. These muscles can be strengthened using exercises, but in the course of lifting, grasping, and pulling on handles and weights, they get a fair amount of training.

Two muscles that work when the elbow is flexed or extended are the biceps and the triceps. The *biceps brachii* is actually two muscles, the prefix *bi* refers to the fact that it has two heads. Both the long and short biceps muscles originate at the scapulae, but at different points. At their insertion, they share a common tendon that crosses the elbow joint and attaches to the radius. The biceps muscle is referred to as a triarticulate muscle because it works across three joints (the shoulder, the elbow, and the radioulnar joints).

The long biceps muscle assists the anterior deltoid and the pectoralis muscles (the uppermost fibers) in raising the arm up in front of the body. The short biceps muscle is mostly involved with one of the most important functions of the biceps muscle: supinating the forearm. Although the forearm does have a muscle designed specifically to supinate the wrist called the supinator, this muscle relies heavily on the biceps muscle to perform this action, particularly when the load is heavy.

Between the biceps muscles and the humerus is the brachialis, a thick band of tissue that attaches to the ulna. The main responsibility of this muscle is to assist the biceps in elbow flexion when the hand is in neutral (facing the side of the body) or when the palm is pronated (facing backward). The brachialis also has an assistor called the brachioradialis. This muscle is considered a forearm muscle, originating near the elbow and attaching to the wrist. It too plays a major role in elbow flexion.

It is important to understand which muscles are working, depending on the position of the hands (prone, supine, or neutral). Grip can make a huge difference in how these muscles work together. When performing exercises for the biceps with a supinated or underhanded grip (palms faceup), the biceps brachii are the main performers. When the grip changes to neutral (palm faces in, also called hammer style) or prone (palm faces down), the brachialis and the brachioradialis are involved with the lift much more. Even if you start a biceps curl in a neutral position and then rotate your hand out (supinate), you change the way you recruit the muscle fibers.

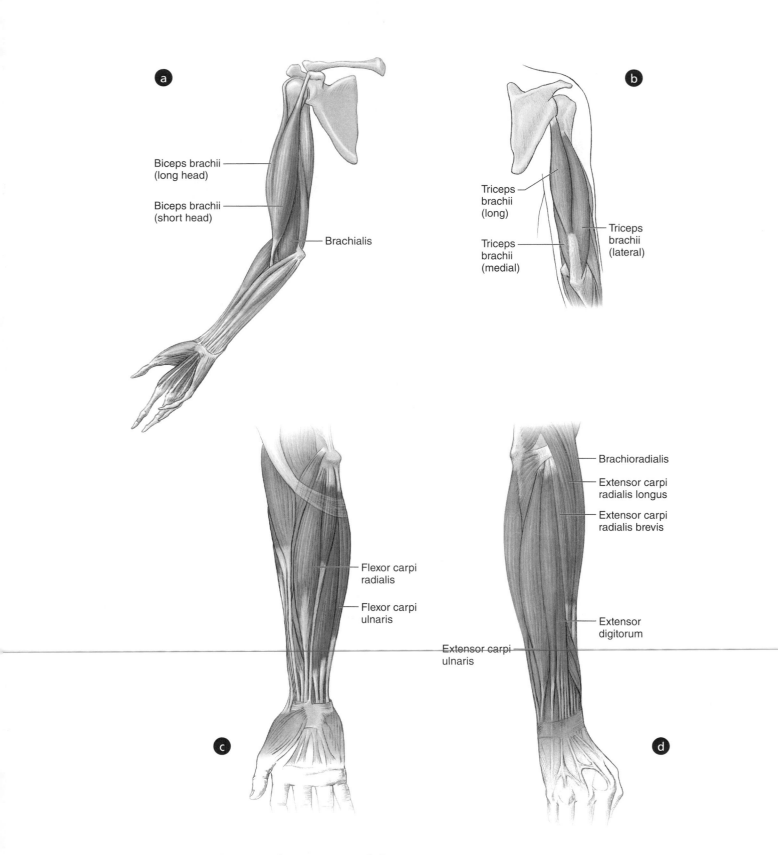

FIGURE 5.5 Muscular structure of the arms.

Grip width also matters. When holding on to a bar with a narrow grip, the long head (outer) gets more work. As the grip gets wider, fibers from the shorter (inner) head are recruited. These are important facts to remember because to change your exercise progressions and recruit fibers in a variety of ways, you need to not only vary the loads, but also change your grip.

The *triceps* are actually the larger of the two muscles on the humerus, making up almost 66 percent of the upper arm. The triceps are made up of three muscles: the lateral (this is most obvious on the outside of the upper arm), the middle, and the long muscles. The lateral muscle is located on the outside of the posterior arm and creates that horseshoe-looking shape you can sometimes see on a well-developed triceps. The rest of that horseshoe shape is muscle that is located on the back of the upper arm. The medial part of the triceps muscle is the thickest part and is located just above the elbow. Both the lateral and medial muscles originate at the humerus; the long part of the muscle originates at the scapula. All three muscles join at a tendon that attaches to the ulna. You might note that the biceps muscle attaches to the radius (the bone in the lower arm on the same side as the thumb), whereas the triceps muscle attaches to the ulna, or the bone on the side of the lower arm closer to the pinky finger.

Although focusing specifically on the triceps muscles is an efficient way to train them, particularly for beginners, the triceps are best put to use in heavy lifts. Developing them can help you perform multijoint exercises (i.e., those that involve the shoulder, the elbow, and the wrist) with greater loads and intensities, especially those that work the chest and shoulders. So when you lift heavy weights for the upper body, the triceps muscles really contribute to the effort. Therefore, if you want to get the triceps strong and lean, load them up with heavy weights.

UPPER BODY EXERCISES

When selecting exercises to perform for the upper body, consider your particular objective, the equipment available, and the time you have to train. Then, select the exercise sequence that suits you best. Also, exercise the most important muscle groups early in the exercise session. This will allow you to target the muscle groups that will help you achieve your goals before fatigue sets in.

The following sections describe upper body exercises in detail. Part III leads you through routines and offers suggestions and recommendations for training loads (i.e., how heavy the weights should be), training volume (i.e., how many sets and repetitions to perform for each exercise), and frequency (i.e., how often to train).

DUMBBELL CHEST PRESS

This exercise targets the chest, anterior deltoids, and triceps. Lie faceup on an exercise bench with your knees bent and your feet flat on the floor. Holding a dumbbell in each hand, position them along the sides of your chest with your elbows bent at a 90-degree angle and your palms turned toward your knees (see figure *a*). Press the weights upward above your body, until your arms are fully extended (see figure *b*). Try not to hold the weights above your eyes; rather, hold them over your chest. Fully extend your elbows, and then slowly lower them to the start position.

BARBELL CHEST PRESS

This exercise targets the chest, anterior deltoids, and triceps. Lie on an exercise bench with your feet flat on the floor. Hold the barbell with your hands slightly wider than shoulder-width apart and straight above your chest (see figure *a*). Slowly lower the barbell toward your chest but not quite touching it (see figure *b*); then press the bar straight back up and repeat.

DUMBBELL CHEST FLY

This exercise targets the chest, shoulders, and serratus anterior muscles. Lie on your back on a flat bench with your feet on the floor. With a dumbbell in each hand, raise your arms straight above your chest with your palms facing each other (see figure *a*). Slowly lower the dumbbells in an arc, so your hands end up out to the sides of your body and your elbows are bent just slightly as if you are wrapping your arms around a large tree trunk (see figure *b*). Slowly raise the weights back up in the same arc until they are together above your chest. Repeat.

STANDING CABLE CHEST FLY

This exercise targets the chest, shoulders, and serratus anterior muscles. Begin by positioning your body in the middle of the cable crossover machine and adjust the pulleys so that they are at about shoulder height. Standing in the middle of the machine with a staggered athletic stance, lower your center of gravity and lean slightly forward (see figure a). Much of the effort used in this exercise will come not only from your arms and chest, but also from the muscles of your legs and core. Hold a cable handle, one in each hand, and extend your arms directly out from your shoulders, palms facing in and elbows soft. Slowly open your arms in an arc in front of your body and move them out to your sides as far as is comfortable (see figure b). Maintain the same arc and return the hands to the start position.

DECLINE BARBELL PRESS

This exercise targets the lower fibers of the pectorals, shoulders, and triceps. Lie faceup on a decline bench with your head at the low end and your feet either on the floor or secured at the high end. Hold the barbell in an overhand grip slightly wider than shoulder width above your head, perpendicular to the floor (see figure *a*). Slowly lower the barbell toward your chest (see figure *b*), and then press the barbell back up above your chest, fully extending the elbow joints and repeat.

PUSH-UP

This exercise targets the chest, anterior deltoids, and triceps. Push-ups also require significant core muscle engagement. The following set-up guidelines for the push-up will help you maintain a proper plank pose, as well as initiate the push-up exercise from the proper starting position all the way through the range of motion to the finish.

Position your body facedown on the floor, hands slightly wider than shoulder-width apart. To determine the correct positioning of your hands and arms relative to your body, establish an open-palm hand position on the floor, with fingers spread and facing forward (see figure a). Now, draw an imaginary line between your thumbs, and position your sternum directly over that line. Slowly lower your body toward the floor so that your upper arms are parallel to the floor (see figure b). Keep your head in line with the rest of your spine and push yourself back up. If you struggle with full push-ups, simply open your feet wider on the floor behind you. This open foot position offers a larger base of support, assisting you with pushing your body weight. As you become stronger in this range of motion, bring your feet closer and closer until you can perform push-ups with your feet together.

INCLINE PUSH-UP

This exercise targets the upper pectorals, shoulders, and triceps. Start with your back to a staircase or a step platform; then kneel down and place your hands flat on the floor, shoulder-width apart. Place your feet on the second stair of the staircase or the step platform and adopt a push-up position (see figure a). Lower yourself until your upper arms are parallel to the floor (see figure b); then press your body back up and repeat.

DECLINE PUSH-UP

This exercise targets the lower pectoral muscles, shoulders, and triceps. Kneel on the floor facing a staircase, or set up a step platform, placing your hands on the second step, slightly wider than shoulder-width apart. If there is a bench in the weight room that you can lower to a position that is about the height of the second or third step on a staircase, you can use that. Extend your legs behind you, positioning yourself into a plank position; your body should be in a straight line from head to heels (see figure *a*). Your ab muscles, low back muscles, and side muscles near your waist line should be engaged. All of these muscles should be isometrically contracted, meaning that they are tight and working to hold your position. Lower yourself by flexing your elbows, so that your body is about a fist's distance from the step (see figure *b*). If this is too low for your current level of strength, just lower your body as low as you can while maintaining your form. Once you lower, pause for a breath and then press back up to the start position.

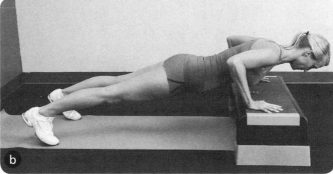

FRONT RAISE

This exercise targets the anterior deltoids. Stand with feet about hip-width apart, toes forward. With dumbbells in each hand, hold your arms at your sides, slightly in front of your body with your palms facing your thighs (see figure *a*). Keep your arms straight as you raise your arms up to shoulder height, parallel to the floor with palms facing down (see figure *b*). Pause at the top and slowly lower your arms back to your sides and repeat.

FRONT CABLE RAISE

This exercise targets the anterior deltoid, the muscle on the front part of your shoulder. Stand with your back to a low pulley station. Place the cable handle in your hand (figure *a*), and then slowly raise your arm up until it is parallel to the floor (see figure *b*). The arm should be fully lengthened, with the elbow and wrist straight. Pause at the top of the lift, and then slowly lower back down to the start position. Because of the nature of cable machines (i.e., typically only one handle per pulley station), you will probably have to perform this exercise one shoulder raise at a time. This is actually a good thing, because you will have to stabilize your core while performing this single-handed move.

LATERAL RAISE

This exercise targets the medial deltoids. Stand with feet shoulder-width apart, toes facing forward. Hold a dumbbell in each hand with your arms straight down by your sides (see figure *a*). Slowly raise your arms straight out to the sides until they are parallel to the floor (see figure *b*). In the raised position your shoulders will make the letter T. Pause at the top of the movement and then slowly lower back down to the start position.

SEATED SHOULDER PRESS

This exercise targets the anterior and medial deltoids and the triceps. Sit on the edge of an exercise bench or a stability ball with your feet on the ground and a dumbbell in each hand. To challenge your balance, bring your feet to shoulder width or narrower. Bring the weights to the sides of your shoulders, palms facing forward, back straight (see figure *a*). The weights should be about earlobe height. Press the weights up over your eyes until your elbows are fully extended (see figure *b*). Slowly lower back down to earlobe level and repeat.

DUMBBELL UPRIGHT ROW

This exercise targets the trapezius and the medial deltoid. Stand upright with your feet shoulder-width apart, holding a dumbbell in each hand. Let your arms hang straight down in front of you so that the dumbbells rest on your upper thighs, palms facing the body (see figure *a*). Slowly draw the weights up toward your chin and then return to the start position (see figure *b*). Keep your scapulae drawn down, opening the chest. Try not to raise the weights higher than shoulder height.

BENT-OVER DUMBBELL ROW

This exercise works the middle back, latissimus dorsi, rhomboids, trapezius, biceps, and brachioradialis. Stand with your feet together, flexed forward at the hips. Your back should be straight and very close to your thighs, and your knees should be flexed. With a dumbbell in each hand, place your hands directly under your shoulders (see figure *a*). Bring the dumbbells up toward your body, squeezing the muscles of your back between your shoulder blades together. Focus on bringing the weights up toward your lowest rib, with your elbows flexing back and upward toward the ceiling behind you (see figure *b*). Lower your arms until your elbows are fully extended.

STRAIGHT BAR UPRIGHT ROW

This exercise targets the trapezius and the medial deltoids. Stand upright with feet shoulder-width apart holding a barbell with your hands placed about 8 to 10 inches (20 to 25 cm) apart with an overhand grip so that your palms face your body. Let your arms hang straight down in front of you, so that the barbell hangs there (see figure a). Slowly draw the barbell straight up allowing your elbows to lead the movement. Allow the bar to come up to chest level (see figure b). Your elbows should be pointed out to the sides. Keep your scapulae drawn down, opening the chest. Slowly lower the barbell and repeat.

LAT PULLDOWN

This exercise works the latissimus dorsi, middle and upper trapezius, and biceps. Sit at a lat pulldown machine, grabbing the bar overhead with an overhand grip. To figure the hand position on the bar, make a V with your arms and then reach up and grab the bar at that width (see figure *a*). Maintain an erect spine and pull the bar toward your body until it reaches the top of your sternum (see figure *b*). Focus on bringing your arms toward the sides of your body as opposed to pulling them back. Slowly let the bar rise back up above your head, resisting the temptation to allow the bar to pull your arms back up. Do not pull the bar behind your back and neck.

PULL-UP

This exercise works the latissimus dorsi, middle back, and biceps. Grab a chin-up bar with your hands slightly wider than shoulder-width apart, palms facing away from you. Let yourself hang with your arms straight, feet off the floor (see figure *a*). Slowly pull yourself up until the bar is directly under your chin, or as high as you can based on your current ability (see figure *b*); then lower yourself back down and repeat.

PULLOVER

This exercise works the upper trapezius, the latissimus dorsi, the lower pectorals, and the triceps. Lie flat on an exercise bench with your feet flat on the floor. Grab a dumbbell and hold it vertically over your chest with both hands, wrapping your hands and fingers around the top base of the dumbbell so the bottom part hangs down in your hands (see figure a). Palms face upward. Slowly lower the dumbbell backward in an arc over your head until you feel a slight stretch in your arms, shoulders, and sides and the weight is over your head (see figure b). Slowly return to the start position (i.e., the weight is back over your chest). Keep your arms fully extended during the exercise, and be sure to control the movement.

SHRUG

This exercise works the trapezius and forearms. Hold a barbell (or a dumbbell in each hand). With the barbell, your hands will be facing toward you; with the dumbbells, the weights will face your sides (figure a). Maintain an erect posture and raise your shoulders as high as you can (see figure b). Pause slowly at the top; then with a slight rollback through the shoulder joint, lower your arms from the shoulder joint allowing a long stretch through the muscles.

REAR DELTOID FLY

This exercise works the posterior deltoids, trapezius, and rhomboids. Start with a dumbbell in each hand, feet together, and knees flexed. Flex your body from your hips to create a reverse arm raise position (see figure *a*). Maintain a head position that is neutral to the spine. Keep your eyes down without dropping your head. Keep an extended spine by tilting your hips back, or posterior. Slowly raise your arms up and out to the sides while keeping the movement smooth and not swinging the weights as you draw the arms in horizontal abduction out to the sides (see figure *b*). Lift and lower, feeling tension in the back of your shoulders, core, and middle back.

SEATED LOW ROW

This exercise works the latissimus dorsi, rhomboids, biceps brachii, and erector spinae. Sit down on a bench attached to a seated row machine and hold the handles with your palms facing down (see figure *a*). Sit with your back straight and your knees flexed, and place your feet against the metal block. Extend your arms feeling your lats stretch. Pull the weight back into your body until the handles touch your abdomen (see figure *b*). Bring your shoulder blades as far back as you can and maintain an erect spine. Slowly return the handles to the start position. There are a variety of handle attachments that can be used for rowing exercises.

SPINAL EXTENSION

There are many ways to perform spinal extension exercises. Because the deep muscles of the spine are small and numerous, you don't have to load them to achieve a training response. Therefore, body weight is often enough as long as you are using proper biomechanics. Following are some exercise examples, and there are many more. Chapter 7, Training the Core, provides more spinal as well as abdominal exercises.

PILATES SWIMMING

Lie facedown on an exercise mat. Keep your legs extended and your feet together. Pull your shoulder blades down, as if you were pulling them into your back pockets, and away from your ears. Extend your arms straight overhead. Pull your abdominal muscles up and in so that you lift your belly button up away from the floor. Reach out from your body's center, and extend your arms and legs so far in opposite directions that they naturally come up off the floor. At the same time, extend the length of your spine so that your head lifts up off the mat as an extension of the reach of your spine (see figure a). Keep your face down toward the mat. Continue to reach your arms and legs out as you alternate right arm/left leg, then left arm/right leg, pumping them up and down in small pulses as if kicking in the water (see figure b). You should feel like you are simulating swimming. Move from your glutes and your shoulder joint. Perform two or three cycles of five counts of moving and breathing. You can increase the intensity of this exercise by adding light hand or ankle weights.

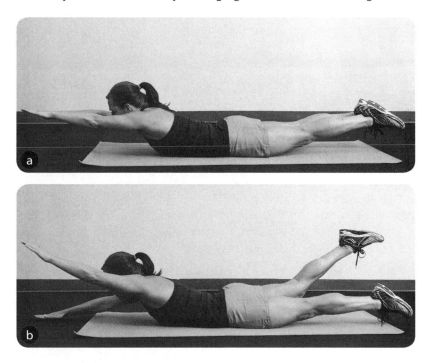

QUADRUPED SPINAL EXTENSION

From a quadruped position (on hands and knees), you will be extending the opposing hip and arm much like swimming, but you will not pulse the moves; instead, you will hold them. To get into proper quadruped position, place your hands directly under your shoulders, palms open, fingers spread (see figure a). Your knees should be directly under your hips, hip-width apart. The spine is in an extended, neutral position. Simultaneously extend the right arm from the shoulder joint and the left leg from the hip (see figure b). Your arm should be extended as much as possible with your biceps and ear lining up. Hold your hand with your thumb up as if you were about to shake someone's hand. Your leg should be held at the height of your hip and no higher. Hold the position for 6 to 10 seconds and then return to the start position, at which point you extend the left arm and right leg.

BICEPS CURL WITH EZ CURL BAR

This exercise works the biceps and forearms. Stand upright with your feet shoulder-width apart, holding an EZ Curl Bar (or dumbbells in each hand) with an underhand grip (see figure a). From a fully extended arm position, slowly curl the bar upward toward your shoulders (see figure b), pause, then slowly lower it back to your thighs, fully extending your elbow joint. Do not swing or use your back to lift the bar.

HAMMER CURL

This exercise works your forearms and biceps. Stand straight with a dumbbell in each hand, arms by your sides and with your palms facing in toward your thighs in a neutral grip (see figure *a*). Slowly curl both dumbbells up toward your shoulders (see figure *b*). Keep your palms facing your sides as you lift up, and try not to turn your wrists. Slowly lower the weights back down.

PREACHER CURL

This exercise works the biceps. Sit at a preacher curl station holding a barbell in both hands, palms facing up, and rest your upper arms on the slanted pad in front of you (see figure *a*). Keep your back straight (don't hunch forward over the pad) and curl the bar up toward your shoulders (see figure *b*). Slowly lower the weight and repeat. If you do not have a preacher curl station, kneel behind a stability ball using the ball the same way you would the preacher curl station.

REVERSE CURL

A reverse curl emphasizes the biceps and forearms. Holding a dumbbell in each hand, hang your arms straight down in front of you with your palms facing the front of your thighs in a prone grip (see figure a). Keeping your back straight and torso upright, slowly curl both dumbbells up toward your shoulders (see figure b). Don't allow your wrists to turn, or "break," as you raise straight up. The backs of your hands should be facing the front of your shoulders at the top of the move. Lower the weights with control.

TRICEPS KICKBACK

This exercise is specific to the triceps muscles located on the back of the upper arms. Stand with your side to an exercise bench and place a dumbbell in your hand on the side away from the bench. Rest your other hand and knee on the exercise bench and bring the hand with the dumbbell in it up to the side of your body (see figure a). Hold it in position alongside your body and press back until the elbow is fully extended (see figure b); then lower the weight to the start position.

TRICEPS DIP

This is a great core and triceps exercise. Sit on a sturdy chair and move forward until your palms are on the edge of the chair, fingers hanging off the front edge and hips in front of the seat of the chair. Keep your hands in place and step forward until your feet are on the floor in front of you (see figure *a*). Keep your arms straight, supporting the weight of your body. Slowly lower your body toward the floor, flexing your elbows behind you and hinging at the hips (see figure *b*), and then press back until your arms are straight, elbows unlocked.

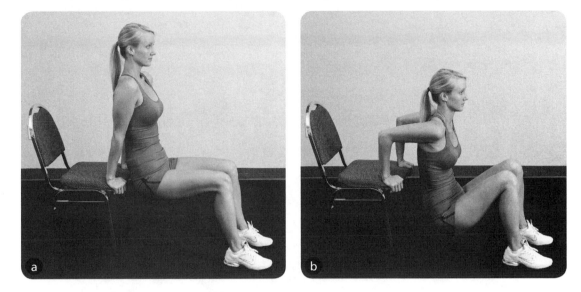

TRX CHEST PRESS

This exercise strengthens the chest, shoulders, triceps, and core. Stand facing away from the TRX anchor point with the straps long, or fully extended. Keep your feet wide to maximize stability, or bring them closer for more intensity. Place your hands into the handles and select an angle for your body to stand in. The steeper the angle, the more challenging and intense the exercise will be. Begin with your elbows flexed (see figure *a*), and press your arms into a straight line (see figure *b*). Keep your hands high enough to prevent the straps from rubbing on your arms. Continue to move through a chest press with core activation. Don't allow your back to sag or your belly to hang in front.

TRX MID ROW

This exercise strengthens the midback, rear deltoids, biceps, and core. Stand facing the TRX anchor point with the straps fully shortened. Keep your feet wide to maximize stability, or bring them closer for more intensity. Place your hands into the handles and select an angle for your body to stand in. The steeper the angle, the more challenging and intense the exercise will be. Begin with your elbows flexed, and pull your arms into a row position (see figure a). As you draw your hands toward your shoulders, keep your elbows in line with your shoulders (see figure b). Continue to move through a row with core activation. Don't allow your back to arch. Note that you can change this exercise simply by changing the rowing positions (e.g., low row or high row) or make it more difficult by creating a steeper angle.

TRX ATOMIC PUSH-UP

This combination of movements creates a high-intensity, total-body exercise, specifically targeting the core, chest, and triceps. Get on the floor with your toes in the foot cradles, facing away from the TRX anchor point and with the straps lengthened to midcalf length (foot cradle about 8 in from the floor). Align your body under and directly in line with the anchor point. Start on your hands with your body in a full plank position (see figure *a*). Drive your tailbone upward, and pull your knees into your chest, creating a rounded spine (see figure *b*). To make the exercise more challenging, move forward or away from the anchor point.

TRX Y DELTOID FLY

This exercise builds strength in the middle and rear deltoids. Stand facing the TRX anchor point with the straps shortened to midlength. Keep your feet offset (as shown) or wide to maximize stability, or bring them closer for more intensity. Place your hands into the handles and select an angle for your body to stand in. The steeper the angle, the more challenging and intense the exercise will be. Begin with your elbows fully extended and your arms raised above your shoulders in a Y position (see figure a). Without dropping your hips, lower your arms to the front (see figure b), and then raise your hands back to a Y position above your head. Don't allow the straps to lose tension. Keep your hands in line with your shoulders with straight elbows. Continue to move through a deltoid raise with core activation. Don't allow your back to arch. Note that you can change this exercise by changing the positions of your arms (e.g., an I deltoid raise if you raise them over your head, or a T deltoid raise if you move them out to the sides).

You are now familiar with the upper body exercises that are listed in the programs outlined later in the book. Following the descriptions and referring to the corresponding photos, you should be able to replicate each exercise easily. Remember, take your time with the exercises, and modify them if you need to. Weight loads, sets, and repetitions will be given to you in later chapters with specific guidelines, but always respect your body and honor your current level of fitness, skill level, competence, and ability. You have plenty of time to learn exercises that may be new to you or especially challenging. Most important, remember that the exercise experience is a journey. Take your time and enjoy it.

Training the Lower Body

Strength training for a great lower body is well worth the effort. The muscles of the lower body (gluteals, hamstrings, quadriceps, hip flexors, adductors, and calves) are easy to target and respond well to a variety of strength exercises, resulting in beautiful and shapely legs, thighs, and gluteal muscles. Many women find that they have to work hard on "trouble spots," including thighs that spread, undeveloped gluteal muscles that are more flat than round, and too much fat on the inner thighs. Some women also have cellulite, an elusive issue, to say the least.

Your genetics and current exercise and eating habits play a large role in determining the amount of fat or muscle mass on your legs, as well as their strength, leanness, and firmness. There is no doubt you will have to decrease your caloric intake and increase your cardio efforts if you want to lose fat mass in your legs. Forget the notion of spot reduction (see chapter 2) with respect to losing weight and gaining strength and leanness in your lower body. No amount of training on a specific muscle or area on the thigh or leg will result in fat loss in that area exclusively. Training the legs requires an "all or none" approach, meaning that you have to perform the right exercises with the right amount of weight to achieve the results you desire. No matter your goal, the exercises here will leave you with a fabulous lower body in a matter of weeks that will give you months and years of strength and beauty.

ANATOMY OF THE LOWER BODY

The muscles of your legs are broken down into anterior and posterior muscle groups. On the top front of the thigh is your largest lower body muscle group: the quadriceps. The inner part of the thigh includes the adductor muscle group, usually referred to as the inner thigh. Behind the thigh are the hamstring muscles, and on the back of the leg, the calf. The gluteal muscles, also located on the posterior portion of the body, are a collection of three muscles (the gluteus maximus, minimus, and medius). The gluteus maximus is the largest muscle on the lower body. Having a good understanding of the muscles of the legs, where they are located, how they work, and the joints they act on will help you select exercises based on your goals.

Gluteals

The muscles that comprise the butt are divided into three groups: the *gluteus maximus*, the *gluteus medius*, and the *gluteus minimus* (figure 6.1). The gluteus maximus is the body's strongest muscle. Originating at the pelvic bone, it inserts at the back of the femur, along a band of tissue known as the tensor fascia lata. The medius and minimus also originate at the pelvis, but they insert along the length of the femur. The gluteus maximus assists the hamstrings to extend the hip, or pull the leg behind when walking or running, and externally rotate the femur in the hip joint.

The gluteus medius and minimus abduct the hip, drawing the leg out to the side. They also flex the hip and internally rotate the femur. These muscles also play a large role in stabilizing the pelvis while the body moves in the sagittal plane (e.g., when walking) and also during kicking. The gluteus medius and minimus must be strong and balanced in their strength to stabilize the pelvis and low back.

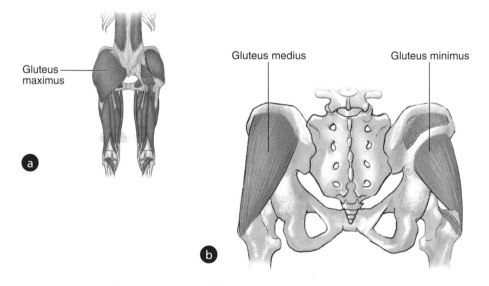

FIGURE 6.1 Muscular structure of the gluteals.

Adductors

The adductor muscles are located on the inside of the femur. These are frequently referred to as the inner thigh muscles. Adduction is the action of bringing the leg closer to the midline of the body. The adductors are actually quite large and surprisingly numerous. Although we don't typically perform many actions that are specific to bringing the leg closer to the middle of the body (kicking a ball in soccer is one example), we do need the large adductors to stabilize the femur and the pelvis during both lateral and sagittal plane motions. The adductors are largely responsible for power and stability at the hip joint and the femur.

The largest of the adductors is the *adductor magnus* (figure 6.2). This muscle originates on the pubic bone and attaches to the lateral side of the femur, right on the inside top of the knee. The *adductor longus* (the longest adductor muscle) and the *adductor brevis* (the shortest) are progressively shorter adductor muscles and attach closer to the hip on the pelvis. Two other adductor muscles are the *pectineus* and the *gracilis*.

Women often try to work the inner thigh muscles in the gym to shrink the size of their legs. This result will never be achieved because spot reduction is not possible (see chapter 2). It is not possible to shrink the size of, or lose fat in, a specific area. Although there are exercises that target the adductors, these muscles respond to the exercises performed for any of the lower body muscles.

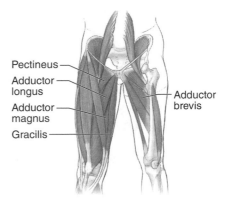

FIGURE 6.2 Muscular structure of the adductors.

Hamstrings

The hamstrings make up the posterior region of the thigh. They cover the femur entirely and are composed of three muscles: the *biceps femoris*, the *semitendinosus*, and the *semimembranosus* (figure 6.3). All originating on the pelvis, these muscles stretch down the length of the femur and insert either on the tibia (shinbone) or on the head of the fibula on the outside of the knee. The three hamstring muscles (with the exception of the short head of the biceps femoris) work to flex the knee joint and extend the hip joint.

The biceps femoris is the outermost posterior thigh muscle. Part of the muscle lies toward the outside of the thigh and originates on the femur. The other part of the muscle originates on the femur and is the only hamstring muscle that doesn't cross the hip joint. This part of the muscle is involved exclusively in knee flexion; it has no role in hip extension.

The semitendinosus is a smaller muscle that originates on the pelvis and shares a tendon with the biceps femoris, running alongside it until it inserts at the tibia on the inside of the knee. The semimembranosus lies alongside the semitendinosus on the inside back of the femur. It originates and inserts in the same place the semitendinosus does, but has a longer tendon at the top and a shorter one at the bottom.

The hamstring muscles have enormous growth potential, but they do not respond well to exercises that attempt to work them at both ends at the same time. Because the hamstring muscles cross the hip joint and flex the knee, they don't respond to exercises that create knee flexion and hip extension at the same time. However, performing these two joint actions separately yields great results in hamstring strength, size, power, and most important, function.

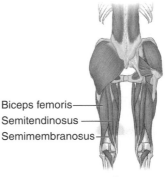

FIGURE 6.3 Muscular structure of the hamstrings.

Quadriceps

There are four quadriceps muscles that perform a simple task: straightening the knee joint once it is flexed. This is a fundamental movement to most actions of the leg, which is why the quadriceps is capable of tremendous strength, as well as endurance.

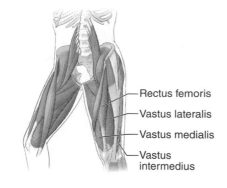

— Rectus femoris

— Vastus lateralis

— Vastus medialis

— Vastus intermedius

FIGURE 6.4 Muscular structure of the quadriceps.

The *rectus femoris* is part of the quadriceps group and plays a major role in hip flexion (figure 6.4). This muscle appears to split down the middle of the thigh, originating at the pelvis and ending along with three other quadriceps muscles in the quadriceps tendon, which crosses the patella (kneecap) and attaches to the tibia. The remaining three quad muscles are commonly referred to as the vastus group. The *vastus lateralis* is a large muscle on the outer portion of the thigh, originating on the outside top of the femur. The *vastus medialis* originates on the inside of the femur attaching vertically along the majority of the bone. It is large and thick at the bottom, and when it is fully developed, it makes a teardrop shape just inside the knee. Beneath the rectus femoris and between the vastus lateralis and vastus medialis lies the *vastus intermedius*, with origination points along the entire front of the femur.

Although it is possible to isolate most of the quadriceps muscles to develop them aesthetically, working them together is the best functional training. Why perform a partial knee extension exercise to target the vastus medialis (located along the inside of the knee joint), when you don't use that muscle exclusive of all the other quadriceps muscles? It makes better sense to train the whole group.

Hip Flexors

The hip flexors are a group of muscles that acts on the femur by pulling it up toward the hip. These muscles are involved in a simple but important movement appropriately called hip flexion. When you lift your leg out in front of your body (if you are sitting, you are already doing this), you are performing hip flexion.

Sometime during the past decade, physical therapists and personal trainers have warned against the overuse of the hip flexors during exercise. The reasoning behind this precaution has to do with lumbar curvature and muscle tightness, and has mainly to do with another hip flexor muscle called the *psoas major* (figure 6.5). This muscle originates on the vertebrae of the low back (lumbar vertebrae) and attaches to the inside top of the femur. When it flexes (shortens), it pulls the vertebrae of the low back into a more pronounced arch, exacerbating lordosis (a significant improper arch in the low back). Strong abdominal muscles are necessary to resist that pull and keep the low back in a neutral position while exercising. Therefore, having sufficient abdominal strength is extremely important when performing exercises such as hanging leg raises, which force the psoas to tug hard on the lumbar vertebrae. If you already have low back pain, you should not risk performing these exercises. The psoas works concomitantly with another muscle called the *iliacus*. This muscle originates on the inside of the pelvis and meets the psoas on the top of the femur. The two muscles share a tendon and are so closely related in proximity as well as role that they are referred to as the iliopsoas.

The largest hip flexor visible to the naked eye is the *rectus femoris*, the only quadriceps muscle that crosses the hip joint. Because it crosses the hip joint, it is largely involved in hip flexion. Another visible hip flexor muscle (in those who are really lean) is the *sartorius*. This is the body's longest muscle; it originates at the outside of the pelvis, crosses the femur diagonally, and attaches to the tibia just below the inside of the knee. When crossing both the hip and knee joints, it acts as a hip flexor to lift the leg to the front. It also works with the gluteals and other hip extensors to abduct the leg from the hip (side leg lift). The sartorius also plays a minor role in knee extension.

The final hip flexor muscle is the *tensor fascia latae*. This muscle is part connective tissue and is located on the front of the femur. This muscle and its connective tissue can play a role in some knee pain and injuries, runner's knee in particular.

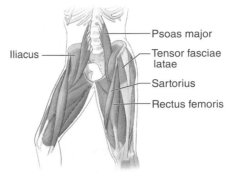

FIGURE 6.5 Muscular structure of the hip flexors.

Lower Leg Muscles

The three muscles on the back of the lower leg are collectively referred to as the calf. The largest and most lateral muscle is the *gastrocnemius* (figure 6.6). This muscle, in very well-developed calves, is easy to distinguish. Because the gastrocnemius originates on the bottom of the femur's epicondyles (the knobs on the inside and outside of the bottom of the femur), the muscle actually crosses the knee joint. Subsequently, when you perform an exercise with knee flexion (e.g., a hamstring curl), you are engaging the gastrocnemius because it helps the hamstrings perform that joint action. Another muscle that helps the gastrocnemius is the *peroneus longus*. It can be seen in very lean legs as a strip of muscle located laterally between the gastrocnemius and the shinbone, or tibia.

The *soleus* is a flat sheath of muscle that lies beneath the gastrocnemius. You can identify this muscle from the back—it lies under the gastrocnemius just above the point where the gastrocnemius and the soleus combine to form the Achilles tendon, which attaches at the heel. Typically, the gastrocnemius and the soleus work together. To isolate the soleus, you could flex the knee joint to 90 degrees and perform a calf raise. The knee flexion cancels out the supporting role of the gastrocnemius, placing all of the effort in the soleus.

The calves are important in the performance of any sport or activity in which the body moves through the sagittal plane (e.g., walking, running, cycling). The calves work with most of the larger lower body exercises (e.g., squats, deadlifts). While the quadriceps work with the knee joint, and the hamstrings and gluteals work with the hips joint to create force and power for the legs to thrust the body forward, the calves work with the ankle joints to provide the final push-off.

The main joint action the calves are responsible for is plantar flexion: the action of pointing the toes so that the heel pulls up closer to the knee joint. The calves are important muscles to develop not only for sports and activity but for aesthetics as well. Like the triceps, the calves develop from performing large-muscle, lower body exercises. However, we will dedicate some exercises to the specific development of this muscle group.

Another set of muscles located on the front of the lower leg are the shin muscles. The largest of these is the *tibialis anterior*. It lies just to the side of the shinbone (tibia). Although it is the largest of the anterior leg muscles, it is still small and thin, originating on the tibia and attaching to the inside top of the foot. Right next to it lies the *extensor digitorum longus*. Both of these muscles (along with a few others) perform ankle dorsiflexion: pulling the toes up toward the shin. The joint actions of both plantar flexion and dorsiflexion are important in the performance of many activities, including the simple act of walking. Maintaining the quality of ankle joint actions is important for preventing foot, ankle, and leg injuries, as well as maintaining the ability to walk with a normal gait pattern. Although we do not specifically perform any exercises for these muscles, they are trained with any exercise that engages the ankle in plantar flexion.

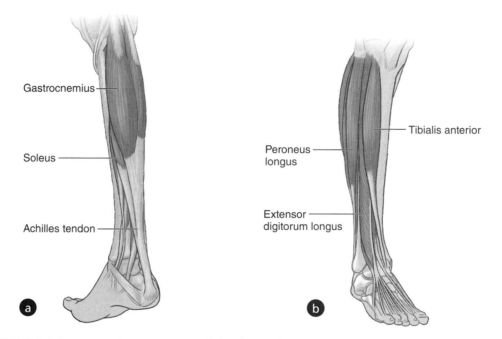

FIGURE 6.6 Muscular structure of the lower leg.

LOWER BODY EXERCISES

When selecting exercises to perform for the lower body, consider your particular objective, the equipment available, and the time you have to train. Then, select the exercise sequence that suits you best. Also, exercise the most important muscle groups early in the session. This will allow you to target the muscle groups that will help you achieve your goals before fatigue sets in.

The following sections describe lower body exercises in detail, including the muscles they work and the equipment you should use to train them. Part III outlines programs in which to plug these exercises along with recommended repetitions and sets and when to do each one based on your goals and needs.

DUMBBELL FRONT SQUAT

This exercise targets the quadriceps and the gluteal muscles. Stand holding a pair of dumbbells with your feet shoulder-width apart and your knees unlocked. Bring the weights up in front of your body, resting each dumbbell on the top of each shoulder (see figure a). Your hands are in a neutral position with your elbows pointing straight out in front. Slowly squat down, lowering your body and flexing your knees and hips until your thighs are almost parallel to the floor (see figure b). Avoid bending forward from the waist. Hold for a brief moment, and then slowly return to the start position.

GOOD MORNING

This exercise targets the gluteals, hamstrings, and low back. Stand in front of a pair of dumbbells with your feet approximately hip-width apart, knees extended but not locked. Flex forward from the waist and reach down to grab the dumbbells with an overhand grip (see figure a). Keep your spine and legs straight. Rise back up to the standing position, bringing the weights to the front of your thighs (see figure b). Resist the urge to pull with your arms. Keep your elbows straight throughout the entire exercise.

SEATED HAMSTRING CURL

This exercise targets the hamstrings and gluteals. Sit at a hamstring curl machine with the appropriate weight selected. Adjust your body so that your knees are aligned with the cam in the machine and your feet are placed over the pad in front of your ankles (see figure *a*). Slowly draw your feet down away from your body, maintaining a stable upper body, flexing your knees, and squeezing your gluteals (see figure *b*). Slowly raise yourself up.

SUPINE STABILITY BALL BRIDGE

This exercise targets the gluteals. Lie supine with your heels on the top of the stability ball and your arms on the floor straight by your sides. Flex your knees, bringing them closer to your chest while keeping your feet on the stability ball (see figure *a*). Slowly press your hips upward, squeezing your glutes (see figure *b*); hold for two seconds, and then slowly return to the start position.

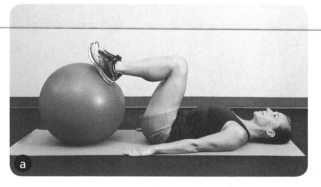

STABILITY BALL GLUTEAL SQUEEZE

This exercise targets the gluteals. Lie facedown on a stability ball. Your fingers and palms should be in contact with the ground, and your toes should be balanced on the floor. Your legs should be fully extended with your body balanced on top of the stability ball (see figure *a*). Use a four-count tempo to raise your legs up while abducted (see figure *b*); bring your heels together (see figure *c*), open your legs, and lower your feet back to the floor (see figure *d*).

FRONT LUNGE

This exercise targets the gluteals and quadriceps. Stand with a dumbbell in each hand using a neutral grip, arms hanging straight down by your sides (see figure *a*). Maintain an erect spine as you step forward with your left foot. Bring your front thigh parallel to the floor, knee flexed straight down behind you (see figure *b*). Push yourself back to the start position, and then forward with the right foot.

REVERSE LUNGE

This exercise targets the quadriceps, gluteals, calves, and hip flexors. Stand with your feet about hip-width apart, a dumbbell in each hand, neutral grip, and arms straight down by your sides (see figure *a*). Maintain an erect spine as you step back onto the ball of your foot, lowering your body until your thigh is parallel to the floor (see figure *b*). Return to the start position and switch legs, step back, and then come back to the start position.

WALKING LUNGE

This exercise targets the quadriceps, gluteals, calves, and hamstrings. Stand with a dumbbell in each hand, feet hip-width apart, arms down by your sides (see figure *a*). Step forward in a long step, lowering your back knee to approximately a 90-degree angle (see figure *b*) while flexing your front knee in the same manner. Without pausing, push off your back foot and bring that leg next to your front leg (see figure *c*). Continue walking forward, alternating legs.

SIDE LUNGE

This exercise targets the quadriceps, gluteals, hamstrings, and calves. Stand tall with feet shoulder-width apart and holding a dumbbell in each hand; hang your arms down by your sides (see figure *a*). Step to the left side with your left foot. Place it on the floor slightly in front of your body and lean into it until your knee is flexed to approximately a 90-degree angle (see figure *b*). Use the quadriceps and push yourself back up to an upright stance; then repeat on the right side.

DUMBBELL SQUAT

This exercise targets your quadriceps and gluteals. There are several ways to perform a squat. We will use dumbbells for this example. Hold a dumbbell in each hand (see figure *a*). Your feet should be approximately hip-width apart. If you feel unstable, or the weight feels really heavy, widen your stance. Moving your base of support (your feet) wider than your spine will give you some additional stability. Keep your arms by your sides, your chest lifted, and your spine straight. Slowly lower your body down toward the floor until your thighs are almost parallel to the floor (see figure *b*). Hold for just a moment, and then return to the upright position.

SINGLE-LEG SQUAT

This exercise targets your quadriceps and challenges balance. Use a pole, pillar, or wall for additional support. Place one hand against the wall and hold a dumbbell or a kettlebell in the other hand. Stand on one leg with the other leg out in front of your body so your heel is just hovering over the floor (see figure *a*). Lower yourself as far as you can (see figure *b*), pause, and return to the start position.

SEATED LEG PRESS

This exercise targets your quadriceps. Sit on the leg press machine with your low back in a neutral position against the back pad. Place your feet on the plate about shoulder-width apart. Press on the foot plate and release the hand brake extending your legs as you do so. Lower the foot plate allowing it to descend as low is as comfortable (see figure *a*). Keep your feet flat on the plate and your back against the pad. Pause briefly; then push the foot plate back until your knees are nearly straight, but still slightly flexed (see figure *b*).

SEATED LEG EXTENSION

This exercise targets your quadriceps. Sit on the leg extension machine with your knee joints on the edge of the seat. Fit yourself into the machine by making adjustments as necessary (see figure *a*). Extend your legs until your knees are straight (see figure *b*). Focus on the contraction of the quadriceps and lower the weight with control without banging the weight plates and repeat.

SEATED CALF RAISE

This exercise targets the soleus. Position yourself on the seated calf machine with the pad across your knees and the balls of your feet on the platform (see figure a). Lower your heels, and then raise them (see figure b). Your feet and ankles will feel the load of this exercise. If you do not have a calf machine, you can hold heavy dumbbells just above each knee.

KETTLEBELL SQUAT

This exercise targets the quadriceps, gluteals, obliques, shoulders, and hamstrings. Start with your feet wider than hip-width apart, knees slightly bent, chest lifted. Hold the kettlebell in your hands with your arms extended in front of your body (see figure a). This is your start position. Hinge forward at the hips and flex your knees as you lower the kettlebell down between your legs (see figure b). This will feel like a squat. As you stand up, thrust the hips and kettlebell forward, straightening up and bringing the kettlebell up and over your head or as high as you can go (see figure c). Return to the start position and repeat.

ANGLE KETTLEBELL SQUAT

This exercise targets the gluteals, abductors, quadriceps, and core. Stand with your feet wider than your hips, with your toes slightly turned out. Hold the kettlebell in front of and at the center of your body with your elbows slightly bent (see figure a). Flex your knees, lowering your body into a squat position (see figure b). As you rise back up, press off your right foot and raise your right leg up, leaning to the left; at the same time, lift the kettlebell overhead (see figure c). Slowly lower back down to the center squat position. Alternate to the right side as the left leg comes up, and repeat the sequence.

KETTLEBELL HIP HINGE

This exercise targets the gluteals. Stand upright with your left leg lifted and your knee flexed at 90 degrees, and hold the kettlebell in your right hand (see figure a). Slowly hinge forward from your hips, extending your spine with your right leg coming up in extension behind you (see figure b). Allow the kettlebell to lower and hang directly over the floor. Stand back up and bring your knee back to the flexed start position. Repeat on the other leg.

SQUAT SEQUENCE WITH CURTSY LUNGE

This exercise challenges the legs and glutes, but also targets the muscles of the core, shoulders, and back. This exercise occurs in a specific sequence, so the repetitions are set for you. This exercise requires 60 repetitions. Begin in a standing position with feet shoulder-width apart and holding a medicine ball in front of you. Lower your body into a squat (see figure *a*), and when you rise back up, bring the ball above your head using straight arms for 10 repetitions (see figure *b*). Continue with the squat and the arm raise, but add a knee lift for 10 repetitions (see figure *c*). Continue with the squat and the knee raise, adding a curtsy lunge for an additional 10 repetitions (see figure *d*). To perform the curtsy lunge from the knee lift position, bring your raised knee behind your supporting leg and the weight will follow the leg in the same direction, crossing in the front of the knee. Once you have successfully completed all 30 repetitions, start again from the squat with the overhead raise and repeat using the other leg for the knee lift and curtsy lunge.

TRX SQUAT

This exercise targets the muscles of the legs including the hamstrings, quadriceps, and gluteal muscles. Stand erect facing the TRX anchor point with the straps adjusted to midlength. Place your hands in the handles with your elbows flexed at about 90 degrees; your toes point forward, and your feet are hip-width apart (see figure a). Lower your body through a squat range of motion, dropping your tailbone down toward the floor (see figure b). Press your glutes behind you on the way down, and engage them on the way up. Drive through the exercise with your legs, allowing your hands to be supported by the straps. Avoid pulling yourself up using the straps.

TRX SINGLE-LEG SQUAT

This exercise challenges core stability while balancing the strength between the right and left legs. The TRX allows for a greater range of motion than you could achieve without the straps. Stand erect facing the TRX anchor point with the straps adjusted to midlength. Place your hands in the handles with your elbows flexed at about 90 degrees; your toes point forward, and your feet are hip-width apart with your left foot centered to the anchor point (see figure a). Flex your right hip and knee to the front of the body, using your quad to hold your leg up (see figure b). Keep your heel on the ground to allow for full leg and gluteal activation. Press your glutes behind you on the way down, and engage them on the way up. Drive through the exercise with your legs, allowing your hands to be supported by the straps; avoid pulling yourself up using the straps. Perform the same amount of time or repetitions on each leg.

TRX STEP BACK LUNGE

This is an effective exercise for the hamstrings and gluteal muscles that will help you progress your single-leg balance and strength. Stand erect facing the TRX anchor point with the straps adjusted to midlength. Place your hands in the handles with your elbows flexed at about 90 degrees; your toes point forward, and your feet are hip-width apart. Step back, as shown in figures *a* and *b*, and then return to the start position, alternating legs each time. Keep your chin lifted with an open chest and avoid rounding your upper back forward.

TRX BALANCE LUNGE

This exercise challenges core stability while lunging with one leg in the TRX. Adjust the straps to midcalf and place one foot into the foot cradles. Lower your body down to the floor in a yoga hinge position (see figure). Slowly rise up to a standing position. Continue this exercise, lowering the body down into a lunge with the back foot in the foot cradle and moving your arms as if moving through the sagittal plane. Repeat on other leg.

TRX HIP PRESS

This exercise challenges the gluteal muscles and activates the core, back extensors, and hamstrings. Lie on the floor facing the TRX anchor point with the straps adjusted to midcalf length. Place your heels in the foot cradles (see figure *a*). Apply even pressure in the foot cradles to avoid a sawing motion at the equalizer loop. Place both arms and hands on the floor alongside your body. Pull your knees into your chest; flex your knees over your hips and press your hips upward (see figure *b*), and then lower them back down. This is a gluteal exercise, so if you are not feeling the work in your glutes, move forward on the floor and bring your body under the anchor point until you feel glute activation.

TRX HAMSTRING CURL

This exercise builds core stability as well as hamstring strength. Lie on the floor facing the TRX anchor point with the straps adjusted to midcalf length. Place your heels in the foot cradles. Lift your hips up and off the floor (see figure *a*). Pull your knees into your chest (see figure *b*) and then press back out again. Maintaining the lifted hip position keeps constant resistance throughout the exercise. Be sure to pull your toes back toward your chin during the exercise.

You are now familiar with the lower body exercises that are listed in the programs outlined in chapters 10 and 11. Following the descriptions and referring to the corresponding photos, you should be able to replicate each exercise easily. Remember, take your time with the exercises, and modify them if you need to. In addition, weight loads, sets, and repetitions will be given to you in the programs in chapters 10 and 11 with specific guidelines, but always respect your body and honor your current level of fitness, skill level, competence, and ability. You have plenty of time to learn exercises that may be new to you or especially challenging. Most important, remember that the exercise experience is a journey. Take your time and enjoy it.

CHAPTER 7

Training the Core

Core work has gained a lot of attention in the past several years. Only recently has the term *core* been used in place of the word *abdominals* to refer to the midsection of the body. Many people are still confused about what the term *core* refers to. How you define the core influences how you integrate exercises into your routines.

Although many consider the core muscles to be the abdominals, this is only partially true. Some experts compare the core muscles to a cylinder. The core muscles extend from the upper two ribs down into the depths of the pelvic floor; the collection of core muscles, spinal cord, tendons, and ligaments all work together in a coordinated way. For example, the muscles of the core are largely involved in each breath you take. When you breathe, your diaphragm lowers; the ribs expand and articulate with the vertebrae of your thoracic spine. The upper two ribs interact with the cervical vertebrae, and the pelvic floor stretches to open up the hip joints.

The important point to remember is that core movements do not require large amounts of effort. In fact, large, forceful movements restrict the body's ability to make these subtle, sensory distinctions. Consider the core muscles as your body's brakes. They are largely responsible for stopping movements, also known as deceleration, and therefore help the brain respond to subtle cues about the position of the body in space. These small, slight movements allow the central nervous system to integrate these faint, more efficient core movement patterns into maintenance of balance and kinesthetic awareness. In other words, the brain knows where the body is in space due to these subtle cues that the core muscles send to the brain. The key is to learn how to become more aware of the muscles that comprise your pelvic floor and their connection to the rest of your body. For more information about becoming more aware of these muscles, see the sidebar Identifying the Muscles of the Core.

Aside from occasional sit-ups, crunches, and push-ups, core exercises are often neglected by a vast majority of habitual exercisers, as well as people new to fitness programs. As a simple definition, any exercise that uses the trunk of the body without external support counts as a core exercise. Therefore, someone who can stabilize their body during exercise is an example of a person who possesses core stability.

Often, a core exercise engages the torso muscles isometrically. The muscles are contracted to stabilize the body, but don't necessarily rely on a joint action to become engaged. Sometimes, the muscles that act as prime movers are stabilized by the smaller, more discrete core muscles. To stabilize the body, all of the muscles of the spine (both anteriorly and posteriorly) have to contract. Sometimes the contractions involve joint actions, and sometimes they don't. This is why many of the core exercises described in this chapter are held for a predetermined period of time, as opposed to involving joint actions and repetitions.

Identifying the Muscles of the Core

To develop the muscles of the core, you must first find them and then engage them. Becoming aware of how your body feels when your core muscles are engaged during exercise will help you use core engagement techniques during exercise. Try the following exercises to develop core awareness; doing so will help with your overall performance.

Shh Breath (Transversus Abdominis)

This exercise will help you become aware of how the abdominal muscles and pelvic floor gradually contract with proper breathing. In a standing position or while lying on your back, place your hands on your midsection, about 2 inches (5 cm) below your navel. Inhale through your nose and allow your abdominal wall to expand in all directions. As you exhale, slowly draw in the space just below your navel and make a "Shhhh" sound.

Snake Breath (Obliques and Quadratus)

This exercise will help you become aware of how the muscles of the core engage when you breathe properly during movement. Lying on your back, place your hands on your rib cage with your elbows resting lightly on the ground. Inhale and allow your ribs to expand. Notice how your hands rise up as your rib cage expands into your hands. Exhale, making a snakelike hissing sound as the rib cage moves away from your hands.

Ha Breath (Intercostals and Diaphragm)

This exercise will help you become aware of how the muscles of the core engage when you breathe properly during movement. While lying on your back, rest your hands on your chest, elbows on the ground, and place your fingertips on your collarbone. As you inhale, allow the breath to rise up into the space under your hands. Exhale and make a "hhhaaaaaaaa" sound. Notice how the sternum softens and the throat expands.

Toe Drop (Transversus Abdominis)

This exercise focuses on the isometric strength and endurance of the transversus abdominis, bringing awareness to the muscle that controls hip movement. In this exercise, you try to lower your leg using your abdominal muscles as opposed to your thigh muscles and hip flexors. Lie supine and engage your pelvic floor with a neutral spine. Bring both knees up to a tabletop position. Slowly drop one foot at a time toward the floor, gently touching the floor with the tip of your big toe. Move your leg by lowering from the hip joint. Slowly return to tabletop and repeat with the other leg. Try this exercise six to eight times with each leg.

When you think about your core, the words *balance* and *stability* should come to mind. A stable core is one that doesn't drift, sag, or sway when movements are performed by the arms, legs, or larger trunk muscles. Core stability is a critical component of a sound fitness program. Targeted core exercises train the small and large muscles in the pelvis, low back, hips, and abdomen to work in harmony and coordination with the spine and the extremities. This leads to enhanced overall strength, better balance, and of course, spinal stability. So whether you work hard on the playing field or just engage in daily activities, core exercises should be part of your fitness program.

ANATOMY OF THE CORE

To build a strong core, you need to exercise a variety of muscles from your hips to your shoulders. It's not enough to do just abdominal crunches and sit-ups. Most people think of a strong core as a nice six-pack or strong abs, but the truth is that this area, which consists of the rectus abdominis muscles, represents a very small part of the core and has a very limited impact on the strength of the core musculature.

What I refer to as the core actually consists of many muscles that stabilize the spine and pelvis and run the entire length of the torso. When these muscles contract, they stabilize the spine, pelvis, and shoulder girdle and create a solid base of support. When this happens, we are able to generate powerful movements of the extremities, not simply for sport or athletic performance, but for functional movements also. This type of fitness is essential to daily living and regular activities. The term *functional fitness* implies that the body has the ability to perform functional movements that are based on situational external and internal forces. Functional movements usually involve movements, such as multiplanar or multijoint, that place demands on the body's core.

The core muscles also make it possible to stand upright and move on two feet. These muscles help us control movements, transfer energy, shift body weight, and move in any direction. A strong core distributes the stresses of weight-bearing loads and protects the back. To be effective, core conditioning exercise programs should target all of these muscle groups. Let's take a closer look at the muscles that we call core, where they are, what they do, and how they are used.

Anterior Core

The four abdominal muscles located on the front of the body are the *rectus abdominis*, the *external obliques*, the *internal obliques*, and the *transversus abdominis* (figure 7.1).

Rectus Abdominis

The main job of the rectus abdominis is to pull the torso closer to the hips, also known as spinal flexion. This is a fairly simple function and the main joint action with respect to performing a crunch. The rectus abdominis is an extremely superficial muscle, meaning that it lies close to the skin's surface. Many strength trainers consider this muscle the most important in terms of aesthetics, but it plays only a minor role in stabilizing the low back and spine.

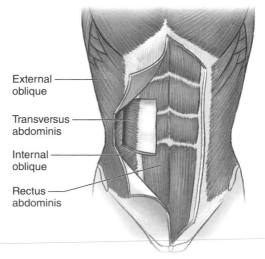

External oblique

Transversus abdominis

Internal oblique

Rectus abdominis

FIGURE 7.1   Muscular structure of the anterior core.

The muscle originates at the pubic symphysis and attaches to the sternum and the cartilage on the fifth, sixth, and seventh ribs.

The rectus abdominis is commonly referred to as a six-pack. The six-pack is the result of the upper abdominal segments being separated by tough connective tissue called fascia. The strip of fascia that runs vertically down the center of the abdominals is called the linea alba. During pregnancy, the linea alba darkens as a result of hormonal changes and is referred to as the linea negra. In pregnancy, this area separates to accommodate for the growth of the fetus and the uterus. In most women, this normal 1- to 3-inch (2.5 to 7.6 cm) separation returns to its prepregnancy state postpartum with some strength training and aerobic exercise. In some women, however (especially those who have multiple pregnancies), this separation becomes larger than 3 inches (7.6 cm), and the division becomes permanent, resulting in a stretched-out and saggy appearance to the abdominal area. This can occur even in the most dedicated exercisers. This condition is known as diastasis recti and often needs to be repaired surgically. Healthy women experiencing normal pregnancies may want to perform abdominal exercises during pregnancy to prevent this condition known as diastasis recti. Muscle strength and endurance exercises encourage the tendons to maintain their strength and can help women return to a prepregnancy state. It is important to follow the Aerobics and Fitness Association of America (AFAA) guideline of performing no more than two minutes at a time of back-lying (supine) exercise after the first trimester.

Many strength trainers look to train both the upper and lower abdominal regions. Others will tell you there is no such thing as lower and upper abdominals, and they are mostly correct. Although it is not possible to train the upper and lower aspects of the rectus abdominis independent of each other, EMG (electromyographic) studies have demonstrated that, in fact, there is a difference in muscle fiber recruitment and activation between the upper and the lower abdominals. These clearly defined muscle segments have their own nerve fiber recruitment patterns. This is why I have exercises that engage the "lower abdominal area" by lifting the feet and legs up in spinal flexion, as well as exercises that focus on flexing the spine from the rib cage, moving the upper body down toward the pelvis. Performing these two spinal joint actions is the best way to fully develop the rectus abdominis.

Deeper Anterior Core Muscles

The *external obliques* are located on the side of the rectus muscles and are some of the widest muscles on the human body. They originate on the lower ribs (ribs 6, 7, and 8) and attach diagonally on the top of the pelvis and to the bottom of the linea alba. They work in tandem with the internal obliques, which lie directly beneath them. They originate on the fascia of the lumbar vertebrae in the low back and the pelvis, and attach to the cartilage of the lowest ribs (ribs 8, 9, and 10), pulling on the top of the linea alba. The external obliques fibers run diagonally down from the middle of the rib cage, whereas the *internal obliques* run diagonally upward from the pelvis.

The external and internal obliques work with the rectus abdominis to rotate the torso from side to side, as well as to flex the torso while in a twisted or rotated position. You can imagine how hard these muscles have to work during rotational exercises at the waist. The oblique muscles are considered postural muscles, because they have to stay in a low-grade, contracted state all day long to keep your torso upright. It is possible to fire these muscles constantly by pulling your abdominal muscles in and actively lifting your rib cage. This action gives you a leaner-appearing midsection and is an important action to maintain proper posture.

The *transversus abdominis* is a thin patch of muscle lying directly under the oblique muscles, with fibers that run horizontally from the pelvis, the cartilage of the lowest ribs, and the thoracolumbar fasciae to the midline of the torso. This muscle does not have a joint action associated with it, and it is has no role in any of the direct actions of the spine, so it contracts only isometrically (i.e., becomes tight without actually requiring movement to occur). Although it doesn't have a direct role in twisting or flexing the spine, the transversus abdominis plays a major role in keeping the intestines and other organs in their proper places and assists with vigorous exhalations, or forceful breaths.

Posterior Core

The posterior muscles of the core consist of two large sets of spinal muscles (one on each side of the spine) called the erector spinae, also known as the spinal erectors. As discussed in chapter 6, these muscles perform all the heavy lifting your back can support. They are located along the segments of the spine and are called the *ilicostalis*, the *longissimus*, and the *spinalis*. The ilicostalis is the outermost muscle that runs along the length of the spine. The longissimus is the middle muscle, and the spinalis is the innermost muscle. These spinal erectors stretch the length of the spine, starting at the lumbar vertebrae and running all the way up to the base of the skull. These muscles allow your spine to move into various positions including extension, flexion, and hyperextension.

The *quadratus lumborum* is also involved in twisting and lateral flexion. This muscle lies just under the lumbar vertebrae, originating at the top of the pelvis and lumbar spinal segments, and then inserts on the lowest rib. This muscle supports the spinal erectors in their job of stabilizing the spine.

Finally, the *multifidus* muscle acts like a strut supporting a bridge, which in this case supports the spinal column. This tiny but crucial stabilizing muscle helps alleviate pressure on the vertebral discs so that body weight can be distributed evenly along the spine. Working with the more superficial muscles of the back (latissimus dorsi and trapezius, for example), keeps our spine straight while the deep muscle groups (such as the multifidus) contribute significantly to the stability of the spine. This is why so many of the exercises performed for core strength are "held" for a short period of time in order to improve muscle endurance, an important component of core strength.

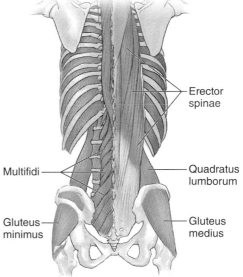

FIGURE 7.2 Muscular structure of the posterior core.

CORE EXERCISES

When selecting exercises to perform for your core, consider your particular objective, the equipment available, and the time you have to train. Then, select the core exercise sequence that suits you best. Each core exercise and progressions are outlined in this section. Part III offers program guidance with respect to repetitions and sets.

Keep in mind that for the exercises for the core muscles, it is not the number of repetitions and sets you perform that is important, but how well and precise you perform them. Be precise and accurate to the best of your ability when working the muscles of the core. These muscles respond to subtle, low-intensity, long-duration movements and movement patterns, so be sure to do each movement and pattern well.

ABDOMINAL PROGRESSION SERIES

The abdominal progression series is a collection of progressively harder exercises. If you find a particular progression too difficult, simply go back to the part of the sequence that you have mastered and slowly begin to incorporate the more difficult moves into the progressions. Do this by trying a few of the harder moves. As you practice one or two, eventually you will work yourself up to three or four, then eventually 10 or 12. The exercises focus on the upper and lower abdominal muscle fibers.

PROGRESSION 1

Lie faceup on a mat. Draw your abdominal muscles into your spine like a brace and place your feet on the floor approximately hip-width apart. Put your fingertips on your head, just behind your ears (see figure *a*). Use a very light touch, because the work should come from the musculature of the abdominal wall, not your hands pulling up on your neck and head. Breathe continuously throughout the exercise. Contract your abdominal wall by bringing your rib cage closer to your hips (see figure *b*). Shorten the distance between your hips and rib cage and count that as one repetition.

PROGRESSION 2

Lie faceup on a mat. Draw your abdominal muscles into your spine like a brace and lift your feet off the floor, holding your knees at a 90-degree angle (see figure *a*). Put your fingertips on your head, just behind your ears. Perform the same exercise as described in progression 1, contracting the abdominal wall (see figure *b*).

PROGRESSION 3

Maintain a faceup position on a mat, but instead, initiate the movement from the lower abdominal area. Hold your legs straight up, toes pointed and arms outstretched in a T position (see figure a). Lift your pelvis as high as you can off the floor while maintaining a vertical orientation with your legs (see figure b). You will not be able to lift your pelvis with control off the floor more than a few inches at the most. Use control as you lift, and don't lift your head or shoulders; focus only on the pelvic lift.

PILATES ROLL-UP

This exercise focuses on the rectus abdominis muscles and the deeper anterior core muscles while simultaneously lengthening the latissimus muscles and the hamstrings. Lie faceup on a mat with your legs straight, arms over your head (see figure a). Keep your shoulder blades anchored in your back, and your ribs down. Don't allow the rib cage to pop out—keep it pulled down. Bring your arms overhead toward your legs and allow your chin to drop down onto your chest while beginning to pull your shoulder blades up, off the mat (see figure b). Think about peeling your spine off the mat in an upward motion, one vertebra at a time. Deepen the curve of your abdominals as you rise up and exhale. Keep your ribs pulled down and together in front, and in one smooth motion, roll your body in an "up and over" motion and reach for your toes. Keep your eyes down and keep your head in line with the curve of your spine. Ideally, your legs should be straight with energy reaching out through your heels; however, an acceptable modification would be to allow your knees to bend slightly.

V-SIT (BOAT POSE)

This exercise improves posture and focuses on the static strength and endurance of the deeper core muscles. While seated on a mat, contract your abdominal muscles and lift your legs up so your hips are at a 45-degree angle, your knees are flexed at 90 degrees, and your palms are prone (see figure a). Reach your arms straight forward or reach up toward your shins (see figure b). Maintain a straight spine. Hold this V position for several seconds. To begin, try three to six seconds, and as you get stronger, hold the position longer, for about 10 to 15 seconds.

STANDING RUSSIAN TWIST

This exercise strengthens the muscles of the core, particularly the obliques, while moving through the transverse plane. Stand with a lightweight kettlebell or medicine ball in your hands (see figure a). Hold the equipment close to your body and twist vigorously with momentum (see figure b). Maintain a long spine and pull your shoulders down into your back. Widen your stance if stabilizing your hips and pelvis is too challenging with a narrower stance. Focus on the motion at the waistline, maintaining a strong and controlled leg position and stable hips.

SIDE PLANK

This exercise engages the muscles of the lateral core and coordinates them with the muscles of the shoulder girdle. Lie on your side on a mat with one hand placed under your shoulder joint and your legs long and stable on top of each other (see figure a). Raise your body up, holding this position for 10 seconds (see figure b). Lower your body and repeat the same exercise on the other side. If staying on your hand is too difficult for your shoulder joint, just lower your body so you are on your elbow and forearm and widen your foot position so your top leg is on the floor in front of your bottom leg.

SUPINE BICYCLE

This exercise engages the oblique muscles and focuses on core control. Lie faceup on a mat with your left knee pulled in toward your chest and your right leg extended (see figure a). Place your fingertips on your head just behind your ears so you have gentle support from your hands and fingers. Then, alternate touching your left elbow to your right knee with your right elbow touching your left knee (see figure b). Move slowly with precision, focusing on moving from your waistline. Try to maintain control in your pelvic area; don't allow your body to move around too much on the floor.

SUPINE CONTRALATERAL BICYCLE

This exercise engages the obliques and the deeper spinal muscles of the core. Lie faceup on a mat with your left knee pulled in toward your chest and your right leg extended (see figure a). Place your fingertips on your head just behind your ears so you have gentle support from your hands and fingers. Then, alternate touching your right elbow to your right knee with your left elbow touching your left knee (see figure b). Move slowly with precision, focusing on moving from your waistline. Try to maintain control in your pelvic area; don't allow your body to move around too much on the floor.

WINDSHIELD WIPERS

This exercise engages the muscles of the core while moving through the transverse plane. Lie faceup on a mat with both legs extended high above your hips and your arms out to your sides. Try to reach for the ceiling with your toes, pointing them up (see figure a). Slowly drop your legs to the right, not quite to the floor but as low as you can and still be able to pull them back up the center (see figure b). Then, alternate your legs to the other side, dropping them almost to the floor. Repeat this leg motion side to side.

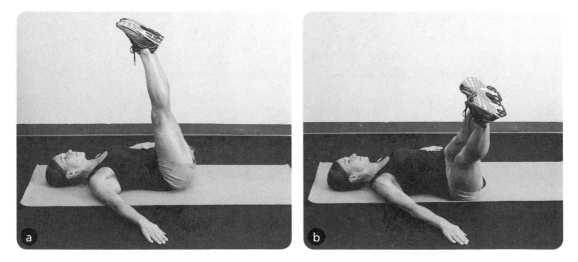

SUPINE CLOCKING

This exercise challenges the coordination of the muscles of the core, the upper and lower abdominal muscles. Lie faceup on a mat with your legs fully extended up, toes pointed toward the ceiling and arms out to the sides (see figure a). Place your hands on the floor for additional support. With your toes pointed, move your feet together in a clockwise circle, as shown in figure b, focusing on starting the toes at 12 o'clock and then moving them precisely to 3 o'clock, then to 6 o'clock, up to 9 o'clock, and ending at 12 o'clock again. Perform the exercise again, but this time move counterclockwise. Control the circular movements of your legs and work from your pelvis and hips.

STABILITY BALL ROLL-OUT

This exercise focuses on the rectus abdominis and the core stabilizers. Start on your knees with a stability ball placed under fisted hands (see figure a). Roll forward, lengthening your body and your elbows (see figure b), and then roll back to the start position.

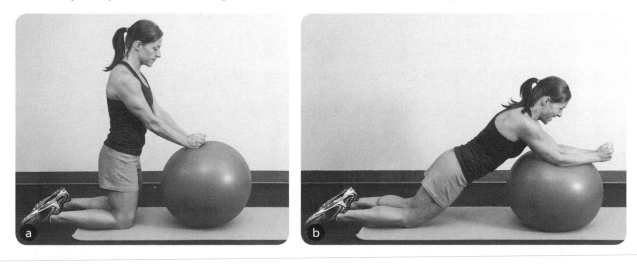

OBLIQUE STABILITY BALL ROLL-OUT

This exercise works the oblique muscles and engages the core. Start on your knees with a stability ball placed under fisted hands (see figure *a*). Roll slightly to the side, lengthening your body at an angle while turning your body toward the ball (see figure *b*), and then roll back to the start position. Repeat this roll out to the other side and return to the start position.

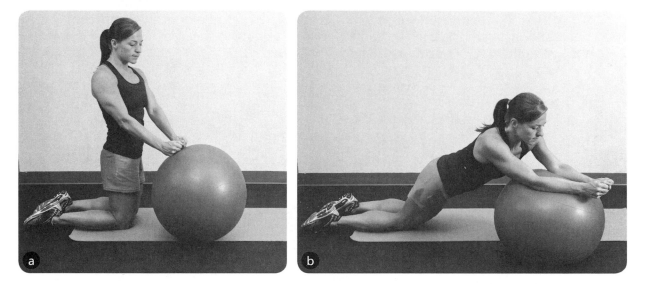

PLANK

This exercise strengthens the arms in relation to the core. Begin on a mat as if you were about to start a full push-up. Draw your torso forward until your shoulders are over your wrists and your whole body is in one straight line from the top of your head to your heels (see figure). Hold this posture without allowing your body to sag in the middle.

PUSH-UP TO PLANK

This exercise integrates the muscles of the chest with the core. Start in plank pose on a mat with your hands placed under your shoulders, fingers spread, elbows long, and feet hip-width apart or together (see figure *a*). Drop your knees to the floor (see figure *b*), perform a push-up (see figure *b*), and then extend your knees and go back to the plank start position.

SUPINE PLANK

This is a very challenging exercise for developing the posterior muscles of the body and increasing flexibility in the chest and shoulders. Sit tall on a mat with your legs extended in front of your body, hands placed slightly behind your body with your fingers pointed forward (see figure *a*). Lift your body up, pressing your hips up toward the ceiling, and fully extend your arms (see figure *b*). Try to create length in your spine as you hold this posture.

TRX PLANK

This exercise builds strength and endurance in the shoulders and the core. Lie facedown on the floor facing away from the TRX anchor point with the straps adjusted to midcalf length. Place your toes in the foot cradles, and place your hands directly under your shoulders. When you are ready, lift your knees off the floor and hold the plank position (see figure). Keep your shoulders pulled back and your core engaged to keep your back from sagging. You may want to start this exercise with your forearms on the floor if the full plank position is too intense.

TRX SIDE PLANK

This exercise offers muscle balance in core strength and challenges the body by placing more demands on the oblique muscles. Lie facedown on the floor facing away from the TRX anchor point with the straps adjusted to midcalf length. Place your toes in the foot cradles with the top foot and leg directly in front of the back foot and leg in a tandem position. Place your elbow directly under your shoulder, and maintain proper body alignment. When you are ready, lift your hips off the floor and hold the side plank position. Keep your shoulders pulled back and your core engaged to keep your back from sagging. You can increase the intensity by getting up onto your hand. To change sides, roll "under" to move to the other side. If you roll "over," your feet will likely come out of the foot cradles. To increase the challenge, place the top leg behind the front heel in a tandem position (see figure).

TRX PIKE

This intense move requires upper body and core stabilization and strengthens the abdominals and shoulders. Lie facedown on the floor facing away from the TRX anchor point with the straps adjusted to midcalf length. Place your toes in the foot cradles, and place your hands directly under your shoulders. When you are ready, lift your knees off the floor and move into the plank position. Pike your hips upward toward the ceiling, activating your quadriceps (see figure). Avoid flexing your knees. Drop your head when in the pike to avoid stressing your neck.

TRX CRUNCH

This exercise tests core and lower body strength with an anaerobic challenge as the tempo of the movements and the repetitions increase. Lie facedown on the floor facing away from the TRX anchor point with the straps adjusted to midcalf length. Place your toes in the foot cradles. Place your hands directly under your shoulders. When you are ready, lift your knees off the floor and come into the plank position. From plank pose, begin to pull your knees into your chest (see figure). Contract your abdominals and lift your hips slightly as you pull your knees in.

TRX OBLIQUE CRUNCH

This exercise is similar to the crunch with respect to execution and core challenge, but the added rotation brings in an additional stability challenge to the chest and shoulders with dynamic core movement. Lie facedown on the floor facing away from the TRX anchor point with the straps adjusted to midcalf length. Place your toes in the foot cradles. Place your hands directly under your shoulders. When you are ready, lift your knees off the floor and come into the plank position. From plank pose, draw your knees in toward your elbows and chest in a controlled manner (see figure). Contract your abdominals and lift your hips slightly as you pull your knees in to fully engage the core.

You are now familiar with the core exercises that are listed in the programs outlined in chapters 10 and 11. Following the descriptions and referring to the corresponding photos, you should be able to replicate each exercise easily. Remember, take your time with the exercises, and modify them if you need to. In addition, weight loads (if appropriate), sets, and repetitions will be given to you in chapters 10 and 11 with specific guidelines, but always respect your body and honor your current level of fitness, skill, competence, and ability. You have plenty of time to learn exercises that may be new to you or are especially challenging. Particularly with the core exercises, technique is more important than how many repetitions you can do or how long you can hold a position. Most important, remember that the exercise experience is a journey. Take your time and enjoy it.

PART III

Strength Training Programs for Women

Starting a Strength Training Program

This chapter explores not only where you are in your current level of fitness, but ways to formulate where you are going with respect to your strength training program. Beginning a well-designed fitness program requires commitment, dedication, and concrete information about the science of exercise to start you off on the right foot. This chapter provides techniques for preparing yourself mentally by setting goals that are measurable, attainable, and realistic and that you can track. Additionally, it outlines assessments you can use to determine your current fitness level, which will help you plan where to go next. You will learn how to take the information you gather from these techniques and use it to track your progress and stay motivated for your workouts.

GETTING YOUR MIND AND BODY READY TO BEGIN

Making the decision to begin a training program is a big step for most women. For many, cardio exercise and some light weightlifting constitute their typical day-to-day workout routines. However, after performing the same cardio and weight routines over and over, they start to notice that their workouts just aren't as effective as they once were. This lack of result—and sometimes burnout—can be discouraging. Even the most successful athletes know that their mental approach plays a strong role in their performance.

Many recreational athletes and fitness enthusiasts realize that, on some level, their thoughts and moods affect their workouts as well as their capacity to stay consistent with a fitness program. It is a big endeavor to start a serious strength training program and be consistent enough to see results. I applaud you for taking this step. The mind (especially the subconscious mind) actually has enormous power to make us stronger, more muscular, more athletic, more powerful, and even happier. Our inner world creates our outer world. Our mind determines what results we will achieve. Therefore, in addition to starting a strength training program to make your body stronger, consider the following to make your mind stronger.

Set goals that are attainable, measurable, action oriented, and realistic.
Begin with fitness tests that give you data about your current fitness level. Based on those data, determine what you want to achieve (e.g., weight loss, increased muscle definition). Use this book to select programming options that will help you attain each of your goals, and then be sure to chart your progress, recording the days you exercise, the exercises you do, the time you spend exercising, and how you feel afterward.

Create a strong, clear mental picture of your goals using visualization and imagery.
See yourself obtaining your ideal physical appearance. Imagine your annual physical exam revealing your enhanced health and vigor.

Reinforce these mental pictures often using positive affirmations.
Write positive statements and post them in your home, your car, or your work space. Keep them simple, so you can use them as mantras. Examples include *I am strong, I am capable, I am determined,* and *I will succeed.*

Maintain a positive focus on your objectives.
Don't allow negative thoughts to stop you from reaching your goals. For example, if you get on the scale and notice that you have gained a pound, or a kilogram, be realistic. Muscle weighs more than fat, so it is highly likely that you have actually lost fat, but gained some muscle. Also, if for some reason you can't make a workout happen one or two days in a row because life gets in the way, don't worry. It takes about six full weeks of inactivity to lose your fitness. All you have to do is stay positive and get back into your workout routine as soon as you can.

Now that we have considered how to prepare mentally for your program, let's take a look at how to prepare physically. The purpose of any exercise program is to stress the body systematically to improve its capacity for exercise. Exercise is beneficial only as long as it forces the body to adapt to the stress of physical effort (more about adaptation in the next section). You will see significant improvements in your performance when you introduce appropriate exercise stresses into your training program. Your current level of physical fitness is largely a reflection of the level of training you are engaging in. You must find out where you are, so you can decide where to go next.

ASSESSING YOUR FITNESS LEVELS

A physical fitness assessment does not address athletic skills or ability; rather, it focuses on specific data about your current fitness level. Whether your goal is better health, more muscle, greater strength, or fat loss, knowing where you are in these areas of fitness will help you change the fitness variables you are currently using if you are not achieving what you want from your fitness program.

The term *fitness testing* refers to the evaluation of the five main areas of fitness, not just strength. The American College of Sports Medicine (ACSM) defines the following components of fitness that should be evaluated prior to beginning a fitness program as well as periodically throughout a regular exercise program to determine progress: *cardiorespiratory function* (both resting and during activity), *muscle strength*, *muscle endurance*, *body composition* (lean mass to fat ratio), and *muscle and joint flexibility*. Checking where you currently stand in relation to standardized fitness levels (which are age and gender norm specific) can offer you a sense of where to begin your fitness program. Testing also helps you measure how far you have come, and perhaps how far you still need to go to achieve your fitness goals.

How Muscles Respond to Strength Training

The most noticeable changes you will experience during your strength training journey will be physiological adaptations such as improved cardiorespiratory fitness, increased muscle strength and endurance, a drop in the percentage of body fat, and a subsequent increase in lean tissue. For example, let's say you are a brand-new runner and you start a running program by alternating bouts of walking with jogging slowly to adapt to the increased intensity and movement. Your body adapts by changing the amount of oxygen your lungs bring into your body, how your muscles respond to the impact of movement, and how it uses energy. As you become more proficient, your muscles adapt by converting oxygen and nutrients into energy more efficiently. As a result, you are able to run for longer periods without becoming winded or fatigued.

Two physiological adaptations to strength training that you can expect are increased muscle strength and increased muscle size, or hypertrophy. Hypertrophy and increased strength often occur together, but it is possible to focus on one over the other. Understanding why certain types of strength training result in increased muscle strength and others result in increased muscle size will help you understand how you get bigger and stronger.

Initially, strength increases are largely due to motor learning, which is a neurological adaptation; the nerves learn how to run the muscles more efficiently. When you are strength training using heavy weights, your muscles become stronger as a result of changes in your nervous system. Repeat performances of these exercises result in more efficient activation of the motor units involved, which is how you continue to get stronger.

The second physiological adaptation you can expect is hypertrophy, or increased muscle size. The two types of hypertrophy are sarcoplasmic and myofibrillar. During sarcoplasmic hypertrophy, the volume of fluid in the muscle cells increases. This type of adaptation occurs when you perform several repetitions (generally 8 to 12) against a submaximal load (this is the type of training most strength trainers and weightlifters do). When you lift a weight a few times and then examine your muscle immediately, you will notice a slight increase in muscle size; this is the result of fluid that has built up around the muscle fibers causing it to appear larger.

The other type of hypertrophy supports the neural adaptations that occur, creating strong muscles, but not as much growth. This is termed *myofibrillar hypertrophy;* the change occurs in the muscle fibers themselves, which are called actin and myosin filaments, proteins that act to contract muscles These contractile proteins increase in number leading to increases in muscle mass and cross-sectional area.

To summarize, the adaptations that occur as a result of strength training are increased muscle strength, which results from increased muscle fiber recruitment as a result of nervous system stimulation, and increased muscle size as a result of either increased fluids in the muscles or increased actin and myosin proteins.

Fitness testing may not provide absolutes in terms of physical fitness and health, but it can offer useful information about your current level of fitness—areas in which you are strong, and areas in which you could stand to improve. You may have good muscle fitness, but need to improve aerobic fitness. You may have a healthy body fat percentage, but want to increase your fat-free mass (muscle). Everyone has a unique entry point into a training program that is based on his or her current fitness level.

Before you begin any of the strength training programming described in chapters 10 and 11, I recommend that you evaluate your current level of fitness using the field tests described next. If you are in any doubt of the current state of your overall health and wellness, check with a medical professional before beginning or progressing any fitness program. Also note that many fitness centers offer cardiorespiratory testing either free of charge or for a nominal fee. At the very least, you may be required to purchase one session from a personal trainer.

Paying a fitness professional to perform a full battery of fitness tests for you can be worthwhile. The initial testing session can spell out your current fitness levels, so you can compare future testing results to these. These baseline data are especially important if you are about to embark on a new training program or are starting a new periodization cycle (periodization is covered in detail in chapter 9). Subsequent tests can be planned for the end or the start of each new cycle. Although I recommend beginning fitness testing with a certified, qualified fitness professional, you should eventually be able to transition to self-evaluation once you establish testing data and become more confident in performing your own fitness testing.

The fitness tests outlined in this chapter will help you evaluate multiple components including cardiorespiratory fitness, muscle strength and endurance, body composition, and flexibility. Having a data-based report on your current fitness levels will put you in a better position to change your overall level of physical fitness.

Cardiorespiratory Fitness Assessment

Cardiorespiratory fitness assessments are also referred to as exercise tolerance testing. Understanding your tolerance for cardio exercise will help you gauge both the high end and the low end of the range in which you can exercise for results. An exercise tolerance test is a worthwhile way to assess your current level of cardiorespiratory fitness prior to progressing your current exercise program; it will help you determine the levels of intensity at which you can and should be working.

An exercise tolerance test allows you to determine your $\dot{V}O_2$max, which represents the maximal rate of aerobic metabolism you experience during exercise. Maximal heart rate is considered the greatest heart rate measured when you are exercising to volitional fatigue (i.e., stopping because you cannot exercise any longer) during a graded exercise test. $\dot{V}O_2$max is usually measured in liters of oxygen per minute, or millimeters of oxygen per kilogram of body weight per minute. Maximal tests are by far the best way to determine the maximal ability of the cardiovascular and respiratory systems under stress. Unfortunately, this type of testing requires expensive facilities and specialized equipment, in addition to a maximal aerobic effort on the part of the examinee. This method is often limited to hospitals and research facilities and is usually performed in the presence of a medical professional trained in advanced cardiac life support.

Because maximal fitness testing can be more difficult to gain access to and then perform, submaximal testing is often used. Several equations have been developed to estimate maximal heart rate using submaximal measures. Thus, submaximal tests provide a reasonably accurate prediction of maximal work capacity to determine the appropriate intensity at which you should be working based on your current level of fitness.

Submaximal tests are based on the linear relationship between an age-predicted heart rate and the cardiorespiratory work being performed. Submaximal heart rate testing is based on the assumption that as the heart rate increases, so does oxygen consumption. Therefore, a maximal heart rate is estimated from this linear relationship. The prediction of maximal heart rate from the submaximal testing is determined via the following formula:

220 – ____ (Your age) = _____ (Your estimated maximal heart rate)

This formula has a margin of error as high as 15 beats for several reasons. One is the fact that the person's resting heart rate is not considered. This is important because resting heart rate takes into account the current level of fitness regardless of age. For example, let's compare a 40-year-old elite marathon runner with a 40-year-old who is severely deconditioned. Both have the same estimated maximal heart rate, which is absurd because they clearly do not have similar fitness levels. Therefore, if maximal heart rate is over- or underpredicted (which frequently occurs when adopting a maximal heart rate number based strictly on age), so are maximal work capacity and maximal oxygen consumption. However, although there may be some error in age-predicted heart rates, submaximal testing has been proven to be accurate and reproducible. Keep in mind, however, that the validity of the results of submaximal fitness tests rests on several assumptions:

- A steady-state heart rate is obtained for each exercise workload.
- A linear relationship exists among heart rate, oxygen uptake, and workload.
- The maximal heart rate for a given age is predictable.
- The biomechanical efficiency of the physical activity performed (i.e., oxygen uptake at a given workload) is the same for everyone.

Unfortunately, it is often quite difficult to conduct a fitness test that meets all the requirements for the four listed assumptions. For example, exercising at a given workload for only a few minutes can be insufficient for many people to achieve a true steady state. To ensure that a steady state has been achieved, the heart rate should be measured after two minutes of exercise at a given workload and again after the third minute of exercise at that workload. These two heart rates should then be compared. If a difference of more than five beats per minute (bpm) between the two is found, the person should continue to exercise at one-minute intervals at the same workload until two successive heart rates differ by less than five beats per minute. It is also important that the submaximal heart rates obtained be between 115 and 150 bpm, because research shows that within this heart rate range, a linear relationship tends to exist between heart rate and oxygen uptake for most healthy adults.

Let's take a look at one excellent submaximal test, the Bruce Protocol Treadmill Test. This should help you find the most appropriate heart rate training zone for your goals.

BRUCE PROTOCOL TREADMILL TEST

The Bruce Protocol Treadmill test is mainly used for evaluating cardiac fitness and function. This test was designed by Dr. Robert Bruce in 1963 and was initially used for assessing patients with heart diseases. This test is a very popular way of testing $\dot{V}O_2$max, which is closely related to aerobic endurance.

This test requires that the person run for as long as possible on a treadmill. The treadmill speed and incline increase in specific increments at timed intervals. Each interval is three minutes long, and at the end of each interval, the speed and incline of the treadmill are increased until the person can no longer complete the exercise. Here is the procedure:

- Before exercise begins, measure resting heart rate, either manually or using a heart rate monitor (see the sidebar Measuring Your Heart Rate for more information).

- Warm your body up by walking on the treadmill at a very slow speed of 1.5 to 1.7 miles per hour (2.4 to 2.7 km/h) for three to five minutes. Do not hold on to the handrails while performing this test.

- Begin the test by setting the treadmill speed at 1.7 miles per hour (2.7 km/h) or at an incline of 10 percent.

- At every three-minute interval, increase treadmill speed and incline by 2 percent, as follows:
  Interval 1: 10% incline at 1.7 mph (2.4 km/h)
  Interval 2: 12% incline at 2.5 mph (4 km/h)
  Interval 3: 14% incline at 3 mph (4.8 km/h)
  Interval 4: 16% incline at 4 mph (6.4 km/h)
  Interval 5: 18% incline at 4.5 mph (7.2 km/h)
  Interval 6: 20% incline at 5 mph (8 km/h)
  Interval 7: 22% incline at 5.5 mph (8.9 km/h)
  Interval 8: 24% incline at 6 mph (9.7 km/h)
  Interval 9: 26% incline at 6.5 mph (10.46 km/h)
  Interval 10: 28% incline at 7 mph (11.3 km/h)

- Stop the test when you are unable to continue, or your heart rate exceeds 85 percent of your maximal heart rate, using the 220 – your age formula provided previously.

- Cool down for three to five minutes, or until your heart rate reaches 100 bpm or lower.

Because the Bruce Protocol Treadmill Test attempts to get you to reach almost maximal levels of intensity, you have to run continuously until you are too tired to continue. $\dot{V}O_2$max is then calculated by entering the total time on the treadmill into a formula (e.g., 9 minutes and 30 seconds is entered into the formula as 9.5). The formula for women is as follows:

$$4.38 \times \underline{\quad\quad} \text{(time)} - 3.9 = \dot{V}O_2\text{max}$$

Using 9 minutes and 30 seconds again as an example, the calculation would be as follows:

$$4.38 \times 9.5 \text{ (time)} = 41.61 - 3.9 = 37.71$$

You can then evaluate your performance by comparing your results to the rankings shown in table 8.1.

TABLE 8.1   Female Cardiorespiratory Fitness Test Norms*

	Age			
	20-29	**30-39**	**40-49**	**50-59**
Superior	>49.6	>47.4	>45.3	>41.0
Excellent	43.9-49.5	42.4-47.3	39.6-45.2	36.7-40.9
Good	39.5-43.8	37.7-42.3	35.9-39.5	32.6-36.6
Fair	36.1-39.4	34.2-37.6	32.8-35.8	29.9-32.5
Poor	32.3-36.0	30.9-34.1	29.4-32.7	26.8-2938
Very poor	<32.2	<30.8	<29.3	<26.7

*Values for $\dot{V}O_2$max in ml/kg/min.

Data reprinted with permission from The Cooper Institute®, Dallas, Texas, from *Physical Fitness Assessments and Norms for Adults and Law Enforcement*. Available online at www.cooperinstitute.org.

Finding Your Training Zone

Getting the most out of your training is linked to your working heart rate, as you may have already done by finding your submaximal working heart rate. When exercising for cardiorespiratory benefits, it is best to exercise within one of three training zones. First determine the intensity of exercise that you consider easy, moderate, and hard and then find the heart rate ranges that correspond to these three training zones.

Opinions vary as to which training zone to exercise in to achieve optimal training results. You need to figure out which training zone is right for you based on your goals. I recommend using a heart rate monitor to monitor your cardiorespiratory training program. There are many reasons to use a heart rate monitor, but an important one is that you can make sure you're not over- or undertraining. Using a heart rate monitor can be motivating, too.

If you don't choose to use a heart rate monitor to determine your training zones, you will have to get out a pen and paper and do the math yourself. In this case, there's a formula you can follow. To calculate your heart rate zones, you will first need to know your true resting heart rate. Although you took a resting heart rate at the start of your treadmill test, it was not a true resting heart rate. The best way to determine a true resting heart rate is to record your heart rate immediately on waking on three consecutive mornings and average the three. If this is not possible, take your resting heart rate during a peaceful, relaxing time of day.

On average, a resting heart rate of 40 to 60 bpm indicates a high fitness level (in the absence of any medications or medical conditions). A resting heart rate of 60 to 80 is average (obviously, the lower within that range, the better). A resting heart rate over 80 bpm usually indicates a sedentary person who may be at risk for certain types of chronic conditions, a smoker, a very deconditioned person, or someone with a disease condition.

Measuring Your Heart Rate

Your heart rate can be taken with a heart rate monitor or manually at any spot on the body at which an artery is close to the surface and a pulse can be felt. The most common places to manually measure heart rate are the neck (carotid artery) and the wrist (radial artery). You should always use your fingers to take a pulse, not your thumb, because you can sometimes feel your own pulse through your thumb.

- To take your heart rate at your *neck*, place your first two fingers on either side of your neck, as shown in figure 8.1*a*. Be careful not to press too hard, and then count the number of beats for a minute.

- To take your heart rate at your *wrist*, place your index and middle fingers together on the opposite wrist, about 1/2 inch (1.3 cm) inside the joint, in line with the index finger, as shown in figure 8.1*b*. Once you find a pulse, count the number of beats you feel in one minute.

For an even more accurate heart rate measurement, you may choose to use a heart rate monitor, as mentioned earlier. Sometimes the motion of the exercise makes manually taking heart rate difficult, and a monitor helps to get clearer results. Heart rate monitors will also record heart rate change over short periods of time.

A heart monitor includes a transmitter attached to a belt worn around the chest and a receiver worn on the wrist. With each heart beat, an electrical signal is transmitted through the skin. The transmitter is placed on the skin near the heart to pick up this signal. It sends the signal containing heart rate data to the wrist receiver, which displays the heart rate. Simple heart rate monitors have the capacity to only show the heart rate at a given time. More elaborate monitors can record time, calculate average and maximal heart rate, and even sound an alarm when a predetermined heart rate zone is reached or exceeded.

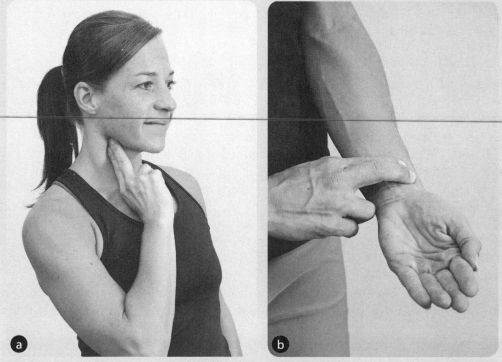

FIGURE 8.1 Measuring your heart rate *(a)* at the neck and *(b)* at the wrist.

Once you have your resting heart rate, you can insert it into the following formula, called the Karvonen Formula, to calculate your training zones (remember, a heart rate monitor will do this work for you!):

220 – ____ (Your age) – ____ (Your resting heart rate)
= ____ (Your heart rate reserve)
× .55 + ____ (Your resting heart rate) = ____ % (Your low-end training zone)

220 – ____ (Your age) – ____ (Your resting heart rate)
= ____ (Your heart rate reserve)
× .70 + ____ (Your resting heart rate) = ____% (Your midrange training zone)

220 – ____ (Your age) – ____ (Your resting heart rate)
= ____ (Your heart rate reserve)
× .85 + ____ (Your resting heart rate) = ____ % (Your high-end training zone)

For example, let's assume a 30-year-old female's maximal heart rate is 190 bpm (220 – 30 = 190). The 220 – age formula fails to determine this woman's heart rate based on her current level of fitness. Therefore, the Karvonen Formula seeks to correct for this by finding the training zone based on her current resting heart rate. Remember, the current resting heart rate is the one you find by taking your pulse on three consecutive mornings and averaging the three.

When first beginning cardio exercise on a regular basis, you should take your pulse at regular intervals during your workout. For example, every three to five minutes to monitor where in your training zone you are exercising. Once you have a sense of how you feel when you are working in the low end of your training zone (i.e., at an easy pace), in the moderate range of your training zone, and in the higher end of your training zone, you will not need to rely on your heart rate as much. You can simply use a method is known as the Rating of Perceived Exertion (RPE), which is a simple, quick, and easy way to gauge your exercise intensity during a workout. It is based on the physical sensations you might experience during physical activity, which include increased heart rate, increased breathing rate, sweating, and muscle fatigue. Although this is a subjective measure, your exertion rating will provide a fairly good estimate of your actual heart rate during physical activity. I frequently use RPE with my clients, because it is easy to extrapolate their actual exercise effort from their feelings of intensity. The RPE scale is shown in figure 8.2.

FIGURE 8.2   RPE Scale

Level 1: No exercise at all
Level 2: Very low intensity—a pace you could maintain all day long
Level 3: Still comfortable, but notice breathing increase
Level 4: Sweating a little bit, but could carry on a conversation easily
Level 5: Just beyond comfortable, are sweating more, and can still talk easily
Level 6: Can still talk, but are slightly breathless
Level 7: Can still talk, but don't really want to
Level 8: Can respond to questions, but can keep this pace up only for a short time
Level 9: Extremely intense pace and cannot withstand for more than seconds, or minutes
Level 10: Absolutely intense pace

For most workouts you will want to be at around level 5 or 6 (moderate intensity). If you're doing interval training, you should recover to around level 4 or 5, and your intensity intervals should be at around level 8 or 9. As you can see from the scale, working at a level 10 wouldn't be recommended for most workouts. For longer, slower workouts, keep your RPE at level 5 or lower.

Training in the Zones

Now that you have a better understanding of how to determine your personal training zones, what your heart rate is when you are in a particular zone, and how being in that zone affects your training, let's explore how to use those zones for improved performance, weight loss, or increased health. Keep in mind that all the training zones offer specific benefits, so you do not have to always achieve zone 3 to obtain great results.

Zone 1

This training zone is reached by walking at a brisk pace, or jogging at a comfortable pace, at a moderate effort level. This zone trains your body to increase the rate of fat release from the cells to the muscles for fuel. Some people call this the fat-burning zone because up to 85 percent of the total calories burned in this zone are fat calories. To burn more total calories (which is critically important to weight loss), you need to exercise longer in this zone. Training in this zone will also develop a base level of endurance that will sustain a higher intensity level and allow you to perform cardio workouts longer without a great deal of fatigue and muscle soreness. Your body can now carry more oxygen to your muscles and break into your fat storage cells to burn more fat calories.

Zone 2

Zone 2 is reached by running at a relatively fast speed for a sustained period of time, say, 45 to 60 minutes. Training in this zone improves your overall physiological functional capacity in a huge way. The number and size of your blood vessels actually increase as you increase your lung capacity and respiratory rate. Your heart muscle increases in size and strength so you can exercise longer before becoming fatigued. You're still metabolizing fat and carbohydrate at about a 50-50 rate, which means that they are burning at about the same ratio. Many people reach this zone and feel as though they have finally arrived at a cardio fitness level that is both challenging and results oriented. I applaud you for reaching this stage, but you will need to venture into the next zone, at least in intervals, for improved performance, increased strength, and powerful fat-loss and endurance adaptations.

Zone 3

This level of intensity is reached by going hard. Training in zone 3 makes you faster and fitter, increasing your heart rate as you cross from aerobic into anaerobic training. At this point, your heart cannot pump enough blood and oxygen to supply the exercising muscles fully, so they respond by continuing to contract anaerobically; as a result, other metabolites are helping with the energy production (ATP-PC and glucose). This is where you may "feel the burn." You can stay in this zone for only a limited amount of time, but as you get more aerobically fit, you will be able to sustain this level longer. This zone will improve speed, strength, and endurance during interval training, which simply means mixing hard training with easier training for determined periods of time. Try to work in zone 3 for the shorter intervals. In my opinion, interval training is one of the best ways to work hard without overtraining.

Muscle Fitness Assessment

Two components of muscle fitness assessment are muscle strength and muscle endurance. Adequate muscle strength and endurance are necessary for optimal health as well as athletic performance, increased lean mass, better aesthetics, and functional daily living. From a health perspective, adequate strength and endurance help us participate in activities of daily living without injury or undue fatigue. From a performance perspective, both are necessary for optimal performance in recreational sports and fitness activities.

Muscle endurance refers to the ability to exert a submaximal force consistently without fatigue over an extended period of time. Muscle strength is the ability of a muscle or muscle group to generate maximal force, or the greatest amount of force that can be produced in a single effort. This is also known as the 1-repetition maximum (1RM). Think of 1RM as the most weight you could move once. We don't typically exercise at our 1RM, because it would be difficult to determine it for every muscle group. But this concept is very important to an Olympic power-lifter, for example, who needs to be able to lift a very heavy load just one time in competition. We want to train to increase our overall strength and stamina, but will do this by estimating our 1RM, and then performing more than one repetition, such as 8 or 10 or even 12 repetitions for the benefits we are searching for, which include increased muscle strength and endurance, improved stamina, and increased muscle size.

The muscle fitness testing included here helps you determine your existing levels of strength and endurance so that you have an initial measure to gauge yourself against when you test again. You will be able to compare your initial testing results with those you achieve as you increase in muscle strength and endurance.

Strength and endurance are specific to the muscle group, speed of contraction, type of contraction, and joint angle being tested. Although muscle strength tests differ from muscle endurance tests, some component of muscle endurance can measure strength to a certain degree. This is important because it is difficult to safely, easily, and quickly determine true muscle strength in 1RM. But, knowing or at least having a good estimation of your 1RM is important for optimizing training. You want to perform your muscle endurance workouts at no less than 75 percent of your 1RM for optimal training benefits. Because getting a good estimate of your 1RM for every muscle group can be difficult, take a look at the sidebar Selecting Your Correct Weight Load for some recommendations.

Two muscle endurance tests that are easy to self-administer are the sit-up test and the push-up test. Both test muscle endurance relative to body weight. Another endurance test is the bench press test; because this test uses a standardized weight, the results do not vary as a function of body weight the way those of the sit-up and push-up tests do.

Selecting Your Correct Weight Load

During your training sessions, you will likely use a combination of equipment, including machines, cables, body weight, and dumbbells. All are effective tools for a beginning strength training routine, and a combination of equipment is recommended to create variety and become comfortable with the equipment. However, you may still question how heavy your weights should be, particularly when using a variety of equipment.

As I mentioned in previous chapters, many women strength train with weights that are too light. For example, if you are prescribed 12 repetitions, and you select a weight that allows you to perform the 12 repetitions easily and another 20 without much effort, the weights are too light. With that said, obviously it is essential to use enough resistance to produce a reasonable degree of muscle fatigue within the limits of the anaerobic energy system. The American Council on Exercise (2011) offers the following recommendation for selecting the correct weight for women: "Training with very light weights that can be performed for two minutes or more is an inefficient exercise technique that has limited benefit for muscle development."

To determine how much weight to use for any piece of equipment, begin with a weight that you can manage with good form and control, and then start experimenting with weights. To build muscle, you need to use more resistance than your muscles are used to. This means that you should be lifting enough weight that allows you to complete the desired number of repetitions, and you should be able to finish your last repetition with difficulty, but also with good form. Recommended starting weights for beginner, intermediate, and advanced exercises are as follows:

Beginner

- Upper body: 8 to 12 pounds (3.6 to 5.4 kg)
- Lower body: 10 to 15 pounds (4.5 to 6.8 kg)

Intermediate

- Upper body: 10 to 15 pounds (4.5 to 6.8 kg)
- Lower body: 12 to 20 pounds (5.4 to 9 kg)

Advanced

- Upper body: 15 to 25 pounds (6.8 to 11.3 kg)
- Lower body: 20 to 40 pounds (9 to 18 kg)

Keep in mind that these are simply suggestions. You may find that a weight load given for intermediates is right for you as a beginner, or you may be ready to start off with weight loads recommended for an advanced exerciser.

SIT-UP TEST

This test measures your ability to perform spinal flexion specifically. In other words, it measures how much muscle endurance you have on your trunk flexor muscles. Ideally, as you get stronger over time, you will improve in this test measure.

To execute the test, lie faceup with your knees flexed and your feet about 18 inches (46 cm) from your hips and your fingertips just behind your ears on each side of your head (see figure 8.3a). Your elbows should touch your knees at the top of the range of motion (see figure 8.3b), and your shoulders should touch the floor upon completion of each sit-up. Don't pull on your head or neck when performing the upward motion of the sit-up. Count how many you can complete in a full range of motion for one minute. Full range of motion means that you can come all the way up with good form and without your feet leaving the ground. Have someone help you by watching the second hand on a clock or using a stopwatch. Refer to table 8.2 for the norms for this test.

FIGURE 8.3 Sit-Up Test.

TABLE 8.2 Female Muscle Endurance Fitness Norms for the One-Minute Sit-Up Test

	Age					
	<20	20-29	30-39	40-49	50-59	60+
Superior	>55	>51	>42	>38	>30	>28
Excellent	46-54	44-49	35-40	29-34	24-29	17-26
Good	36-40	38-42	29-33	24-28	20-22	11-15
Fair	32-35	32-37	25-28	20-23	14-19	6-10
Poor	28-30	24-31	20 -24	14-19	10-12	3-5
Very poor	<25	<18	<11	<7	<5	<0

Data reprinted with permission from The Cooper Institute®, Dallas, Texas, from *Physical Fitness Assessments and Norms for Adults and Law Enforcement*. Available online at www.cooperinstitute.org.

PUSH-UP TEST

The Push-Up Test assesses the strength of the triceps, anterior deltoids, and pectoralis muscles. The push-up position is different for men and women. Women use the modified bent-knee position, but the rest of the testing procedure is the same for both genders. It's important to use the modified version if you want to compare your results using the norms established for women.

To execute the test, get into a modified plank pose: place your hands directly under your shoulders, place your knees on the floor with your feet either lifted or down (see figure 8.4a). Picture an imaginary line between your thumbs and make sure your sternum is directly over that line. Keep your body rigid. Your chest must come within 3 inches (7.6 cm) of the floor for a push-up to be counted as a rep (see figure 8.4b). You can place a small ball or even a partner's fist (if someone is helping you with this test) under your sternum to make sure you come all the way down during each repetition. Count the number of push-ups you can do for one minute. If you need to rest, do so in the up position. Refer to table 8.3 for the norms for females for this test.

FIGURE 8.4 Push-Up Test.

TABLE 8.3 Female Muscle Endurance Fitness Norms for the One-Minute Modified Push-Up Test

	Age				
	20-29	**30-39**	**40-49**	**50-59**	**60+**
Superior	45-70	39-56	33-60	28-31	20
Excellent	36-42	31-36	24-28	21-25	15-17
Good	30-34	24-29	18-21	17-20	12-15
Fair	23-29	19-23	13-17	12-15	5-12
Poor	17-22	11-17	6-11	6-10	2-4
Very poor	9-15	4-9	1-4	0-4	0-1

Data reprinted with permission from The Cooper Institute®, Dallas, Texas, from *Physical Fitness Assessments and Norms for Adults and Law Enforcement*. Available online at www.cooperinstitute.org.

Body Fat: What Are the Risks?

Though for most people *body fat* has negative connotations, fat is critical for good health. The ability to store body fat allowed our ancestors to survive times when food was scarce. Today, fat is still essential for keeping the body functioning, preserving body heat, and protecting the organs from trauma. Therefore, we need a certain amount of body fat.

When our bodies store either too much fat or not enough fat is when we experience health problems such as high cholesterol, hypertension, glucose intolerance, and insulin resistance. Too little body fat puts a woman at risk for serious medical or psychological conditions, or both. Having a very low body fat percentage can result in musculoskeletal problems and osteoporosis. It can also upset the hormonal balance causing loss of menstruation. Striving for extremely low body fat can also result in severe eating disorders such as anorexia nervosa, bulimia, and binge eating, which have significant health implications.

For those who carry too much fat, the especially dangerous type is fat that is stored at the waist, creating what is often called an apple-shaped body. This fat is known as visceral fat, and its main goal is to protect internal organs. Too much of this type of fat places extra stress on the internal organs and has been linked to many disease conditions. Adipose tissue is fat that is located beneath the skin, often stored on the hips and thighs, creating a pear-shaped body and a cellulite appearance on the legs, the thighs, and sometimes the arms.

Body Composition Assessment

Did you know that two people can have the same height and weight, but very different percentages of body fat? Did you also realize that you can be skinny but severely out of shape? Or even heavy and fit? Many people trying to lose weight often turn to the bathroom scale to record their progress. But that is not the only, or most accurate, way to measure body composition, or body fat percentage. Total body mass can be divided into lean mass (also called fat-free mass) and fat mass. Lean mass is composed of bone, muscle, and organs. Fat is composed of adipose tissue—just fat. The assessment of body composition determines the relative percentages of fat-free mass to fat mass.

As discussed in chapter 1, there are a variety of ways to measure the amount of body fat a person is carrying, including underwater weighing, which involves weighing the person on land and then underwater; bioelectric impedance analysis (BIA), which involves placing electrodes on the person's hand and foot to measure a current that is passed through the body; BMI calculation, which measures body fat based on height and weight; skinfold measurement, which involves measuring the thickness of skinfolds at predetermined sites; and handheld body fat monitors that provide body fat readings based on the personal information entered.

Ideal body weight had historically been estimated from height and frame size without considering the composition of body weight. As a result, well-muscled women were often considered overweight, and overfat woman were considered within acceptable ranges. It is not uncommon for an exerciser to lose body fat and gain muscle weight without a change in body weight. Without an assessment of body composition, this favorable change could go unnoticed and lead to frustration on the part of the exerciser. Once you have determined your fat mass percentage using the BMI calculation from chapter 1 (see page 12), or other methods discussed in the previous section, you should use that information to determine your ideal body weight.

Plug your numbers into the following equations to determine your lean body weight:

100% – ___ (Fat percentage) = ___ (Lean body mass percentage)
___ (Body weight) × ___ (Lean body mass percentage)
= ___ (Lean body weight)

To give you an example, let's assume one woman determined that her body fat percentage is 23 percent. To calculate this woman's desired weight for her desired body fat range, you must calculate her lean mass. First, because 23 percent of her body is fat, to determine her lean mass, you simply subtract 23 from 100 for 77, which means that 77 percent of her body is lean body mass. Then, assuming that her total body weight is 140 pounds (63.5 kg), you use the decimal form of this percentage to derive her ideal lean body weight, as follows:

100% – 23 (Fat percentage) = 77 (Lean body mass percentage)
140 (Body weight) × .77 (Lean body mass percentage)
= 107.8 (Lean body weight)

As discussed in chapter 1, ideal body fat levels for most women are between 18 and 22 percent; the average for a healthy woman today is actually about 25 percent body fat. So, if you want to determine what your body weight should be for a desired percentage of fat within this healthy range, first subtract the desired percentage of fat from 100 percent, and then divide the lean body weight by the decimal form of this percentage, as follows:

100% – ____ (Desired percent fat) = ____ (Desired lean percent)
____ (Lean body weight) / _____ (Desired lean percent)
= _____ (Desired body weight)

Remember that muscle weight increases even though body fat is decreasing. Body composition and even girth measurements should be evaluated every six weeks throughout your exercise program (see the sidebar Taking Girth Measurements for more information). The results can be motivating, especially if your weight loss is from fat.

Flexibility Assessment

The sit-and-reach test can be helpful in measuring flexibility, specifically of the low back and hamstring muscles. This test is helpful because tension in this area can play a large role in low back pain and muscle tightness. As one of several fitness tests used to measure flexibility, the sit-and-reach test can be easily reproduced to assess your improvement in this area later. However, this testing technique is limited because it measures flexibility only in the low back and hamstrings. It doesn't address the flexibility of other joints and muscles in the body.

Taking Girth Measurements

Easy and inexpensive to complete, girth measurements have been used alone or in conjunction with body composition measures to determine weight loss in women. As body composition changes as a result of increased lean mass and decreased fat mass, girth measurements can be a good indicator of progress. Whether you are looking to increase muscle size or see changes in the size of your thighs as a result of fat loss and muscle gain, girth measures are a sure way to see results. Grab a friend and have her use a tape measure, held with adequate tension, at the following sites to measure your girth (see figure 8.5):

- *Arm*—Measure directly over the largest part of the upper arm.
- *Chest*—Measure across the nipple line.
- *Waist*—Measure around the narrowest part of the midriff.
- *Navel*—Measure directly over the belly button.
- *Hips*—Measure across the top of the buttock cheeks.
- *Thigh*—Measure about 8 inches (20 cm) from the top of the kneecaps, standing with feet together.
- *Calf*—Measure at the maximal circumference of the right leg.

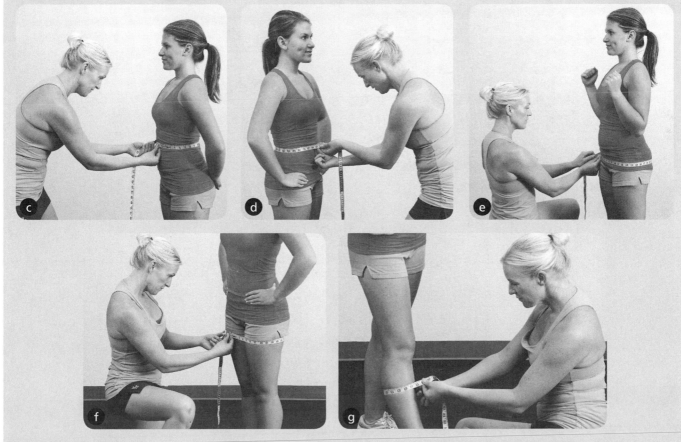

FIGURE 8.5 Girth measurement sites: *(a)* arm, *(b)* chest, *(c)* waist, *(d)* navel, *(e)* hips, *(f)* thigh, and *(g)* calf.

SIT-AND-REACH TEST

Although this test is often conducted using a sit-and-reach box, it doesn't require one. In the example here, we use a cloth tape measure (the same one used for the girth measurements) secured to the floor with tape so that it lies flat. Place a piece of tape at the 15-inch (38 cm) mark on the tape measure. This is where you will place your heels when you are ready to take the test.

To perform the test, be sure to warm up and then sit on the floor with your shoes off and your legs stretched out straight ahead, over the cloth tape measure. Place your feet at the 15-inch (38 cm) mark on the tape measure (figure 8.6a). Both knees should be locked and pressed flat to the floor, or as straight as possible. Your back should be straight. If necessary, you can sit with your back against a wall. Lean forward slowly as far as possible with your hands stacked on top of each other and your fingertips level, keeping the legs flat (figure 8.6b). Your head and shoulders can come away from the wall now. Do *not* jerk or bounce to reach further.

Slowly reach along the length of the tape measure as far as possible and hold the stretch for two full seconds so that a partner can read your measurement. To measure your score, your partner should look directly below where your fingertips are able to reach to on the tape measure. You are attempting to reach past the 15-inch (38 cm) mark on the tape measure, where your heels are situated. Repeat the reach three times, and compare your longest reach with the norms in table 8.4.

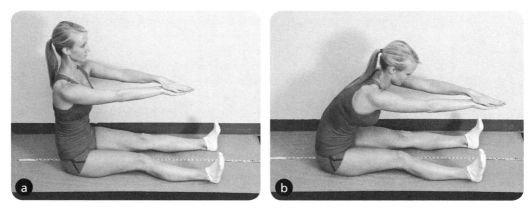

FIGURE 8.6 Sit-and-Reach Test.

TABLE 8.4 Female Flexibility Fitness Norms for the Sit-and-Reach Test

	Age					
	<20	**20-29**	**30-39**	**40-49**	**50-59**	**60+**
Superior	>24.3	>24.5	>24.0	>22.8	>23.0	>23.0
Excellent	22.5-24.3	22.5-23.8	21.5-22.5	20.5-21.5	20.3-21.5	19.0-21.8
Good	21.5-22.3	20.5-22.0	20.0-21.0	19.0-20.0	18.5-20.0	17.0-18.0
Fair	20.5-21.3	19.3-20.3	18.3-19.5	17.3-18.5	16.8-18.0	15.5-17.0
Poor	18.5-20.0	17.0-19.0	16.5-17.8	15.0-17.0	14.8-16.0	13.0-15.2
Very poor	<14.5	<14.1	<12.0	<10.5	<12.3	<9.2

Data reprinted with permission from The Cooper Institute®, Dallas, Texas, from *Physical Fitness Assessments and Norms for Adults and Law Enforcement*. Available online at www.cooperinstitute.org.

TRACKING YOUR PROGRESS

Physical assessments are a critical starting point for your fitness program. Using your initial results to determine the areas you need to focus on and the areas in which you are already doing well and do not need as much attention will really help you stay focused and on track with your programs. In addition to this, baseline data allow you to track your progress to determine whether your training program is helping. Without baseline data, you are basically running blind and cannot know whether you are getting the results you want.

Identifying Your Goals

As with any kind of planning, the question *What do you want?* should come before anything else. What you want is the source of your training goals, which should drive every training decision you make. This will ensure that you progress at an appropriate pace. As you begin, take the time to set some goals so you will be sure to get what you want out of the time you spend training. Having concrete fitness assessment information will help you set specific goals. From my experience, the best training goals have the following qualities:

- *Clearly understood and specific.* For example, if you are 30 years old and scored only 25 on the sit-up test, you can establish a performance goal of achieving a higher number, or performing in a better category.

- *Believable and realistic.* For example, if you are 39 years old and have a body fat percentage of 31 percent, it would be unrealistic and unhealthy to set a goal of decreasing your body fat to 21 percent in four weeks. This goal is not only unrealistic, but also unhealthy. A more appropriate goal could be that percentage achieved in a longer time frame, more like 9 to 12 months of intensive, dedicated training.

- *Time based, or within a specific time frame.* A four-week time frame for achieving a 10 percent reduction in body fat is not based in reality. A more appropriate time frame would take into consideration your ability to exercise as frequently as daily, as well as to significantly change your diet.

- *Measurable using fitness assessments.* Appropriate goals address things that can be measured. A goal to increase the number of push-ups you can do in one minute can be evaluated by retesting after six weeks to see if you have improved.

Be sure to write your goals down, and ensure that they meet all of the preceding requirements. For instance, you can improve a vague goal such as wanting to be more fit by focusing on an aspect of fitness (becoming better at aerobic activities, having stronger legs, being more flexible) and transform your vague goal into something concrete and measurable.

Recording Your Data

When participating in a strength training program, you need to also record your data to monitor your progress. Figure 8.7 is a form you can copy and use to record not only your initial results, but also those that come later. You could also purchase a simple notebook (pen and paper method) and record your results that way. Some women use computer programs such as Excel or other electronic techniques to track their assessment results.

Whatever method you choose, be sure to always include the date and time of day that you are testing. Try to perform fitness tests at the same time of day each time. This is important because your body tends to follow certain patterns with respect to fatigue, hunger, and stress levels. If you don't leave yourself enough time to assess yourself, you may rush through the tests and not be as thorough as you could have been.

FIGURE 8.7 Strength Training Progress Form

	Date: Time:	Date: Time:	Date: Time:	Date: Time:	Date: Time:	Date: Time:
Cardiorespiratory Fitness Test Results						
Bruce Protocol Treadmill Test	Interval #: Ranking: Heart rate:	Interval #: Ranking: Heart rate:	Interval #: Ranking: Heart rate:	Interval #: Ranking: Heart rate:	Interval #: Ranking: Heart rate:	Interval #: Ranking: Heart rate:
Muscle Fitness Test Results						
Sit-Up Test	# of sit-ups: Ranking:	# of sit-ups: Ranking:	# of sit-ups: Ranking:	# of sit-ups: Ranking:	# of sit-ups: Ranking:	# of sit-ups: Ranking:
Modified Push-Up Test	# of push-ups: Ranking:	# of push-ups: Ranking:	# of push-ups: Ranking:	# of push-ups: Ranking:	# of push-ups: Ranking:	# of push-ups: Ranking:
Flexibility Test Results						
Sit-and-Reach Test	# of inches: Ranking:	# of inches: Ranking:	# of inches: Ranking:	# of inches: Ranking:	# of inches: Ranking:	# of inches: Ranking:
Body Composition Test Results						
	Weight: Lean body mass %:	Weight: Lean body mass %:	Weight: Lean body mass %:	Weight: Lean body mass %:	Weight: Lean body mass %:	Weight: Lean body mass %:

From I. Lewis-McCormick, 2012, *A woman's guide to muscle and strength* (Champaign, IL: Human Kinetics).

Also, stress can increase your heart rate falsely. This will make a difference when you are taking the treadmill test for cardio capacity. To prepare for fitness tests, be sure to be well hydrated and well rested and to have eaten early enough before your evaluation that digestion will not interfere with the test. Assessing yourself at the same time of day may be an easy way to remember this guideline.

Also, be sure to retest every six weeks for the first six months. After you are satisfied with your results, you can move to a twice-yearly testing cycle (every six months). The initial six-week intervals provide a reasonable amount of time for your body to transform and for you to see results and determine whether you are on the right track.

Knowing When to Move Forward in Your Fitness Program

When starting a strength training program, design your workouts based on the results of your fitness assessments and the categories you fall into (e.g., excellent, good, poor). The categories you fall into will also lead you toward the correct weight loads, exercise duration, training intensity, number of repetitions and sets, and type of cardio training. Chapter 9 covers important fitness training components to help you create a fitness program that works for you. It will help you determine how long each exercise session should be and how hard you should work. Chapter 9 explains how the programs are set up using periodization and how specific training variables come into play to give you a deeper understanding of the fitness journey you are about to embark on.

There is actually no cut-and-dried data about when you should progress to the next weight load, cardio intensity, and so on. It depends on how hard you have been training, where you are in the progressions, how much recovery you have been allowing yourself, and how you feel about increasing the training volume. Chapters 10 and 11 outline programs that break your training cycles down so you can easily understand what you need to do and when. These programs are designed to gradually improve your fitness by using built-in rest periods and time gaps in which you will achieve the strength gains and cardio success necessary for moving forward. The workouts are designed this way to make your progression from beginner to intermediate to advanced easy and stress free.

The discoveries made during your fitness assessments should prepare you both physically and mentally for your new strength training program. Physically, you will be in a better position to set reasonable long- and short-term goals. Some of your test results may even motivate you by creating a desire to improve or instilling confidence knowing you are doing well in certain areas. Fitness assessments can also help you see the value of doing a variety of exercises rather than just the ones you know; this is important because variety is key to sustaining a fitness program over the long term. Therefore, your commitment toward your new strength and fitness training will likely be one of success in terms of goal attainment.

CHAPTER 9

Developing a Workout

This chapter introduces you to specific training essentials and explains how to use them to create a program that produces a manageable, progressive, long-term approach to training. Also, by learning how to adjust these training essentials at various time frames, you'll learn how to develop a periodized training program that will result in continuous strength improvements, increased muscle definition, and consequently, greater levels of health, self-confidence, and well-being.

CONCEPTS OF A PERIODIZATION PROGRAM

Because the human body adapts quickly to strength training programs, you must make changes at regular intervals to achieve continual progress. To help you achieve the best results, this book uses a concept known as periodization. Periodization resulted from research done by Hans Selye, a young Hungarian physician who observed that when the human body was subjected to stress, it responded in predictable stages. Periodization, then, involves a progressive cycling of various aspects of a training program, in this case a strength training program, during a specific period of time. Periodizing your strength workouts can help you avoid strength training plateaus and prevent overuse injuries. This helps you create workouts that result in improvements in strength, power, muscle size, endurance, and athletic performance.

At the beginning of a periodization program, you will lift light weights using a high volume of repetitions and sets. This is followed by a low volume of repetitions and sets accompanied by progressively heavier weights, all planned over phases, or specific time frames. The main benefit of periodization training is the deliberate increase in stress on the body, which places a constant demand on the muscles in a predictable, organized, and understandable progression. Let's examine each phase in a periodization program and take a look at the volumes and loads you might use during each of them.

Periodized training is divided into segments of time referred to as macrocycles, mesocycles, and microcycles. The overall time frame for a program is the *macrocycle*. This may be as short as 6 months or as long as 1 year. The macrocycle helps you establish a long-range goal and then prepare a plan of action for attaining that goal. This is done by dividing the macrocycle into manageable chunks of time of shorter duration called *mesocycles*. For example, you may divide a 6-month macrocycle into two 3-month mesocycles. Because these mesocycles are still long-term time frames for attaining a specific goal, we use the term *microcycle* to refer to the weeks within each mesocycle.

Periodizing your training is the key to avoiding plateaus and keeping your motivation high. This is particularly important after the initial pleasure of seeing body changes occur rapidly at the start of a new program. Instead of doing the same routine week after week and month after month, you can make appropriate changes at regular intervals to keep your body working harder, while still giving it adequate rest and recovery. Once your body has adapted to the routine, you will want to manipulate the program variables again. This way, you will continue to see changes in your muscle fitness.

STRENGTH TRAINING PROGRAM ESSENTIALS

In 2002, the American College of Sports Medicine (ACSM) published a position stand on strength and conditioning variables for active, healthy adults. The position stand provided the recommended quality and quantity of exercise for developing and maintaining cardiorespiratory and muscular fitness and flexibility in healthy adults. Although this statement was based in research and supported by the entire scientific community, as well as being the basis for all professional fitness trainers' strength programs, it did not consider all the research on strength training over the preceding decade. This early version of the ACSM position stand for exercise recommendations for healthy adults also did not offer any information on how to progress fitness programs. This opened up a lot of opportunity for people to enter the strength training arena with all kinds of opinions and training protocols without collective agreement as to the best methods to achieve overall fitness. You can imagine how confusing all of this information has become. It is no wonder so many women were led astray and consequently left to sift through literally thousands of exercise programs and routines on their own.

Although the 2002 ACSM position stand provided an outstanding framework for the best practices for strength trainers, the ACSM updated the statement in 2009 to reflect the numerous studies on strength training that had taken place since 2002. This updated position stand is for fitness professionals and those other enthusiasts who want to use strength training research for results-based outcomes. Specifically, the updated guidelines make several modifications to the 2002 position stand to better meet the needs of those who are looking for significant muscle development beyond minimal strength gains. The updated ACSM position stand addresses several more variables, as well as the importance of progressive adaptations (i.e., periodization) to increased muscle strength and performance.

The 2009 ACSM document indicates that people looking for increased strength and better health by decreasing fat mass and increasing lean tissue through resistance training should follow strength-specific programs. These should include the use of concentric (muscle shortening), eccentric (muscle lengthening), and isometric muscle actions and bilateral and unilateral, as well as single- and multiple-joint exercises. Programs should also address weight selection, exercise selection and order, the ideal number of sets and repetitions for attaining particular goals, the frequency of exercise, and recovery, all of which are covered next in this section.

The 2009 ACSM guidelines can help decrease training plateaus and significantly improve performance to achieve a higher level of muscle strength, endurance, and overall fitness. Any woman new to strength training should follow these guidelines. She can then expect to take this information forward into intermediate and advanced training.

Frequency

The frequency of exercise refers to how often you need to train to see the results you are looking for, without compromising your recovery time between training sessions. Remember that the body needs to go through a process of rebuilding and repairing to replenish the energy reserves that are consumed during exercise. Frequency is actually a balance between providing just enough stress for the body to adapt to the resistance, and allowing just enough time for recovery and repair to occur.

The appropriate frequency between strength workouts depends on the periodization phase you are in (this is covered later in this chapter) and the type of workout you are performing. Frequency also has to take into account the training variable known as volume (covered later in this section) because how often you exercise depends on the type of program you are using. In general, though, the recommendation for training frequency is two or three days per week for beginning levels, three or four days per week for intermediate, and four or five days per week for advanced. Your frequency for cardio training can be daily, but you will need to change the intensity of the cardio workouts frequently, particularly as you become more fit. The guideline for cardiorespiratory training is a minimum of three sessions per week, and the guideline for flexibility training is no less than two sessions per week.

Remember that each time you complete a strenuous strength training session (regardless of the body part), you are taxing your body as a whole—including all of the physiological systems and major organs. Keep in mind that your body does not distinguish days of the week. It only understands time between sessions. You may need more recovery between sessions depending on how hard you work, as well as your level of fitness.

Intensity

Intensity refers to the amount of effort invested in a training program, or in any one training session. The weight you lift should challenge you. It should be heavy enough that you feel muscle exhaustion as you approach your last two repetitions. *Exhaustion* means that your muscles are so tired that you can't do another full repetition in good form or without assistance. Many women do not lift heavy enough, or in other words, to exhaustion. This is mostly because they don't know that they are supposed to! They tend to simply perform the number of repetitions that they think is good, or they choose light weights because of that age-old myth of getting too big as a result of lifting heavy weights.

In resistance training, the workload is the primary measure of intensity. The workload can be determined by any one of the following:

- The amount of weight lifted during an exercise
- The number of repetitions completed for a particular exercise
- The length of time to complete all exercises in a set, or the total training session time

You may choose to increase your workload by lifting heavier weights or by performing more repetitions with the same weight. Another option is to lift the same weight for the same number of repetitions, but decrease the rest time between sets. As a general rule, increase the intensity using only *one* of the previous three parameters. For example, don't increase weight and decrease rest time in the same session. This will only serve to prefatigue you and may result in injury.

Also, you should sequence your exercises to optimize intensity. For example, perform large muscle group exercises before small ones, multiple-joint exercises before single-joint ones, and higher-intensity exercises before lower-intensity ones.

Time

Time in this context refers to the length of time of your overall training session. The common consensus for the duration of resistance training sessions is no longer than 60 minutes. Any longer than that can set you up for boredom and burnout. Cardio training should last 30 to 45 minutes, and flexibility training, 20 to 30 minutes. As you become more advanced and your intensity increases, your sessions will become shorter. Particularly grueling strength training sessions should last only 20 to 30 minutes. Regardless of the time frame you need to achieve your goals, you should approach each exercise session with focus and purpose.

Many women fail to take full advantage of their training time. They allow themselves to be distracted and use their time poorly. If you are in the gym to work out, that should be your primary goal. Do not allow anyone or anything to limit you or sidetrack you from accomplishing your goal.

Interval-Based Exercise Training

Interval training is a unique and powerful way to train that is time efficient and burns more total calories than regular training. It involves the performance of higher-intensity exercise followed by recovery periods in a very specific time frame. The purpose of performing short bouts of high-intensity exercise is to reach overload, or uncomfortable intensity levels, throughout your training routines. Obviously, it would be impossible to exercise at such high intensity levels for an entire 30-minute workout. This is why there are built-in rest periods—not enough to allow you to fully recover, but enough to challenge you appropriately during these quick-paced, time-efficient workouts.

The interval training formulas outlined here are based on the body's energy systems (anaerobic and aerobic) to offer you a scientific approach to interval training. The best ratios are those that are related to the ATP-PC, anaerobic glycolysis, and aerobic energy systems. Because these systems become depleted in very specific time frames, we use ratio intervals to follow their energy depletion and consequent recovery. The *work* in *work-to-rest ratio* is anaerobic; that is, you work until you become breathless or close to it (this uses the ATP-PC, or anaerobic glycolysis, system), and then recover aerobically so you can catch your breath enough to prepare you for the next interval.

Most important with interval training is to remain consistent. If you decide to run on the treadmill at a 2:1 work-to-rest ratio, you need to stay true to the intervals and not decide halfway through that you need more time to rest or can wait another minute. The training benefit comes from the overload that results from the consistency of the ratios. For example, if you decide that the hard part will take two minutes and your recovery will take one minute, stick with that routine during the entire workout to the best of your ability.

You have the flexibility to select any work-to-rest interval range you would like within any of the three heart rate zones. Use the following ratios to determine which works best for you depending on how long you need to work hard and how long you need to recover. Also included are some examples of activities using the ratios. If you understand the work-to-rest ratio design, however, you can devise your own ratios and choose any activity you like (e.g., cycling, outdoor walking, or jogging).

1:1 Work-to-Rest Ratio

A 1:1 work-to-rest ratio means that you work and recover for the same amount of time. Following are sample 1:1 work-to-rest ratio activities:

- *Treadmill:* Alternate five minutes of running (at 5 mph, or 8 km/h, or faster) with five minutes of walking (at 3.5 to 4 mph, or 5.6 to 6.4 km/h) for a total of 30 to 45 minutes.
- *Elliptical trainer:* Alternate two minutes at a high intensity (as hard as you can work while still maintaining good form, posture, and control) with two minutes at a moderate intensity for a total of 30 to 45 minutes.

2:1 Work-to-Rest Ratio

A 2:1 work-to-rest ratio means that you work for twice as long as you recover. Following are sample 2:1 work-to-rest ratio activities:

- *Treadmill:* Alternate three minutes of running (5 to 7 mph, or 8 to 11.3 km/h) with 90 seconds of jogging (5 to 5.5 mph, or 8 to 8.9 km/h) for a total of 30 to 45 minutes.
- *Elliptical trainer:* Alternate 40 seconds at a high intensity (as hard as you can work while still maintaining good form, posture, and control) with 20 seconds at a moderate intensity for a total of 25 to 30 minutes.

3:1 Work-to-Rest Ratio

A 3:1 work-to-rest ratio means that you work three times as long as the recovery. Following are sample 3:1 work-to-rest ratio activities:

- *Treadmill:* Alternate 15 minutes of running (5 to 6 mph, or 8 to 9.7 km/h) with five minutes of jogging (6 to 7 mph, or 9.7 to 11.3 km/h) for 30 to 45 minutes.
- *Elliptical trainer:* Alternate nine minutes at a high intensity (as hard as you can work while still maintaining good form, posture, and control) with three minutes at a moderate intensity for 30 to 45 minutes.

Remember, too, that you can change the work-to-rest ratio into a rest-to-work ratio, if you need to. For example, if working hard for two minutes with only one minute of recovery (2:1) is too much for you, simply flip it and use the ratio as a rest-to-work ratio instead—working for one minute and then recovering for two minutes (1:2).

Type

This may seem rather obvious, but it's worth saying anyway: the best exercise to perform to achieve a goal is exercise that will achieve that goal. For example, to increase strength, perform strength training; to attain cardio goals, run, cycle, use an elliptical trainer, or take a fitness class; for flexibility, do yoga or Pilates or take a stretching class. All components of fitness are important, so be sure to spend an adequate amount of time addressing each one specifically to achieve a balanced approach (see the principle of specificity later in this chapter).

Volume

Training volume refers to the cumulative work completed not only during a single training session, but also over the course of a training phase. Volume refers to the number of muscles and muscle groups worked, the exercises selected, and the number of sets and repetitions performed. Keep in mind that the periodization model will guide you in deciding how often to strength train, how many sets to perform, and how many repetitions to do. However, you should understand how volume affects your overall strength training performance and goals.

Training volume is one of the variables you will change on a regular basis to optimize periodization in your strength training program. When you first begin a strength training program, the volume (of the first mesocycle in particular) should be on the lower end of the continuum. This means that you should not start out with too much, too soon, including too much weight, too many exercises, or sessions that are too long (longer than 60 minutes). Beginning slowly is important because it allows you to adapt gradually to the new training program, the training stimulus, and the new stresses that your body will experience. Maintaining a low volume initially will allow you to feel successful after accomplishing your goals in each new microcycle. Training volume can be gradually increased as your muscles are subjected to more time under tension and repetitions and sets increase. You will develop a commitment to the program as you become stronger and more confident.

You can also use your training volume to estimate the number of calories you burn during a training session, because there is a high correlation between the amount of weight lifted and the number of calories burned.

Training Load

Many experts say that a weight you cannot control throughout a set (say, eight repetitions) is too heavy. If you pick up two 20-pound dumbbells, place one in each hand, and proceed to perform 10 repetitions of biceps curls but cannot get past repetition 5, the weights are too heavy. But how exactly do you know what weight to choose?

Choosing the correct weight loads for every set of exercises is a tricky and often changing process. However, the process can be simplified by knowing what you are trying to do; that is, what goal you are trying to accomplish. Microcycles are very helpful in this regard, because each microcycle outlines a short-term goal that is very specific and easy to understand. For example, in microcycle 1, you are simply attempting to get through an entire workout, focusing on form and technique. The weight loads do not need to be heavy at this point. There is plenty of time to improve your strength, but form and technique need to be correct from the start. In microcycle 2, the weight loads might be heavier because the goals of the sessions have changed.

Let's take a look at a variety of methods you can use to figure out just how much weight you need to be using. Keep in mind that as the training intensity increases (i.e., the weights become heavier), volume will decrease (i.e., reps and sets become shorter). This is because performing many repetitions and sets with heavy weights is harder. The opposite is also true: if the weight loads are lighter, you will be able to perform higher volumes (i.e., more sets and repetitions).

Novice strength trainers (those who are untrained and have no resistance training experience or those who have not trained for several years) should perform 8 to 12 repetitions. Intermediate-level strength trainers (with approximately six months of consistent resistance training experience) and advanced strength trainers (with two or more years of resistance training experience) should use a wider loading range (from 1 to 12 repetitions) in a periodized fashion with an eventual emphasis on heavy loading (1 to 6 repetitions) using three- to five-minute rest periods between sets performed at a moderate contraction velocity (taking one to two seconds for the concentric, or shortening, phase of the contraction and one to two seconds for the eccentric phase of the contraction). When training at a specific RM load, people who can perform the current workload for one or two repetitions over the desired number of repetitions in the prescribed set should increase the load (i.e., the weight) by 5 to 10 percent. Keep in mind that the repetition guidelines are just that—guidelines. Take the liberty to increase your repetitions or increase your weight loads as necessary to complete the sets safely.

Never lift super heavy loads when you are strength training alone. If you were to drop a weight on your foot or another body part, you could be in trouble. When strength training using very heavy weights, have a lifting partner or a personal trainer with you in case you need assistance. This person should be strong enough to handle a heavy weight without your assistance in case of an emergency.

Progressive Overload

Progressive overload is the gradual increase in exercise stress placed on the body during training. Progressive overload is quite specific to the area of fitness you are seeking to improve (e.g., a gradual increase in cardio training to improve cardio fitness or a gradual increase in weight loads to improve muscle strength and endurance). When you are new to strength training, you will likely experience results relatively quickly. However, without a continual manipulation of the training variables, you will plateau quickly, meaning that you will stop seeing results from the same training regimen. By systematically increasing the demands you place on your body, you will continue to see strength and cardiorespiratory improvements. For further improvement to take place, you must manipulate at least one of the following variables: exercise intensity (i.e., weight loads), the number of repetitions, the speed at which you move the weights, or the rest periods between exercises.

Since 2002, many research studies have demonstrated that to improve muscle strength over the long haul, you must engage in a program that progressively manipulates a variety of training variables. The fact is, you will stop seeing strength training results after about the first four to six weeks of performing the same routine. To achieve a higher level of muscle fitness, you have to change the training variables, such as the exercises, the number of sets, the frequency of training, and the weight loads. By manipulating these variables, you will avoid training plateaus and achieve a higher level of muscle fitness.

Specificity

Training improvements and adaptations are extremely specific to the training you perform. For example, to improve your ability to perform full push-ups, you must practice full push-ups. Although chest presses and bent-knee push-ups do strengthen the chest and triceps, and there is some carryover to the full push-up, only practicing full push-ups will improve your ability to perform full push-ups. The principle of specificity is that precise. The most effective strength training programs target specific training goals.

With respect to results-based training, the most current ACSM position stand (2009) highlights two goals of people who perform strength training. The first is to continually achieve greater fitness gains. The second is to maintain the muscle fitness they have achieved, preserving their health and appearance. The first goal is most important to the beginner exerciser. The amount of improvement you can expect to see will come from the manipulation of several variables. For this reason, applying the principle of progressive overload is very important for a beginning strength trainer.

Recovery

Recovery is perhaps one of the most important principles of training. It sounds so simple, and yet it's so powerful and frequently neglected. Proper recovery from your workouts will help you avoid overtraining, needless injuries, and exercise burnout, and it will help you achieve amazing training results.

Exercising too frequently and too intensely hinders the body's ability to recover and adapt. Keep in mind that the harder you train, the more recovery you should allow for yourself. Unfortunately, many athletes don't have this luxury; but fortunately, you do. Without adequate recovery, you are left feeling fatigue, which results in disrupted homeostasis, or physical imbalance. However, adequate recovery from each training session (as well as between training programs) will yield the benefits of the training effect.

You can assess your recovery by considering the following: if you cannot exceed the load or repetitions on the same exercise that you performed in the same sequence the last time you did that particular workout (all things being equal), then you have not fully recovered.

Recovery in strength training refers to both short-term and long-term recovery. Short-term recovery refers to the days between workouts. You should rest for a minimum of 48 hours between strength workouts. This should give your body time to get ready to perform the next strength workout. Keep in mind that alternating training days regardless of whether you change the muscle groups is inadequate for full recovery between workouts. Therefore, changing muscle groups on a consecutive training day is not enough recovery time between workouts. You can perform flexibility training, low-intensity cardio exercise, or nothing on your recovery days between strength workouts.

As mentioned previously, the central nervous system controls the entire body. Energy systems, metabolism, the endocrine system—all require a certain amount of time to regenerate between workouts, even if you are alternating muscle groups. This is true because the human body is connected as a whole—the mind and the body work together and cannot be separate from one another.

The 48-hour guideline for recovery between workouts is just a guideline, however. If you find that you need even more rest between workouts, honor your body by giving yourself more time to recover. There's nothing wrong with taking an additional day off if you need it.

Long-term recovery refers to the weeks between the stages of a mesocycle or a macrocycle, or the time between the end and beginning of a new periodization program, as discussed earlier in this chapter. The periodization programs in chapters 10 and 11 have built-in recovery cycles. I suggest that you take a week off at the end of each mesocycle (i.e., at the end of each 12 weeks of exercise, or each three-month phase). If you want to see results, you need to trust me on the week-off plan. It will benefit you enormously by decreasing your risk of injury due to overtraining or overuse, offer you the opportunity to try a new exercise modality, and energize you for the upcoming mesocycle. It is already worked into your periodization programs, so you don't have to worry about planning for it. I also suggest alternatives to strength training that you can take part in during your recovery. You may discover that you really look forward to these breaks.

As you can see, a well-rounded, comprehensive strength training program addresses a number of components. Having a solid operational knowledge of these components will mean the difference between simply working out versus following a fitness plan that yields the results you want. The following chapters contain specific information about your next steps, helping you create a program that will make a difference. The information in this chapter will help you accomplish your goals as you start your beginner, intermediate, or advanced strength training program with confidence and practical know-how.

Beginner and Intermediate Strength Programs

The workouts outlined in this chapter for beginners and intermediate-level exercisers will get you started with a strength training program that makes sense and is manageable. You should have a fairly good understanding of program expectations, training variables, and periodization training phases from earlier chapters. Now it's time to take that foundational knowledge one step further.

In this chapter, you will learn that exercise movements, equipment, and weight loads are not randomly selected. Rather, they are systematically chosen to build the skills you need to move to an advanced training program. An understanding of why you start with certain exercises and certain equipment will help you progress in your strength training.

MOVING FROM BEGINNER TO INTERMEDIATE

To progress from beginner to intermediate workouts, you need to gain the core strength and stability required to perform exercises safely, as well as increase your overall capacity for more intense exercise. The American Council on Exercise (ACE) has outlined a very safe and effective beginning strength training program, with the intent of moving forward to an intermediate, and eventually an advanced, training level. This program is intended to prepare your body for higher levels of intensity by creating a more stable and functional you. The workouts outlined in this chapter will help you perform exercises with proper form and technique, increase your core strength and (as a result) movement stability, and improve your overall functional strength. Moving into the next phases of strength training should be an easy transition if you work hard and stay consistent with your program (ACE 2010).

You will initially perform strength training exercises twice a week for three microcycles (six weeks), incorporating total-body workouts in each session. After three microcycles, you should be able to exercise more than two days per week.

As you move into intermediate programming, you will progress to strength workouts three days per week. Microcycles 1-6 are the beginner workouts and miscrocycles 7-12 are the intermediate workouts.

Workouts begin with circuits, which are complete sets of a certain number of exercises for each of the major muscle groups of the body. A variety of exercises are incorporated into circuits that are appropriate for your current level of fitness and experience. Keep in mind that you will still track your workouts with the periodization programming (the macro-, meso-, and microcycles) that you read about in chapter 9. Those training phases, as well as recovery periods, will not change with any of the programs (beginner, intermediate, advanced, and endurance) throughout this book. This periodization training, as presented in chapter 9, is the foundation of your exercise programming.

The circuits consist of 8 to 10 exercises performed for a specified number of repetitions; each completed circuit is referred to as a set. The sequence of exercises allows you to rest certain body parts as you are working others, or when moving from one exercise station to the next. Preparing for each new exercise by setting up the machine or selecting the dumbbells provides a natural break. So in theory, you should be able to move from one exercise to the next without having to take significant rest breaks in between. You will want to move quickly from one exercise to the next, however, so that you can complete up to three full sets (circuits) within a 60-minute time frame.

Workouts later in the program include timed repetitions with heavier loads rather than a specific number of sets. This means that you will have a specific number of repetitions to complete at each station prior to moving on. You should complete these repetitions in a timely fashion as a beginner, but the expectation is that you will be able to perform a specific set of repetitions in a set time frame, and that your time frame will decrease as your loads increase.

Finally, at the end of each set or circuit, take a one-minute recovery period to drink water and take a short rest. The goal is to complete each circuit two or three times through for approximately 12 to 15 repetitions at each station. Beginner workouts 1 and 2 offer the choice of either two or three sets. If three sets are too much, simply do what you can. Ideally, you will perform two sets of each exercise as indicated, log the exercises you perform, and make an effort to increase your ability to maintain as many exercises within each circuit as you can during each workout. If you stick with the beginner strength phase for the first three months, within just a few weeks of consistent training, you should be able to perform the entire three-set circuit in 60 minutes and also see noticeable improvements in your body, how you feel, and how you look.

The upside of circuits is that they are quick, provide exercises for all the major muscle groups, and can easily be set up and performed in a short time frame. The downside is that even though you can take more time to complete the assigned repetitions (within reason) at each station, because you are exercising the entire time, there is not a lot of opportunity for rest. And, even though you are changing the muscle groups each time you move to another station, you are still taxing the central nervous system throughout. Because the exercise is continuous, you will not be able to lift heavy loads, because the training volume at this stage is already high (recall that training volume refers to the number of sets and repetitions you are performing). However, the ideal training situation for a beginning strength trainer is high training volume with low loads, so you are actually following the plan well using these training circuits. The bottom line, all those things considered, is that circuit training is a really good plan for a beginner strength trainer because it increases stamina for the next challenge—intermediate circuits.

Overcoming Distractions in the Gym

It is really important that you not get sidetracked and distracted from your circuits. A friend or someone you know may want to interrupt your training to say hello and shoot the breeze, taking critical minutes away from your routine. This is a common occurrence at the gym.

The component of your conditioning program that allows you to move from beginner to intermediate status is your training time. You need to experience the winded feeling and overcome the fatigue your body is experiencing by allowing your body to adapt to the progressive overload. If you are not experiencing overload because of distractions that are taking you away from your training routine, you will not progress, nor will you experience the training effect you are working toward.

Let people you might see or know understand that you are in the middle of a circuit and can chat after you are finished. If you don't take your training time and program goals seriously, you will not get the results you want. Results are entirely earned, so make sure you are not disrupted. You may be able to avoid distractions by working out in the gym at downtimes, by wearing headphones, or by simply not engaging in conversation at all.

THE PROGRAM

The macrocycle for the beginner-to-intermediate strength training program is six months long, which is broken down into two mesocycles—three months of beginner workouts followed by three months of intermediate workouts. Each mesocycle is then broken down further into 6, two-week microcycles. The goal of the first mesocycle, which is your beginner program, is to increase overall fitness and strength as well as create a comfort level with the techniques and make regular strength training and cardio exercise part of your lifestyle. The goal of the second mesocycle, your intermediate program, is to further increase stamina and endurance and establish a consistent routine to prepare you to move to an advanced program. Following is a more detailed explanation of what you will do in each of the microcycles. Note that you should be sure to take a 1-week break between the beginner phase and the intermediate phase.

Microcycles 1-3 (Weeks 1-6)

In the first three microcycles (weeks 1-6), you will do workouts 1 and 2 each week. For example, during week 1, perform workout 1 once, and workout 2 once. During week 2, perform workout 1 once, and workout 2 once. Continue this plan for the first three microcycles (6 weeks). Within each microcycle, you should also perform at least three cardio workouts each week on the days you do not strength train. Spend 30 to 40 minutes on a cardio machine of your choice working between 5 and 7 on the Rating of Perceived Exertion (RPE) scale (this time includes a five-minute warm-up and a five-minute cool-down). Stretch after each strength workout and after each cardio workout. Also, allow at least 48 hours between strength workouts.

Microcycles 4-6 (Weeks 7-12)

In microcycle 4 (weeks 7 and 8), perform workout 3 two times each week and in microcycle 5 (weeks 9 and 10), perform workout 4 two times each week. Finally, in microcycle 6 (weeks 11 and 12), perform each workout (3 and 4) one day each week. For example in week 11, you would perform workout 3 on Tuesday, and then workout 4 on Friday.

Throughout these microcycles, you should also perform three or four cardio workouts each week on the days you do not strength train. Spend 30 to 45 minutes on a cardio machine of your choice working between 5 and 7 on the RPE scale (this time includes a five-minute warm-up and a five-minute cool-down). Stretch after each strength workout and after each cardio workout. Also, allow at least 48 hours between strength workouts.

Microcycles 7-9 (Weeks 13-18)

In microcycle 5, perform workout 5 three times per week and in microcycle 6, perform workout 6 three times per week. In microcycle 7, perform workouts 5 and 6 three times per week. You can decide if you want to perform workout 5 twice in one week and workout 6 once, vice versa. During these microcycles, perform at least three cardio workouts each week on the days you do not strength train. Spend 30 to 45 minutes on a cardio machine of your choice working between 5 and 7 on the RPE scale (this time includes a five-minute warm-up and a five-minute cool-down). Stretch after each strength workout and after each cardio workout. Also, allow at least 48 hours between strength workouts.

Microcycles 10-12 (Weeks 19-24)

In microcycle 10, perform workout 7, three times per week. In microcycle 11, perform workout 8, three times per week. In microcycle 12, perform workout 7 and 8, three times per week. You can decide if you want to perform workout 7 twice in one week and workout 8 one time, or workout 8 twice and workout 7 once. During these microcycles, perform at least three cardio workouts each week, on the days you do not strength train. Spend 30 to 45 minutes on a cardio machine of your choice working between 5 and 7 on the RPE scale (this time includes a five-minute warm-up and a five-minute cool-down). Stretch after each strength workout and after each cardio workout. Also, allow at least 48 hours between your strength workouts for adequate recovery.

BEGINNER WORKOUT 1

Warm-up	Warm up for 5 to 7 minutes on a treadmill, elliptical trainer, or stationary bike before beginning the workout.			
	Exercise	**Sets***	**Reps**	**Muscles worked**
	Seated pelvic tilt on stability ball	2	8	Lower body, core
	Seated hip circles on stability ball	2	4	Lower body, core
	Lateral stretch	2	2	Lateral spine
	Knee lift with medicine ball	2	2	Legs and low back
	Body ball reach	2	2	Spine, lower body
	Standing figure four	2	2	Hips, low back
Lower and upper body	Since you are just starting out, try and keep your weight loads low, and focus on learning the correct form and technique. You will have plenty of time to add weight after you get the technique down.			
	Exercise	**Sets***	**Reps**	**Muscles worked**
	Front lunge with lateral squat	1	10 (right and left)	Lower body
	Dumbbell front squat	2-3	15	Hamstrings, gluteals, quadriceps
	Dumbbell chest press	2-3	15	Chest, shoulders
	Stability ball gluteal squeeze	2-3	25	Gluteals
	Lat pulldown (Perform bent-over dumbbell row if machine is not available.)	2-3	15	Midback
	Leg extension (Perform squat if machine is not available.)	2-3	15	Quadriceps
	Seated shoulder press	2-3	15	Shoulders
	Incline push-up	2-3	10	Chest, shoulders, core
	Seated hamstring curl (Perform deadlift if machine is not available.)	2-3	15	Quadriceps
	Pilates swimming	2-3	10	Posterior muscles
	Biceps curl with EZ Curl Bar	2-3	15	Arms
Core	**Exercise**	**Sets***	**Reps**	**Muscles worked**
	Supine stability ball bridge	2	5	Core
	Abdominal progression series	1	10 each exercise	Core
Flexibility	**Exercise**	**Sets***	**Reps**	**Muscles worked**
	Seated hip circles on stability ball	2	5 (right and left)	--
	Lateral stretch	2	2	--
	Spinal extension	2	2 (right and left)	--
	Standing figure four	2	2 (right and left)	--

*Take 60 seconds of rest between sets.

BEGINNER WORKOUT 2

Warm-up	Warm up for 5 to 7 minutes on a treadmill, elliptical trainer, or stationary bike before beginning the workout.			
	Exercise	**Sets***	**Reps**	**Muscles worked**
	Seated pelvic tilt on stability ball	2	8	Lower body, core
	Seated hip circles on stability ball	2	4	Lower body, core
	Lateral stretch	2	2	Lateral spine
	Knee lift with medicine ball	2	2	Legs and low back
	Body ball reach	2	2	Spine, lower body
	Standing figure four	2	2	Hips, low back
Lower and upper body	Since you are just starting out, try and keep your weight loads low, and focus on learning the correct form and technique. You will have plenty of time to add weight after you get the technique down.			
	Exercise	**Sets***	**Reps**	**Muscles worked**
	Good morning	2-3	12	Hamstrings, gluteals
	Dumbbell chest fly	2-3	12	Chest, shoulders
	Front lunge	2-3	12 (alternating right and left)	Gluteals, hamstrings
	Bent-over dumbbell row	2-3	12	Midback
	Single-leg squat	2-3	12 (right and left)	Quadriceps
	Dumbbell upright row	2-3	12	Shoulders
	Seated leg press (Perform squat if machine is not available.)	2-3	12	Gluteals, hamstrings
	Push-up	2-3	10	Chest, core, triceps
	Pullover	2-3	12	Lats, trapezius
	Hammer curl	2-3	12	Biceps, forearms
Core	**Exercise**	**Sets***	**Reps**	**Muscles worked**
	Supine stability ball bridge	3	10 (each exercise)	Spine
	Push-up to plank	3	10	Core
	Stability ball roll-out	3	10	Anterior core
	Supine clocking	2-3	10	Anterior core
Flexibility	**Exercise**	**Sets***	**Reps**	**Muscles worked**
	Standing cat and cow	2	4	--
	Standing knee flexion and extension with ankle dorsiflexion	2	4 (right and left)	--
	Front lunge with lateral squat	2	4 (right and left)	--
	Body ball reach	2	4 (right and left)	--

*Take 60 seconds of rest between sets.

BEGINNER WORKOUT 3

Warm-up	Warm up for 5 to 7 minutes on a treadmill, elliptical trainer, or stationary bike before beginning the workout.			
	Exercise	**Sets***	**Reps**	**Muscles worked**
	Plié with medicine ball lift	2	8	Lower body, core
	Front lunge with lateral squat	2	4	Lower body, core
	Lateral stretch	2	2	Lateral spine
	Standing knee flexion and extension with ankle dorsiflexion	2	2	Legs, low back
	Spinal extension	2	2	Spine, lower body
	Standing figure four	2	2	Hips, low back
Lower and upper body	Now that you are becoming more accustomed to the workouts, you can begin to increase your weight loads, but continue to focus on learning the correct form and technique. Give the techniques 100% of your attention while strength training.			
	Exercise	**Sets***	**Reps**	**Muscles worked**
	Walking lunge	3	50 (alternating legs)	Hamstrings, gluteals, quadriceps
	Lat pulldown (Perform bent-over dumbbell row if machine is not available.)	3	12	Chest, shoulders
	Good morning	3	12	Gluteals
	Decline push-up	3	12	Anterior deltoid, chest, triceps
	Pull-up	3	5	Biceps, lats, core
	Side lunge	3	12 (right and left counted as 1)	Lateral leg muscles, gluteals
	Seated calf raise	3	12 (each leg)	Calves
	Front cable raise (Use dumbbells and perform a front raise if machine is not available.)	3	10	Anterior deltoid, chest, core
	Bent-over dumbbell row	3	12	Midback, biceps
	Rear deltoid fly	3	12	Posterior deltoid, posture muscles
Core	**Exercise**	**Sets***	**Reps**	**Muscles worked**
	Windshield wipers	2	10	Core
	Abdominal progression series	2	10 each exercise	Core
	Quadruped spinal extension	2	10 (right and left)	Core, balance
Flexibility	**Exercise**	**Sets***	**Reps**	**Muscles worked**
	Full-body stretch	2	2	--
	Low back stretch	2	2	--
	Spinal twist	2	2	--
	Hamstring stretch	2	2 (right and left)	--

*Take 60 seconds of rest between sets.

BEGINNER WORKOUT 4

Warm-up	Warm up for 5 to 7 minutes on a treadmill, elliptical trainer, or stationary bike before beginning the workout.			
	Exercise	**Sets***	**Reps**	**Muscles worked**
	Plié with medicine ball lift	2	8	Lower body, core
	Front lunge with lateral squat	2	4	Lower body, core
	Lateral stretch	2	2	Lateral spine
	Standing knee flexion and extension with ankle dorsiflexion	2	2	Legs, low back
	Spinal extension	2	2	Spine, lower body
	Standing figure four	2	2	Hips, low back
Lower and upper body	Now that you are becoming more accustomed to the workouts, you can begin to increase your weight loads, but continue to focus on learning the correct form and technique. Give the techniques 100% of your attention while strength training.			
	Exercise	**Sets***	**Reps**	**Muscles worked**
	Walking lunge	5	10	Quadriceps, gluteals, hamstrings
	Squat sequence with curtsy lunge	6	10	Legs, hamstrings, quadriceps, gluteals
	Seated calf raise (Use dumbbells and perform calf raise if machine is not available.)	3	10	Calves
	Push-up	2	10	Chest, triceps, anterior deltoid
	Decline push-up	2	10	Chest, triceps
	Standing cable chest fly (Use dumbbells and perform chest fly if machine is not available.)	2	10	Chest, core
	Lat pulldown (Perform bent-over dumbbell row if machine is not available.)	2	10	Back, biceps
	Pullover	2	10	Back, deltoids
	Bent-over dumbbell row	2	10	Back, biceps
	Lateral raise	2	10	Shoulders
	Dumbbell upright row	3	10	Shoulders
	Seated shoulder press	2	10	Shoulders, triceps
	Rear deltoid fly	2	10	Shoulders, postural muscles
	Biceps curl with EZ Curl Bar	2	10	Forearms, biceps
	Hammer curl	2	10	Forearms, biceps
	Triceps kickback	2	10	Forearms, triceps
	Pilates swimming	5	10	Entire chain of posterior muscles

Core	Exercise	Sets*	Reps	Muscles worked
	Pilates roll-up	3	10 (right and left)	Core
	Side plank	4	30 seconds (right and left)	Core
	Knee lift with medicine ball	4	2 (right and left)	Core
	Stability ball roll-out	2	10	Core
	Oblique stability ball roll-out	2	5 (right and left)	Core
Flexibility	Exercise	Sets*	Reps	Muscles worked
	Child's pose	1	30 seconds	--
	Standing shoulder horizontal adduction	3	2 (front and back)	--
	Shoulder rotation with bands	2	1	--
	Low back stretch	2	2 (right and left)	--
	Hamstring stretch	2	2	--
	Forward bend	2	2	--
	Forward bend with a twist	2	2	--

*Take 60 seconds of rest between sets.

BEGINNER WORKOUT 5

	Warm up for 5 to 7 minutes on a treadmill, elliptical trainer, or stationary bike before beginning the workout.			
Warm-up	**Exercise**	**Sets***	**Reps**	**Muscles worked**
	Plié with medicine ball lift	2	8	Lower body, core
	Front lunge with lateral squat	2	4	Lower body, core
	Lateral stretch	2	2	Lateral spine
	Standing knee flexion and extension with ankle dorsiflexion	2	2	Legs, low back
	Spinal extension	2	2	Spine, lower body
	Standing figure four	2	2	Hips, low back
Lower and upper body	*Now that you are becoming more accustomed to the workouts, you can continue to increase your weight loads, but stay focused on continued learning. Understanding the correct form and technique will allow you to move into more advanced techniques.*			
	Exercise	**Sets***	**Reps**	**Muscles worked**
	Dumbbell squat	3	10	Quadriceps, gluteals
	Single-leg squat	3	10	Hamstrings, quadriceps, core
	Seated leg press (Perform squat if machine is not available.)	3	10	Hamstrings, quadriceps, gluteals
	Seated hamstring curl (Perform deadlift if machine is not available.)	3	10	Hamstrings
	Standing cable chest fly (Perform chest press if machine is not available.)	3	10	Chest, anterior deltoid, core
	Dumbbell chest fly	3	10	Chest, anterior deltoid
	Lat pulldown (Perform bent-over dumbbell row if machine is not available.)	3	10	Back, biceps
	Pullover	3	10	Back, anterior deltoid, core
	Side plank	2-3	10 on right and 10 on left side	Core
	Seated shoulder press	3	10	Shoulders, triceps
	Straight bar upright row	3	10	Shoulders
	Preacher curl	3	10	Forearms, biceps
	Hammer curl	3	10	Forearms, biceps
	Triceps kickback	3	10	Forearms, triceps

Core	Exercise	Sets*	Reps	Muscles worked
	Pilates roll-up	5	10	Core
	Plank	3	30 seconds	Chest and core
	Knee lift with medicine ball	1	10 (right and left)	Core
	Supine contralateral bicycle	2	25	Core
	Push-up to plank	1	10	Core
Flexibility	Exercise	Sets*	Reps	Muscles worked
	Child's pose	1	30 seconds	--
	Low back stretch	1	2	--
	Hamstring stretch	2	2 (right and left)	--
	Spinal twist	2	2 (right and left)	--
	Quadruped cat and cow	2	2	--
	Downward-facing dog	4	2	--

*Take 60 seconds of rest between sets.

BEGINNER WORKOUT 6

Warm-up	Warm up for 5 to 7 minutes on a treadmill, elliptical trainer, or stationary bike before beginning the workout.			
	Exercise	**Sets***	**Reps**	**Muscles worked**
	Plié with medicine ball lift	2	8	Lower body, core
	Front lunge with lateral squat	2	4	Lower body, core
	Lateral stretch	2	2	Lateral spine
	Standing knee flexion and extension with ankle dorsiflexion	2	2	Legs, low back
	Spinal extension	2	2	Spine, lower body
	Standing figure four	2	2	Hips, low back
Lower and upper body	Now that you are becoming more accustomed to the workouts, you can continue to increase your weight loads, but stay focused on continued learning. Understanding the correct form and technique will allow you to move into more advanced techniques.			
	Exercise	**Sets***	**Reps**	**Muscles worked**
	Dumbbell squat	3	10	Hamstrings, gluteals, low back
	Reverse lunge	3	10	Hamstrings, quadriceps, gluteals
	Side lunge	3	10	Hamstrings, quadriceps, gluteals
	Kettlebell hip hinge	2	10 (right and left)	Legs, core
	Push-up	3	10	Chest, triceps, core
	Barbell chest press	3	10	Chest, anterior deltoid
	Lat pulldown (Perform bent-over dumbbell row if machine is not available.)	3	10	Back, biceps
	Pullover	3	10	Back, core
	Seated low row (Perform biceps curl if machine is not available.)	3	10	Back, posterior deltoid, biceps
	Lateral raise	3	10	Shoulders
	Dumbbell upright row	3	10	Shoulders
	Reverse curl	3	10	Forearms, biceps
	Triceps kickback	3	10	Forearms, triceps

Core	Exercise	Sets*	Reps	Muscles worked
	Pilates roll-up	5	30 seconds (right and left)	Core
	Side plank	2	5 (right and left)	Core
	Supine clocking	2	10	Core
	Supine bicycle	2	25	Core
Flexibility	Exercise	Sets*	Reps	Muscles worked
	Child's pose	1	30 seconds	--
	Low back stretch	1	2	--
	Hamstring stretch	1	2 (right and left)	--
	Spinal twist	2	2 (right and left)	--
	Standing cat and cow	2	2	--
	Downward-facing dog	2	2	--
	Forward bend	2	2	--
	Forward bend with a twist	2	2 (right and left)	--

*Take 60 seconds of rest between sets.

BEGINNER WORKOUT 7

Warm-up	Warm up for 5 to 7 minutes on a treadmill, elliptical trainer, or stationary bike before beginning the workout.			
	Exercise	**Sets***	**Reps**	**Muscles worked**
	Plié with medicine ball lift	2	8	Lower body, core
	Standing cat and cow	2	4	Lower body, core
	Lateral stretch	2	2	Lateral spine
	Standing knee flexion and extension with ankle dorsiflexion	2	2	Legs, low back
	Spinal extension	2	2	Spine, lower body
	Standing figure four	2	2	Hips, low back
	Knee lift with medicine ball	1	8	Lower body, core
Lower and upper body	Now that you are becoming more accustomed to the workouts, you can continue to increase your weight loads, but stay focused on continued learning. Understanding the correct form and technique will allow you to move into more advanced techniques.			
	Exercise	**Sets***	**Reps**	**Muscles worked**
	Walking lunge	5	10	Hamstrings, gluteals, quadriceps
	Decline push-up	3	10	Chest, shoulders, triceps
	Good morning	3	10	Hamstrings, gluteals, low back
	Seated low row	3	10	Back, biceps
	Seated leg extension	3	10	Quadriceps
	Pullover	3	10	Lats, shoulders, core
	Kettlebell squat	3	10	Lower body
	Front cable raise	3	10	Shoulders, core
	Standing cable chest fly	3	10	Chest, core
	Angle kettlebell squat	3	10	Lower body, hips, core
	Rear deltoid fly	3	10	Shoulders, core
	Hammer curl	3	10	Forearms, biceps
	Triceps kickback	3	10	Forearms, triceps

Core	Exercise	Sets*	Reps	Muscles worked
	Abdominal progression series	2	10 each exercise	Core
	Supine bicycle	2	10	Core
	Supine contralateral bicycle	2	10	Core
	Standing Russian twist	2	10	Core
Flexibility	Exercise	Sets*	Reps	Muscles worked
	Child's pose	1	30 seconds	--
	Low back stretch	1	2	--
	Hamstring stretch	1	2 (right and left)	--
	Spinal twist	2	2 (right and left)	--
	Quadruped cat and cow	2	2	--
	Downward-facing dog	2	2	--
	Forward bend	2	2	--
	Forward bend with a twist	2	2 (right and left)	--

*Take 60 seconds of rest between sets.

BEGINNER WORKOUT 8

Warm-up	*Warm up for 5 to 7 minutes on a treadmill, elliptical trainer, or stationary bike before beginning the workout.*			
	Exercise	**Sets**	**Reps**	**Muscles worked**
	Plié with medicine ball lift	2	8	Lower body, core
	Standing cat and cow	2	4	Lower body, core
	Lateral stretch	2	2	Lateral spine
	Standing knee flexion and extension with ankle dorsiflexion	2	2	Legs, low back
	Spinal extension	2	2	Spine, lower body
	Standing figure four	2	2	Hips, low back
	Knee lift with medicine ball	1	8	Lower body, core
Lower and upper body	*Now that you are becoming more accustomed to the workouts, you can continue to increase your weight loads, but stay focused on continued learning. Understanding the correct form and technique will allow you to move into more advanced techniques.*			
	Exercise	**Sets***	**Reps**	**Muscles worked**
	Squat sequence with curtsy lunge	3	10 (right and left)	Hamstrings, gluteals, quadriceps, core
	Seated hamstring curl	3	10	Hamstrings
	Good morning	3	10	Hamstrings, quadriceps, gluteals
	Seated leg press	3	10	Lower body
	Pilates swimming	5	10	Core, posterior muscles of body
	Barbell chest press	3	10	Chest, anterior deltoid
	Lat pulldown	3	10	Back, biceps
	Dumbbell chest press	3	10	Chest, triceps, shoulders
	Bent-over dumbbell row	3	10	Back, biceps, core
	Straight bar upright row	3	10	Shoulders
	Seated calf raise	3	10	Legs
	Biceps curl with EZ Curl Bar	3	10	Forearms, biceps
	Triceps dip	3	10	Chest, triceps, core

Core	Exercise	Sets*	Reps	Muscles worked
	Stability ball roll-out	5	5 (right and left)	Core
	Oblique stability ball roll-out	5	5 (right and left)	Core
	V-sit (boat pose)	5	10 seconds	Core
	Push-up to plank	2	10	Core, chest, triceps
Flexibility	Exercise	Sets*	Reps	Muscles worked
	Full-body stretch	2	30 seconds	--
	Low back stretch	2	10 seconds each leg	--
	Hamstring stretch	2	10 seconds each leg	--
	Spinal twist	2	2 (right and left)	--
	Quadruped cat and cow	2	2	--
	Child's pose	2	30 seconds	--
	Foam roller shoulder extension	2	2	--

*Take 60 seconds of rest between sets.

Advanced and Endurance Strength Programs

I f you have progressed through the beginner-to-intermediate program in chapter 10, then you have experienced increases in muscle strength, size, and endurance. After preparing your body through those foundational programs, you should be ready to perform even more challenging routines as you seek to improve each fitness variable (power, speed, balance, and agility). In the programs outlined in this chapter, you will be working harder than you were in the beginner-to-intermediate program, not because you are performing new exercises, but because of changes in the way you train.

The training changes in this chapter include supersets (i.e., performing an exercise and then, without stopping or resting, performing another that uses the same muscle or opposing muscle group), small circuits that include cardio-based activity, and "quick workouts," which typically include high-intensity cardio intervals. You will continue to use circuits, but slightly different from the way you used them in the beginner-to-intermediate program. Circuits in these programs are made up of sets of four exercises performed for one minute each, with a minute of rest between sets.

This chapter also outlines a program for women who focus primarily on endurance training. This chapter maybe particularly useful for women who perform cardiorespiratory training exclusively, with no part of their fitness program incorporating strength training. Women with this focus often miss the powerful benefits that resistance training and increased core strength can contribute to their weight loss efforts, running economy, speed (if competitive: 5K, 10K, half marathon, marathon, or triathlon), endurance, and stamina, as well as injury prevention. Research published in the *Scandinavian Journal of Medicine & Science in Sports* (Hoff, Gran, and Helgerud 2002) demonstrated that endurance athletes who increased their strength improved their aerobic endurance significantly.

The strength programs in this chapter follow the same periodization schedule as used in chapter 10, featuring the 6-month macrocycle that is broken down into two, 3-month mesocycles, each one consisting of six, 2-week microcycles, with one week of rest between mesocycles for recovery.

ADVANCED STRENGTH PROGRAM ROUTINES

If you want to continue to improve your performance and maintain your strength levels by training at a higher intensity level, these advanced programs will be especially helpful. This chapter includes strength training workouts, a variety of core and flexibility workouts, as well as several variations of cardiovascular training protocols. This chapter also includes a number of exercises using the TRX suspension training system. The advanced workouts are for those women who have been strength training for no less than six months continually. If you have been participating in endurance training programs exclusively and are a dedicated endurance athlete, I suggest you start with the beginner programs in chapter 10 before moving into the endurance workouts in this chapter. This way you will have the opportunity to develop a strong baseline strength level before embarking on these more advanced programs.

As a beginner, you likely experienced rapid gains in strength and muscle growth, particularly in the first six months of consistent training. Over time, your body likely adapted to the stimulus, making it more difficult to obtain results. Advanced programs stimulate muscle growth and promote further increases in muscle size and strength.

Some of the workouts focus on the upper body, some focus on the lower body, and some are full-body routines. Some include bouts of high-intensity cardio exercise such as five, 1-minute jump rope sequences or three, 1-minute jump squats (using just body weight) between exercise sets. Regardless of the routine you follow, be sure to allow for adequate recovery between sessions. As you recall from chapter 9, recovery is necessary because the entire body is taxed and challenged during every exercise session. Keep in mind that you may need more time between workouts than suggested, so listen to your body regarding appropriate recovery intervals.

On the days you are not performing one of these routines, you should perform flexibility training. You can use the stretches I have included in chapter 4. They are part of each workout and are also included in specific routines at the end of this chapter, or you can take a yoga class or follow a yoga DVD. You should also perform cardio sessions such as using a treadmill, walking outdoors, running, using an elliptical trainer, cycling, or swimming on your days off from strength training. Also, take one full day of recovery each week to focus simply on hydration and rest.

The macrocycle for the advanced strength training program is 6 months long (24 weeks) which is further broken down into two, 12-week programs called mesocycles which are 3 months each. The first 3-month mesocycle is the initial advanced programming workouts. The second 3-month mesocycle includes even more intense, advanced workouts. Each mesocycle is then broken down further into 2-week microcycles. The goal of the first mesocycle (microcycles 1-6) is to increase intensity and work with the strength you acquired from the beginner-to-intermediate strength training program (chapter 10). The goal of the second mesocycle (microcycles 7-12) is to further challenge your body through intense endurance and strength training programming.

Note that you should take one entire week off for active recovery between mesocycles 1 and 2. The purpose of this week is to give your body time to prepare for the next phase, as well as to take a much needed break. I recommend that you stretch daily and take short, easy walks either outdoors or in, but stay out of the gym to avoid the temptation to exercise this week.

Mesocycle 1, Microcycles 1 and 2 (Weeks 1-4)

Microcycles 1 and 2 will take you four weeks to complete. These microcycles prepare you for longer, more intense strength workouts using fewer exercises; the workouts are divided into upper and lower body exercises. Be sure to take the time to recover between sets. Recommendations for recovery times and days between workouts are given as you begin these more strenuous workouts, but you may need to adjust them based on your hydration level, how much recovery you have taken between workouts, your sleep cycles (i.e., whether are you getting adequate rest), and your nutritional intake (i.e., how well you are eating).

To warm up for these workouts, walk, jog, or run on a treadmill or get onto the elliptical trainer for no less than 10 minutes. Wait until after the workout to stretch, but if you feel tightness, you can perform easy stretches for areas you would like to loosen up. Prior to the workout, if you choose to stretch, do not hold the stretches long; simply move into them as you feel comfortable, performing three to five light stretches on any muscle group you feel you need to. Another option is to wait until after the workout to perform the stretch routine noted at the end of the workout.

Mesocycle 1, Microcycles 3 and 4 (Weeks 5-8)

Microcycles 3 and 4 continue to challenge your strength and endurance levels. These microcycles also take your cardio workouts to another level. You will work for shorter bouts at much higher intensity levels. Also, you will want to increase your weight loads by 10 percent from your previous microcycles when you begin these microcycles. To warm up for these workouts, walk, jog, or run on a treadmill or elliptical trainer for no less than 10 minutes. Wait until after the workout to stretch, but if you feel tightness, perform easy stretches for areas you would like to loosen up. Prior to the workout, if you choose to stretch, do not hold the stretches long; simply move into them as you feel comfortable, performing three to five light stretches on any muscle group you feel you need to. Another option is to wait until after the workout to perform the stretch routine noted at the end of the workout.

Mesocycle 1, Microcycles 5 and 6 (Weeks 9-12)

Microcycles 5 and 6 continue to challenge your cardio training, but your strength workouts are going to pick up a notch. You will begin to use pyramid-style workouts, in which the weight loads stay the same, but the repetitions change each set. Work harder by increasing your weight loads by 10 percent for these microcycles.

To warm up for these workouts, walk, jog, or run on a treadmill or get onto an elliptical trainer for no less than 10 minutes. Wait until after the workout to stretch, but if you feel tightness, perform easy stretches for areas you would like to loosen up. Prior to the workout, if you choose to stretch, do not hold the stretches long; simply move into them as you feel comfortable, performing three to five light stretches on any muscle group you feel you need to. Another option is to wait until after the workout to perform the stretch routine noted at the end of the workout.

Mesocycle 2, Microcycles 1 and 2 (Weeks 14-17)

Microcycles 1 and 2 in mesocycle 2 continue to challenge your cardio training while your strength workouts pick up a notch by adding supersetting strength training techniques. These techniques target specific muscle groups. Work harder by increasing your weight loads by 10 percent for these microcycles.

To warm up for these workouts, walk, jog, or run on a treadmill or get onto an elliptical trainer for no less than 10 minutes. Wait until after the workout to stretch, but if you feel tightness, perform easy stretches for areas you would like to loosen up. Prior to the workout, if you choose to stretch, do not hold the stretches long; simply move into them as you feel comfortable, performing three to five light stretches on any muscle group you feel you need to. Another option is to wait until after the workout to perform the stretch routine noted at the end of the workout.

Mesocycle 2, Microcycles 3 and 4 (Weeks 18-21)

Microcycles 3 and 4 include cardio training that levels off, allowing you to perform longer cardio workouts at lower intensities. You continue to use pyramid-style workouts in which the weight loads stay the same, but the repetitions change each set. Your strength workouts gain an endurance focus by adding TRX suspension training to the mix. Work harder by increasing your weight loads by 10 percent for these microcycles.

To warm up for these workouts, walk, jog, or run on a treadmill or get onto an elliptical trainer for no less than 10 minutes. Wait until after the workout to stretch, but if you feel tightness, perform easy stretches for areas you would like to loosen up. Prior to the workout, if you choose to stretch, do not hold the stretches long; simply move into them as you feel comfortable, performing three to five light stretches on any muscle group you feel you need to. Another option is to wait until after the workout to perform the stretch routine noted at the end of the workout.

Mesocycle 2, Microcycles 5 and 6 (Weeks 22-25)

Microcycles 5 and 6 include superset strength techniques, ascending and descending pyramids, body weight workouts, and TRX suspension training. These two microcycles have a lot of variety. Maintain your last microcycle's weight loads for these microcycles.

To warm up for these workouts, walk, jog, or run on a treadmill or get onto an elliptical trainer for no less than 10 minutes. Wait until after the workout to stretch, but if you feel tightness, perform easy stretches for areas you would like to loosen up. Prior to the workout, if you choose to stretch, do not hold the stretches long; simply move into them as you feel comfortable, performing three to five light stretches on any muscle group you feel you need to. Another option is to wait until after the workout to perform the stretch routine noted at the end of the workout.

MESOCYCLE 1, Microcycles 1 and 2 (Weeks 1-4)

Day 1: Lower body	Exercises	Sets	Reps
Choose one of the following two options: ***Option 1:** Perform each exercise, recovering for twice as long as it takes to perform the set. For example, if it takes you 45 seconds to complete a set of 10 front squats, allow yourself 90 seconds, or a minute and a half, of recovery before beginning another set. If this is not long enough, take more time as necessary. ***Option 2:** Perform a set of exercises, and then between sets, perform 1 set of the core-specific exercises as indicated in this workout. This will minimize downtime and keep the workouts moving.	Dumbbell front squat	3	10
	Reverse lunge	3	10
	Side lunge	3	10
	Single-leg squat	3	10
	Standing calf raise	3	10
	Abdominal progression series	3	10 (each exercise)
	Side plank	2	10 (right and left)
	Pilates swimming	5	10 (end each set with a child's pose)

Day 2: Cardio, core, and flexibility	Run 3 miles (4.8 km) on a treadmill at alternating intensities at two different speeds. For example, walk for 5 minutes at 4 mph (6.4 km/h), and then run at 5.5 mph (8.9 km/h) or higher for 5 minutes. Complete this pattern for a total of 3 miles (4.8 km). Follow with the core exercises at the end of this table and flexibility training using stretch workout 1 on page 203.		

Day 3: Upper body

Perform each exercise in sequence (e.g., cable chest fly, triceps kickback, dumbbell upright row, lat pulldown, hammer curl). After you complete each set, do it again, and then one more time for a total of 3 sets.

Exercises	Sets	Reps
Standing cable chest fly	3	10
Triceps kickback	3	10
Straight bar upright row	3	10
Lat pulldown	3	10
Hammer curl	3	10

Day 4: Cardio, core, and flexibility	Run for 30 minutes either on the treadmill or outdoors. If on the treadmill, try to find a pace you can tolerate for 30 minutes. Try to maintain a consistent pace, training in heart rate training zone 3. Follow with the core exercises at the end of this table and flexibility training using stretch workout 2 on page 203.		

Day 5: Quick workout

This workout intersperses treadmill running with exercise sets. For each set, perform the complete sequence of exercises for the repetitions indicated one time through; then run on the treadmill for 5 minutes at 6.5 miles per hour (10.5 km, or as high as you can work without having to stop or slow down). Choose a speed you can maintain.

Exercises	Sets	Reps
Kettlebell squat	3	15
Push-up to plank	3	15
Side lunge	3	15
Pull-up	3	5
5 minutes of treadmill running	3	Allow yourself 1 minute of recovery after the cardio segment and before you begin the next set of four exercises.

Day 6: Cardio, core, and flexibility	Run for 30 minutes either on the treadmill or outdoors. If on the treadmill, try to find a pace you can tolerate for 30 minutes. Try to maintain a consistent pace, training in heart rate training zone 3. Follow with the core exercises at the end of this table and flexibility training using stretch workout 2 on page 203.		

Day 7: Day off for recovery

Core exercises	Exercises	Sets	Reps
	Abdominal progression series	1	10 (each exercise)
	Pilates roll-up	1	10
	Bridge	1	10
	Standing Russian twist	1	10
	Side plank	1	30 seconds (right and left)
	Quadruped back extension	1	30 seconds (right and left)

MESOCYCLE 1, Microcycles 3 and 4 (Weeks 5-8)

Day 1: Total body	Exercises	Sets	Reps
Perform each exercise, recovering for twice as long as it takes to perform the set. For example, if it takes you 45 seconds to complete a set of 10 seated cable rows, allow yourself 90 seconds, or a minute and a half, of recovery before beginning another set. If this is not long enough, take more time as necessary.	Walking lunge	5	10
	Bent-over dumbbell row	3	10
	Stability ball gluteal squeeze	2	25
	Dumbbell chest fly	3	10
	Seated cable row	3	10
	Incline push-up	3	10
	Seated leg extension	3	10
	Seated shoulder press	3	10
	Biceps curl with EZ Curl Bar	3	10
	Seated calf raise	3	10

Day 2: Cardio, core, and flexibility	Run on the treadmill for 45 minutes. Walk at a comfortable pace for 5 minutes; jog at a mildly uncomfortable pace for 5 minutes; run at a challenging pace for 5 minutes. Continue this cycle with these techniques for 45 minutes. Follow with the core exercises at the end of this table and flexibility training using stretch workout 1 on page 203.

Day 3: Upper body	Exercises	Sets	Reps
Perform all sets of each exercise before moving to the next exercise. For example, do 3 sets of lat pulldowns before moving on to the cable chest fly. Rest for 90 seconds to 3 minutes between sets.	Push-up	3	10
	Lat pulldown	3	10
	Cable chest fly	3	10
	Lateral raise	3	10
	Biceps curl with EZ Curl Bar	3	10
	Triceps dip	3	10

Day 4: Cardio, core, and flexibility	For this cardio workout, work on a treadmill. Using the distance on the display, change your running speed every quarter mile. For the first quarter mile (0 to .25), run at a comfortable pace; for the second quarter mile (.25 to .5), speed up; for the third quarter mile (.5 to .75), decrease your speed to allow yourself the opportunity to recover; for the fourth quarter mile (.75 to 1.00) run at the hardest pace you can handle for the entire duration. Continue to change your speeds each quarter mile until you reach 3 miles. Follow with the core exercises at the end of this table and flexibility training using stretch workout 2 on page 203.

Day 5: Lower body	Exercises	Sets	Reps
	Stability ball gluteal squeeze	3	10
	Side lunge	3	10
	Dumbbell front squat	3	10
	Seated leg press	3	10
	Kettlebell hip hinge	3	10
Day 6: Cardio, core, and flexibility	Run 3 miles (4.8 km) on a treadmill at alternating intensities at two different speeds. For example, walk for 5 minutes at 4 mph (6.4 km/h), and then run at 5.5 mph (8.9 km/h) or higher for 5 minutes. Complete this pattern for a total of 3 miles (4.8 km). Follow with the core exercises at the end of this table and flexibility training using stretch workout 1 on page 203.		
Day 7: Day off for recovery			
Core exercises	Exercises	Sets	Reps
	Push-up to plank	1	10
	Stability ball roll-out	1	10
	Oblique stability ball roll-out	1	10
	Windshield wipers	1	5 (right and left counted as 1)
	Supine clocking	1	10

MESOCYCLE 1, Microcycles 5 and 6 (Weeks 9-12)

Day 1: Lower body	Exercises	Sets	Reps
This workout uses a descending pyramid technique (i.e., repetitions decrease as you fatigue). You may need more recovery between these sets as the intensity gets harder and the sets get shorter. Recover between sets for 1 to 3 minutes (5 minutes is too long). Make sure you are using weight loads that fatigue you by the time you get to set 4, and that you are performing only 4 repetitions.	Squat sequence with curtsy lunge	1 set of each rep amount	10, 8, 6, 4
	Reverse lunge	1 set of each rep amount	10, 8, 6, 4
	Side lunge	1 set of each rep amount	10, 8, 6, 4
	Single-leg squat	1 set of each rep amount	10, 8, 6, 4
	Standing calf raise	1 set of each rep amount	10, 8, 6, 4

Day 2: Cardio, core, and flexibility	
	Run 3 miles (4.8 km) on a treadmill at a consistent speed. Increase the incline every quarter mile, starting at a .5% incline. Continue to increase the incline every quarter mile until you cannot continue to increase and maintain your speed. Follow with the core exercises at the end of this table and flexibility training using stretch workout 1 on page 203.

Day 3: Upper body	Exercises	Sets	Reps
This workout uses a descending pyramid technique (i.e., the workout gets harder even though the repetitions decrease). You may need more recovery between sets as the intensity gets harder and the sets get shorter. Recover between sets for 1 to 3 minutes (5 minutes is too long).	Dumbbell chest press	1 of each rep amount	10, 8, 6, 4
	Push-up to plank	1 of each rep amount	10, 8, 6, 4
	Seated low row	1 of each rep amount	10, 8, 6, 4
	Lat pulldown	1 of each rep amount	10, 8, 6, 4
	Hammer curl	1 of each rep amount	10, 8, 6, 4
	Triceps kickback	1 of each rep amount	10, 8, 6, 4

Day 4: Cardio, core, and flexibility	
	Perform a 30-minute elliptical training workout at a pace you can tolerate for the full 30 minutes. Try to maintain a consistent pace, training in heart rate training zone 3. Follow with the core exercises at the end of this table and flexibility training using stretch workout 2 on page 203.

Day 5: Lower body	Exercises	Sets	Reps
This workout also uses a descending pyramid technique (i.e., the workout gets harder even though the repetitions decrease). You may need more recovery between these sets as the intensity gets harder and the sets get shorter. Recover between sets for 1 to 3 minutes (5 minutes is too long).	Angle kettlebell squat	1 of each rep amount	10, 8, 6, 4
	Reverse lunge	1 of each rep amount	10, 8, 6, 4
	Side lunge	1 of each rep amount	10, 8, 6, 4
	Single-leg squat	1 of each rep amount	10, 8, 6, 4
	Seated calf raise	1 of each rep amount	10, 8, 6, 4

Day 6: Day off for recovery	

Day 7: Upper body	Exercises	Sets	Reps
You may need more recovery between sets as the intensity gets harder and the sets get shorter. Recover between sets for 1 to 3 minutes (5 minutes is too long).	Dumbbell chest press	1 of each rep amount	10, 8, 6, 4
	Push-up to plank	1 of each rep amount	10, 8, 6, 4
	Seated low row	1 of each rep amount	10, 8, 6, 4
	Lat pulldown	1 of each rep amount	10, 8, 6, 4
	Hammer curl	1 of each rep amount	10, 8, 6, 4
	Triceps kickback	1 of each rep amount	10, 8, 6, 4

Day 1: Superset total body workout

These supersets require you to perform each exercise for the same muscle groups three times in a row. Once you have completed the chest sequence, move on to the back sequence. Follow this with the leg sequence, and then finish with the arm sequence. After you complete each sequence, perform a one-minute interval of jumping rope. If you don't have a jump rope, simply jump in place.

Exercises	Sets	Reps
Chest sequence: 1. Dumbbell chest press 2. Push-up 3. Triceps kickback	3 of each exercise (1, 2, 3); then repeat	10 (each exercise)
Back sequence: 1. Lat pulldown 2. Seated low row 3. Dumbbell upright row	3 of each exercise (1, 2, 3); then repeat	10 (each exercise)
Leg sequence: 1. Front lunge 2. Side lunge 3. Dumbbell squat	3 of each exercise (1, 2, 3); then repeat	10 (each exercise)
Arm sequence: 1. Biceps curl with EZ Curl Bar 2. Hammer curl 3. Lateral raise	3 of each exercise (1, 2, 3); then repeat	10 (each exercise)

Day 2: Cardio, core, and flexibility

Treadmill tempo run: Run, jog, or walk 1 mile (1.6 km) at an easy pace. Run your second mile (1.6 km) at a pace that feels mildly uncomfortable (a pace you can tolerate, but that challenges you). For mile 3 (third 1.6 km), run at a comfortable pace. Follow with core exercises at the end of this table and flexibility training using stretch workout 1 on page 203.

Day 3: Kettlebell body weight workout

Incorporate a one-minute squat jump segment between each set. You should complete three sets of one-minute jump squat intervals within this workout.

Exercises	Sets	Reps
Kettlebell squat	3	15
Angle kettlebell squat	3	15
Pull-up	3	5
Triceps dip	3	10
Standing Russian twist	3	10

Day 4: Cardio, core, and flexibility

Long treadmill run: Run on a treadmill for 55 minutes at a very easy pace. Follow with the core exercises at the end of this table and flexibility training using stretch workout 2 on page 203.

Day 5: Quick workout 3

This is a combination of exercises you are already familiar with. They are grouped to create fatigue. Take the time you need between exercise sequences to rehydrate and recover.

Exercises	Sets	Reps
Squat sequence with curtsy lunge	2	10 of each exercise for a total of 60 repetitions
Shoulder sequence: 1. Lateral raise 2. Front raise 3. Seated shoulder press	2	8, 4, 2

(continued)

Day 5: Quick workout 3, *continued*	Exercises	Sets	Reps
	Deadlift to bent-over dumbbell row	2	Perform 10 deadlifts; then 10 rows
	Standing cat and cow	2	6-8
	Incline push-up/push-up	2	20 (10 incline push-ups; then 10 push-ups)
Day 6: Cardio, core, and flexibility	Intensity run: Start running on a treadmill at a comfortable pace at an incline of .5 %. Increase your incline by 1 to 2% every 5 minutes for a total of 30 minutes. Follow with the core exercises at the end of this table and flexibility training using stretch workout 2 on page 203.		
Day 7: Day off for recovery			

Core exercises	Exercises	Sets	Reps
Perform five one-minute intervals of jumping rope within this workout. You can perform them all at once, a minute at a time, interspersed within the workout, or between exercise sets.	Side plank	2	30 seconds (right and left)
	Pilates roll-up	2	10
	V-sit	2	10
	Supine bicycle	2	10
	Supine contralateral bicycle	2	10
	Pilates swimming to child's pose	5	10

MESOCYCLE 2, Microcycles 3 and 4 (Weeks 18-21)

Day 1: Circuit workout	Exercises	Sets	Reps
For this workout, perform these exercises in an ascending pyramid, and then run on the treadmill for 5 minutes in heart rate training zone 3. Perform this circuit four times. As you recall, the ascending pyramid technique means that you perform more repetitions each set, but use the same weight load.	Good morning	4	8, 10, 12, 14
	Decline barbell press	4	8, 10, 12, 14
	Reverse lunge	4	8, 10, 12, 14
	Straight bar upright row	4	8, 10, 12, 14
	Push-up to plank	4	8, 10, 12, 14
	Seated low row	4	8, 10, 12, 14
Day 2: Day off for recovery			

Day 3: TRX suspension training workout 1 Increase to 3 sets for microcycle 4.	Exercises	Sets	Time
	TRX squat	2	30 seconds
	TRX chest press	2	30 seconds
	TRX crunch	2	30 seconds
	TRX step back lunge	2	30 seconds
	TRX mid row	2	30 seconds
	TRX plank	2	30 seconds
Day 4: Cardio, core, and flexibility	Intensity run for 25 minutes: Warm up for 5 minutes at a comfortable pace. Run at a hard pace for 5 minutes. Recover for 5 minutes at a comfortable pace. Run for 5 minutes at a hard pace. Recover for 5 minutes at a comfortable pace. Follow with the core exercises at the end of this table and flexibility training using stretch workout 1 on page 203.		
Day 5: TRX suspension training workout 2 Increase to 3 sets for microcycle 4.	Exercises	Sets	Time
	TRX single-leg squat	2	30 seconds
	TRX side plank	2	30 seconds each side
	TRX crunch	2	30 seconds
	TRX balance lunge	2	30 seconds
	TRX hamstring curl	2	30 seconds
	TRX atomic push-up	2	30 seconds
Day 6: Cardio, core, and flexibility	Run on a treadmill or outdoors for 50 minutes at a comfortable pace. Follow with the core exercises at the end of this table and flexibility training using stretch workout 2 on page 203.		
Core exercises	Exercises	Sets	Reps
	Quadruped back extension	2	4 on right and left
	Supine plank	2	Hold 30 seconds each
	Abdominal progression series	2	Perform 10 of each movement
	Quadruped cat and cow	2	About 10 seconds in each posture
	Push-up to plank	2	5
Day 7: Day off for recovery			

Day 1: Lower body workout	Exercises	Sets	Reps
Perform these exercises using the descending pyramid technique. You may also choose to perform these exercises using an ascending pyramid technique (i.e., more repetitions each set using the same weight). If so, just reverse the reps so the number increases for each set. Take 30 to 60 seconds of recovery between exercises.	Dumbbell front squat	4	12, 10, 8, 6
	Deadlift	4	12, 10, 8, 6
	Side lunge	4	12, 10, 8, 6
	Seated leg press	4	12, 10, 8, 6
	Seated calf raise	4	12, 10, 8, 6

Day 2: Cardio, core, and flexibility	
	Elliptical trainer cardio workout using a 2:1 interval ratio: After you warm up for 5 minutes, perform 40 seconds of hard training (going as fast as you can with control); then recover for 20 seconds (going at a pace that allows you to catch your breath). Continue this program for 20 minutes. Follow with the core exercises at the end of this table and flexibility training using stretch workout 2 on page 203.

Day 3: Upper body workout	Exercises	Sets	Reps
Superset each exercise by performing both sets back to back for each muscle group before moving to the next muscle group. Try not to take much rest between the two exercises in each set.	Rhomboids, lats, and posterior deltoid sequence: 1. Seated low row 2. Bent-over dumbbell row	2	8 of each exercise
	Lats, posterior deltoid, and trapezius sequence: 1. Lat pulldown 2. Pullover	2	8 of each exercise
	Chest and anterior deltoid sequence: 1. Dumbbell chest press 2. Incline push-up	2	8 of each exercise
	Middle deltoid and trapezius sequence: 1. Seated shoulder press 2. Shrug	2	8 of each exercise
	Arms sequence: 1. Preacher curl 2. Triceps kickback	2	8 of each exercise

Day 4: Cardio, core, and flexibility	
	Run on a treadmill or outdoors for 50 minutes at a comfortable pace. Follow with the core exercises at the end of this table and flexibility training using stretch workout 1 on page 203.

Day 5: Quick workout 4 (total body weight interval workout)	Exercises	Sets	Time
Take no more than 10 seconds to transition between exercises. Take 1 minute for recovery between sets.	Pull-up	4	1 minute
	Dip	4	1 minute
	Push-up to plank	4	1 minute
	Side plank	4	30 seconds (right and left)
	Single-leg squat	4	30 seconds (each leg)

Day 6: Day off for recovery			
Day 7: TRX workout 3 Increase your sets to 3 for microcycle 6.	**Exercises**	**Sets**	**Time**
	TRX chest press	2	45 seconds
	TRX mid row	2	45 seconds
	TRX Y deltoid fly	2	45 seconds
	TRX pike	2	45 seconds
	TRX plank	2	45 seconds
	TRX oblique crunch	2	45 seconds
Core exercises	**Exercises**	**Sets**	**Reps**
	Supine clocking	3	5
	Windshield wipers	3	5
	Supine plank	3	30 seconds
	Push-up to plank	3	5
	Pilates swimming	3	5

ENDURANCE STRENGTH PROGRAM ROUTINES

Many runners and other endurance-trained females neglect strength training. This is a major mistake because strength training decreases the risk of lower body injuries (e.g., runner's knee and IT band syndrome), increases joint stability (tendons and ligaments at the ankle, knee, and hip stay strong and flexible), and decreases the risk of repetitive stress injuries (shin splints and low back pain) that are often the result of many miles of endurance training activities. Strength training helps you run faster, longer, and more efficiently without as much need for long recovery. This is due to the increase in lean mass, which assists the body in fuel production. The more lean mass you have, the greater your ability to create and maintain mitochondria, the component of muscle cells that uses oxygen to produce energy. Producing more energy and reducing your risk of injury will help you perform better, stronger, and faster.

Another important benefit of strength training for the endurance-trained female is increased core strength. The ability to draw power from the center of the body is critical for long-term efficiency and endurance. A strong core helps you move through the motions of running (i.e., sagittal plane motions) with stability and control. Additionally, increased core strength improves running economy, speed, and power.

The endurance programs in this section are TRX suspension training workouts. If you recall, specific TRX exercises for the upper body, lower body, and core were outlined in chapters 5, 6, and 7, respectively.

TRX Suspension Training Guidelines

When using the TRX Suspension Trainer, always maintain a strong and stable body. Although some of the exercises focus on either the upper body or lower body, all the exercises require a stable core. You can keep your core muscles engaged by drawing in your abdominal wall and maintaining a rigid posture. Set the TRX Suspension Trainer up by attaching it to a strong anchor point (follow the Basic Use DVD and guidebook that comes with the product, if possible). The equalizer loop should be about 6 feet (2 m) from the floor when the TRX Suspension Trainer hangs straight down from the stable anchor point.

You can increase the intensity of many of the exercises by changing the angle at which you are standing while performing the exercise. For example, when performing the row exercise, you can make the work harder by walking forwards, bringing your body under the anchor point (conversely, you can make the work easier by walking backwards). The length of the straps should be adjusted depending on the exercise you are performing (i.e., short, mid-length, long, and mid-calf length).

The orientation to the TRX when preparing to perform each exercise is referred to as facing the anchor point (e.g., for the squat) or facing away from the anchor point (e.g., for the chest press). The same terminology is used with exercises that take you to the floor. Make sure when you perform each exercise that you keep the straps tight by maintaining tension throughout the entire exercise; try not to let them sag.

TRX Suspension Training Program

The upper body, lower body, and core exercises in the following workouts are described in chapters 5, 6, and 7, respectively. You can perform each workout with weights and other equipment, or by itself for a quick, unique, and powerful TRX workout. Because TRX exercises enhance endurance, time is important. Try to perform them two or three times weekly, interspersed within your running program. The workouts should take 30 to 45 minutes total. Most of the exercises are presented according to time, but you can also use the repetition method if you prefer. Be sure to allow for adequate recovery when performing your strength workouts in combination with your running program.

I recommend using TRX workouts in a "pick and choose" manner. Each workout addresses the upper body, lower body, and core, so no matter which one you choose, you will cover all areas of the body. Definitely alternate the workouts, however, for the sake of balance and variety.

TRX ENDURANCE WORKOUT 1

The exercises in this workout address the lower body, upper body, and core. Perform each exercise as grouped for the total time recommended. Then move onto the next group of exercises.

Exercise	Sets	Time
Group 1		
TRX squat	2	30 seconds
TRX chest press	2	30 seconds
TRX crunch	2	30 seconds
Group 2		
TRX step back lunge	2	1 minute (alternating legs)
TRX mid row	2	30 seconds
TRX plank	2	30 seconds

TRX ENDURANCE WORKOUT 2

The exercises in this workout address the lower body and core. Perform each exercise as grouped for the total time recommended. Then move onto the next group of exercises.

Exercise	Sets	Time
Group 1		
TRX single-leg squat	2	30 seconds
TRX side plank	2	30 seconds
TRX crunch	2	30 seconds
Group 2		
TRX balance lunge	2	30 seconds (each leg)
TRX hamstring curl	2	30 seconds
TRX atomic push-up	2	30 seconds

TRX ENDURANCE WORKOUT 3

The exercises in this workout address the upper body and core. Perform each exercise as grouped for the total time recommended. Then move onto the next group of exercises.

Exercise	Sets	Time
Group 1		
TRX chest press	3	30 seconds
TRX mid row	3	30 seconds
TRX Y deltoid fly	3	30 seconds
Group 2		
TRX pike	3	30 seconds
TRX plank	3	30 seconds
TRX oblique crunch	3	30 seconds

TRX ENDURANCE WORKOUT 4

The exercises in this workout address the core. Perform each exercise as grouped for the total time recommended. Then move onto the next group of exercises.

Exercise	Sets	Time
Group 1		
TRX hip press	2	45 seconds
TRX hamstring curl	2	45 seconds
TRX crunch	2	45 seconds
Group 2		
TRX pike	2	45 seconds
TRX oblique crunch	2	45 seconds
TRX plank	2	45 seconds

TRX ENDURANCE WORKOUT 5

The exercises in this workout address the lower body and core. Perform each exercise as grouped for the total time recommended. Then move onto the next group of exercises.

Exercise	Sets	Time
Group 1		
TRX squat	2	45 seconds
TRX step back lunge	2	45 seconds
TRX balance lunge	2	45 seconds
Group 2		
TRX atomic push-up	3	45 seconds
TRX oblique crunch	3	45 seconds
TRX plank	3	45 seconds

TRX ENDURANCE WORKOUT 6

The exercises in this workout address the upper body and core. Perform each exercise as grouped for the total time recommended. Then move onto the next group of exercises.

Exercise	Sets	Time
Group 1		
TRX chest press	3	45 seconds
TRX mid row	3	45 seconds
TRX Y deltoid fly	3	45 seconds
Group 2		
TRX atomic push-up	3	45 seconds
TRX oblique crunch	3	45 seconds
TRX pike	3	45 seconds

FLEXIBILITY WORKOUTS

Flexibility, in the form of stretches and other range of motion movements, is important in fitness and sport because it creates more movement, either in a muscle group or about a joint, helping you stay strong and even reducing your chance of getting injured. When you try to perform a movement that your body cannot perform, your muscles respond by contracting, which further inhibits your ability to move into that position. Some people get injured when they try to place their joints (shoulder, knee, elbow, wrist, hip) into positions that the supporting soft tissues (muscle, tendons, and ligaments) cannot tolerate.

Many fitness enthusiasts hold the erroneous belief that having adequate flexibility dramatically decreases the risk of getting injured, or that stretching diminishes soreness following a hard workout. Stretching does not decrease soreness, nor will having flexibility in muscles or a good range of motion about a joint protect you from injury. If you try to perform movements that your muscles or joints cannot support, because they are either are not strong enough or not flexible enough, you will likely get injured. However, don't misunderstand and believe that flexibility training is not important. Muscles that have adequate amounts of flexibility allow other parts of the body (joints in particular) to move through ranges of motion without pain, tightness, or premature fatigue. Therefore, having adequate flexibility supports your strength and endurance training efforts.

General flexibility refers to the muscles themselves, whereas flexibility at the joints (e.g., shoulder or hip) addresses range of motion. Consistent and regular stretching routines will increase flexibility and range of motion, as well as help you conserve and maintain the flexibility you already have. Because adequate flexibility will support your strength efforts, you should practice stretching on a regular basis.

The following stretch workouts are referenced in the preceding microcycle workouts. These routines should take 10 to 15 minutes to complete. The best time to perform stretches is after your strength or cardio workouts. Cold muscles and joints do not respond to stretches the same way that warm muscles and joints do. In fact, it is not recommended that you stretch muscles unless they are warm. Some research has shown that stretching prior to a workout can actually decrease performance. If you have warmed up properly, you should have begun to sweat. This simple signal will help you know whether your body is ready to perform a stretch routine. If you have completed the workout and perhaps the cardio segment recommended for each microcycle, you will definitely be ready to perform the stretch sequence recommended at the end of each workout.

STRETCH WORKOUT 1

Exercise	Sets	Time
Lateral stretch	3	Reach up and hold the stretch for about 8 to 10 seconds on each side.
Spinal extension	2-4	Hold the stretch for about 5 to 7 seconds.
Standing knee flexion and extension with ankle dorsiflexion	2-4	Extend and flex the knee, holding the stretch for about 2 to 4 seconds each time.
Standing figure four	2-4	Hold the stretch for about 5 to 8 seconds on each side.
Forward bend	2-4	Reach down for the toes/feet, holding the stretch for 5 to 8 seconds each time
Forward bend with a twist	2-4	Reach down for the toes/feet, holding the stretch for 5 to 8 seconds each time.
Standing cat and cow	3-5	Flex and extend the spine and hips holding the stretch for 4 to 6 seconds each time.
Standing shoulder horizontal adduction	2-4	Hold the stretch for 4 to 6 seconds on each side.
Full-body stretch	2-4	Lengthen and hold for about 5 to 8 seconds each time.
Bridge	2-4	Lift and hold; then slowly roll down for about 5 to 8 seconds.
Foam roller spinal extension (optional)	2-4	Move through a consistent range of motion at a controlled pace.
Foam roller shoulder extension (optional	2-4	Move through a consistent range of motion at a controlled pace.

STRETCH WORKOUT 2

Exercise	Sets	Time
Full-body stretch	2-4	Lengthen and hold for about 5 to 8 seconds each time.
Bridge	2-4	Lift and hold; then slowly roll down for about 5 to 8 seconds.
Low back stretch	2-4	Hold each leg for 6 to 10 seconds.
Hamstring stretch	2-4	Hold each leg for 6 to 10 seconds.
Spinal twist	2-4	Hold each leg for 6 to 10 seconds.
Quadruped cat and cow	3-5	Flex and extend the spine and hips holding the stretch for 4 to 6 seconds each time.
Child's pose	1-2	Hold posture for 10 to 30 seconds.
Downward-facing dog	2-4	Hold posture for 4 to 6 seconds.
Forward bend	2-4	Reach down for the toes/feet, holding the stretch for 5 to 8 seconds each time
Forward bend with a twist	2-4	Reach down for the toes/feet, holding the stretch 5 to 8 seconds each time.
Foam roller spinal extension (optional)	2-4	Move through a consistent range of motion at a controlled pace.
Foam roller shoulder extension (optional)	2-4	Move through a consistent range of motion at a controlled pace.

This chapter outlined advanced and endurance strength training programs that you can use to increase your muscle strength and further develop your muscle size. Be certain that you move into these advanced programs only after you have developed your muscles by adhering to the beginner-to-intermediate strength program. Throughout this book, I have suggested ways to train, shown what progress you can expect, and explained how to improve muscle fitness, cardiorespiratory endurance, and flexibility. I have also encouraged you to use the periodization method of training to improve performance and incorporate recovery to minimize your chance of injury.

You can maintain your newly gained strength for up to six weeks after the cessation of a consistent training program by performing a lower volume and frequency of training, as long as the intensity (resistance) remains the same. One strength training session per week will help you maintain strength for six weeks or more. Two sessions per week will ensure maintenance for a prolonged period, depending on the level of strength you achieved before beginning the maintenance program. If your circumstances change and you are not able to train on a regular basis, you will retain half the strength you have gained for up to one year.

You now know enough to design and carry out a muscle fitness program that will improve your appearance, health, and everyday performance. You have also decreased your risk of age-related muscle strength declines that can result in conditions such as osteoporosis, loss of mobility, and general age-related muscle loss. Therefore, go forward in your training program with confidence and expect outstanding, long-term results.

References

CHAPTER 1

Donnelly, J.E., S.N. Blair, J.M Jakicic, M.M. Manore, J.W. Rankin, and B.K. Smith. 2009. Appropriate Physical Activity Intervention Strategies for Weight Loss and Prevention of Weight Regain for Adults. *Medicine & Science in Sports & Exercise* 41: 2, 459-471.

Fagard, R.H. 2001. Exercise Characteristics and the Blood Pressure Response to Dynamic Physical Training. *Medicine & Science in Sports & Exercise* 33: S484-S492.

Kohrt, W.M., S.A. Bloomfield, K.D. Little, M.E. Nelson, V.R. Yingling, and American College of Sports Medicine. 2004. American College of Sports Medicine Position Stand: Physical Activity and Bone Health. *Medicine & Science in Sports & Exercise* 36 (11): 1985-1996.

Marks, Derek, and Len Kravitz. 2000. Growth Hormone Response to an Acute Bout of Resistance Exercise in Weight-Trained and Non-Weight-Trained Women. *Journal of Strength and Conditioning Research* 14 (2): 220-227.

Marx, J.O., N.A. Ratamess, B.C. Nindl, L.A. Gotshalk, J.S. Volek, K. Dohi, J.A. Bush, A.L. Gomez, S.A. Mazzetti, S.J. Fleck, K. Hakkinen, R.U. Newton, and W.J. Kraemer. 2001. Low-Volume Circuit Versus High-Volume Periodized Resistance Training in Women. *Medicine & Science in Sports & Exercise* 33 (4): 635-643.

Ormsbee, M.J., J.P. Thyfault, E.A. Johnson, R.M. Kraus, M.D. Choi, and R.C. Hickner. 2007. Fat Metabolism and Acute Resistance Exercise in Trained Men. *Journal of Applied Physiology* 102: 1767-1772.

Pollock, Michael L., Barry A. Franklin, Gary J. Balady, Bernard L. Chaitman, Jerome L. Fleg, Barbara Fletcher, Marian Limacher, Ileana L. Piña, Richard A. Stein, Mark Williams, and Terry Bazzarre. 2000. Resistance Exercise in Individuals With and Without Cardiovascular Disease: Benefits, Rationale, Safety, and Prescription, An Advisory From the Committee on Exercise, Rehabilitation, and Prevention, Council on Clinical Cardiology, American Heart Association. AHA Science Advisory. *Circulation* 101: 828. doi: 10.1161/01.CIR.101.7.828. © 2000 American Heart Association, Inc.

CHAPTER 2

American College of Sports Medicine. October 2007. The female athlete triad. *Medicine & Science in Sports & Exercise* 39 (10): 1867-1882.

Hillman, C.H., K.I. Erickson, and A.F. Kramer. 2008. Be Smart, Exercise Your Heart: Exercise Effects on Brain and Cognition. *Nature Reviews Neuroscience* 9 (1): 58-65.

CHAPTER 4

Astrand, P. and K. Rodahl. 2003. *Textbook of Work Physiology*, 4th ed. New York: McGraw-Hill.

Green, D.J. 2010. American Council on Exercise. *ACE Personal Trainer Manual*, 4th ed. San Diego, CA. p.372-374.

CHAPTER 8

American Council on Exercise. 2011. *ACE Personal Trainer Manual*, 4th ed. San Diego, CA: American Council on Exercise. p. 361

Medicine & Science in Sports and Exercise. 2009. Special Communication Position Stand: Progression Models in Resistance Training for Healthy Adults.p. 689-690.

CHAPTER 9

American College of Sports Medicine. 1998. ACSM Position Stand: The recommended quality and quantity of exercise for developing and maintaining cardiorespiratory and muscular fitness, and flexibility in healthy adults. *Medicine & Science in Sports and Exercise*. 30: 975-99

American College of Sports Medicine. 2009. ACSM Position Stand: Progression Models in Resistance Training for Healthy Adults. *Medicine. & Science in Sports and Exercise* 41(3). p. 687-708.

CHAPTER 10

Green, D. 2010. ACE Personal Trainer Manual. 4th Edition. *American Council on Exercise*. San Diego, CA.

CHAPTER 11

Hoff, J., Gran, A., and Helgerud, J. 2002. "Maximal Strength Training Improves Aerobic Endurance Performance." *Scandinavian Journal of Medicine & Science in Sports* 12: 288-295.

About the Author

Irene Lewis-McCormick, M.S. is a personal trainer, an international presenter, an author, and a 25-year fitness veteran. She holds a Master's of Science degree in Exercise and Sport Science with an emphasis in Physiology from Iowa State University. She holds professional certifications from NSCA-CSCS, ACE, AFAA, YogaFit, Pilates, and AEA.

She is a frequent contributor to consumer and fitness publications including *IDEA Health & Fitness Journal*, *Fitness Management*, *Shape*, *Oxygen*, *MORE* magazine, *Diabetic Living*, and *Heart Healthy Living*. Irene is on the editorial advisory board of *Diabetic Living* magazine and is a subject matter expert and exam writer for the American Council on Exercise.

Irene presents for IDEA, SCW, Fitness Anywhere, DCAC, Fitness Fest, the Mayo Clinic, YMCA, and many regional venues. She is a master TRX course instructor and master training for JumpSport® Trampoline Fitness. She has been a featured presenter in several DVDs including programs for pre- and postnatal exercise, water fitness, strength training, step, Pilates, and foam roller exercise.